WORLDPROOFING
YOUR KIDS

WORLDPROOFING YOUR KIDS

≋

*Helping Moms Prepare Their Kids to
Navigate Today's Turbulent Times*

LAEL F. ARRINGTON

CROSSWAY BOOKS • WHEATON, ILLINOIS
A DIVISION OF GOOD NEWS PUBLISHERS

Worldproofing Your Kids

Copyright © 1997 by Lael F. Arrington

Published by Crossway Books
      a division of Good News Publishers
      1300 Crescent Street
      Wheaton, Illinois 60187

Cover design: D^2 DesignWorks

Cover illustration: John Ceballos

First printing 1997

Printed in the United States of America

Library of Congress Cataloging-in-Publication Data
Arrington, Lael F., 1951-
   Worldproofing your kids : helping moms prepare their kids to
navigate today's turbulent times.
      p.   cm.
   Includes bibliographical references and index.
   ISBN 0-89107-956-4
   1. Child rearing—Religious aspects—Christianity. 2. Parenting—
Religious aspects—Christianity. 3. Mother and child—Religious
aspects—Christianity. I. Title.
BT78.F54 1996
649'—dc20   96-12499

06	05	04	03	02	01	00	99	98			
15	14	13	12	11	10	9	8	7	6	5	4	3

For my friend Norma Jeter
who "supplied what was lacking"
in my hands that could not type
and in many, many other ways

CONTENTS

FOREWORD

MOST PARENTS IN AMERICA ARE RUNNING SCARED. BUT MOTHERS particularly are ill at ease because they know intuitively that they place a unique rudder in children's minds. Fathers generally represent the world outside, but moms teach how to be a person in that world. As children move away from their mother, they carry part of her with them. Eminent Professor Louise J. Kaplan has written, "a young child's sense of well-being comes from having enough good-mother and good self-experience to permit him to continue functioning as a separate self . . ." (*Oneness and Separateness*). The quiet question persists, am I steering my child properly?

In our increasingly complex and rapidly changing world, how can a mother know the correct setting for the compass, especially if she herself has reeled in the confusing classroom and the harsh business world? Lael Arrington moves to front and center with thoughtful answers to this dilemma. Hers is no pat-answer, pollyanna response. Here is a hiker in the cultural jungle, hacking a path through the issues of abortion, euthanasia, evolution, animal rights, and mothers in the marketplace. She, like all of us, has seen too many children get lost in the intellectual woods.

Who should read this book? *Worldproofing* is a sturdy discussion, a challenge for every mom (and dad), every pastor, every person who knows and cares about the influence of a mother. It is also an instruction manual with creative suggestions for putting big ideas into bite-size portions.

Lael is a real-life been-there-done-that woman. Although she is a cogent thinker, her human emotions show through. She is funny—with a myriad of chuckles from lawyer jokes to the embarrassment of finding herself on the front row of a fashionable wedding ceremony with a price tag blatantly visible on her new suit. She is poignant, disclosing her own battle with serious illness, her own downers with disappointments.

The solutions found in these pages spring from a biblical base. They are solid, practical explanations of issues confronting our contemporary world. At a time when many of us are disoriented, squinting into our foggy hodgepodge of ideas, here are bright, readable direction signs. They will light up Christian homes, church libraries, and the desks of youth leaders. This compelling guidebook can bring in-depth understanding of complex issues, and it can also furnish on-the-spot guidance. A needed volume, it is thought-provoking, delightfully engaging—a heads-up choreography for our part in these challenging, turbulent times.

—Howard and Jeanne Hendricks,
Center for Christian Leadership,
Dallas Theological Seminary

THE "WITHOUT WHOM" DEPARTMENT

I ACKNOWLEDGE
MY GREAT APPRECIATION TO:

My husband and son—Jack and Zach Arrington—and Cal and Mollie Axtell and Dave and Patty LaRoche. When I first shared my plans to write a book, each asked: "Are you going to put my name in it?" Yes.

I do wish to thank you, my wonderful husband, Jack, and my fine son Zach, without whom this book truly would not have been possible: Jack for ever-ready, always thoughtful theological support, computer support, daily and deadline support, and faithful, loving leadership; Zach for being the lab where so much of this "lecture" was developed and for contributing his pages to the project. He keeps us challenged with his great mind and laughing with his great humor.

THEN THANKS TO:

All the dear friends whose feedback over the past three and a half years has shaped the final product, especially Mollie, Helen Durham, Kathy Graumann, Melvin Hawkins, Dick Frey, and the rest of our Rosehill Writers' Guild. I'm sure you can all find the sentences you helped to craft.

Mom and Dad, Erin, Shirley, and Shirley Ann, and so many of our Tomball Bible Church family who have given their prayers and encouragement and have shared their stories, which brought my story to life.

And all the dear friends who have typed and typed and retyped. Thanks to Sue Donovan, Pat Stevens, Penny Jennings, and especially Norma Jeter who took one of the last handwritten manuscripts in America and made it a book. Thanks, Norma, for offering to type in the beginning and launching the whole project—then keeping it going with your great research.

Lindsey O'Connor—if you had not walked into my class and my life, I would not have known how to write or market a book. Thank you for being God's gift to mentor me along and for believing in me—that my gifts were sufficient to the task. I missed writing together on the phone when you finished your book before I finished mine!

Dr. Francis Schaeffer and then Chuck Colson for mentoring me through their writings. Also Texas State Board of Education member Donna Ballard, and Professors Marvin Olasky and Phillip Johnson, whose books have been so helpful and who took the time to look at my chapters. My deepest thanks to Professor Johnson for speedy assistance and words of encouragement that really helped at deadline time.

I feel as if I had the blessing of having three editors: John Eldredge from Focus on the Family, who challenged me to think higher and deeper through his thoughtful commentary on my manuscript; Patty LaRoche who helped me make it accessible without dumbing it down (while "laughing all the way"); and Lila Bishop at Crossway who took me even farther in both directions. What a joy to have an editor who makes me sound like me, only better, and in whose heart and ideas I found such a kindred spirit.

And finally, Lord, You have charted the course of this life from which this book flows. You know all the doors You opened and the gifts You gave me, and I have journaled them for my own remembrance. I have no idea what You plan to do with this strange hybrid of cat stories, lawyer jokes, presuppositions, and postmodernism. May it all be for Your glory. I know You will continue to surprise me.

YOU KNOW YOU NEED
THIS BOOK IF . . .

➤ you think a multiculturalist is someone who subscribes to the symphony, the ballet, *and* the opera.

➤ you stand on the rim of the Grand Canyon and feel tempted to cave in to Charles Darwin and Carl Sagan.

➤ you picked up one of Francis Schaeffer's books to read, and by the fourth page you found yourself wondering if the socks you just put in the wash were going to bleed on your husband's favorite T-shirt.

➤ you read that the *Time* movie critic described *Mission Impossible* as "postmodern," which you thought described a line of home furnishings at Pier One.

➤ you think all true Christians are Democrats.

➤ you feel that monitoring your children's entertainment choices is harder than playing Whack the Mole at the pizza parlor—you settle on a movie choice, and up pops a scary book they want to read; you make a call on the book, and up pops a hot new record they just have to have; pop-whack! pop-whack!

➤ you think all true Christians are Republicans.

➤ the cultural voices and ideas contending for your children's hearts and minds are no longer just background noise, but rock-strewn rapids that tilt and smack your family's life raft and propel you faster downstream. You can't see the river ahead, but you can see the canyon narrowing, and you can hear a distant roar.

> you could use some help worldproofing your kids and preparing them to navigate today's turbulent times—at least as much as any mom can.

When you sit at the beauty salon or the PTA meeting and hear someone carry on about truth being "whatever works for me," do you sit there uneasily, thinking, _I know that she's wrong, and I don't believe that,_ but you are unable to articulate why she's wrong? When Johnny is asked to prepare for a debate on animal "rights," do you know what principles are involved and where to find biblical support for your values? Can you help Johnny understand why we draw a line between animal life and human life and how he can communicate that to his class and teacher? This book offers practical help to teach your children a Christian view of the world, especially in key areas of cultural debate.

In a sort of handbook form, each chapter in this book takes up a different cultural issue and helps you see how this got to be an issue, what God's Word says about it, and how you can discuss it with those who reject the Bible's authority. Specific teaching strategies, learning activities, and resources on the issues equip you to teach God's truth about each issue to your children. And best of all, in the last part, Bible studies written to accompany each chapter guide you through your _own_ study of Scriptures that speak to these issues. I humbly acknowledge that many books have been written about each of these topics. If you would appreciate help from a summary that respects their complexity but tries to convey their substance to moms with Little League, a checkbook to balance, a house to run, and perhaps a job outside the home, then here it is.

In order to navigate our life rafts around the half-submerged rocks of Darwinian evolution or avoid getting sucked into the entertain-me-to-death whirlpool, we can take a cue from the sons of Issachar. First Chronicles 12 lists those outstanding leaders of Israel who helped David establish his kingdom after Saul's death. Thousands of brave skilled warriors are listed, all prepared to do battle. In the middle of the list, 200 men from the tribe of Issachar are honored—"men who understood the times and knew what Israel should do." (I'm sure they had smart wives!)

This book will help *you* understand today's turbulent times—times when the meaning seems to be leaking out of people's lives. The first part deals with the most abstract but most important larger issue: the meaning of truth in a culture that is no longer Christian. What *is* truth? If white is "true for me" and black is "true for you," and everyone else "feels" rather gray, how do we teach our children to cling to what is *really* true, especially in a world of endless options and opinions?

Part Two deals with *personal value*. What does "personhood" mean? Your answer has everything to do with what you believe about how the world began. If there is no Creator, then there is no image of God, only "rights"—animal "rights," abortion "rights," the "right" to die. But if there is no Creator, who gives the "rights"?

Work, leisure, and the richer life are addressed in Part Three. How shall we invest the time and talent God gives us in a meaningful way? The Entertainment Culture beckons to our children, "Jump on the treadmill! Work is only the means . . . the end is money and the cool things and entertainment it can buy. 'Must go faster!'"

And finally, Part Four looks at our *citizenship*—our sense of belonging. How does our destination impart meaning to our lives? As we observe our social fabric fraying at the edges, do we panic, withdraw? Or does the increasing chaos make us feel even more "homesick at home" (G. K. Chesterton)?

Through it all we try to keep our sense of humor. It is a challenge but also a joy to see our children learn to paddle and spot the dangers. We may wish God had launched us down Lazy River, but it's here on Thunder River that He plans an adventure to strengthen our faith and grow our character. The wettest, wildest amusement park thrill rides pale in comparison.

TRUTH

*Okay, what happened
to the map?*

AS THE WORLD CHURNS

1

≈

Understanding
Our Turbulent Times

IT WAS DEFINITELY DEAD, THEY DECIDED.

Clutching their Dillard's shopping bags, Ellen and Kay woefully gazed down at the ex-cat in the mall parking lot. Obviously a recent hit—no flies, no smell.

"What business could that poor kitty have had here?" murmured Ellen.

"Come on, Ellen, we've got to just . . ."

But Ellen had already grabbed her shopping bag and was explaining, "I'll just put my things in your bag, and then I'll take the tissue . . ."

She dumped her purchases into Kay's bag and then used the tissue paper to cradle and lower the former feline into her own Dillard's bag and cover it. They continued the short trek to the car in silence, stashing their goods in the trunk. But it occurred to both of them that if they left Ellen's burial bag in the trunk, warmed by the Texas sunshine while they ate, Kay's Lumina would soon lose that new-car smell.

They decided just to leave the bag on top of the trunk, and they headed over to Luby's Cafeteria. After they cleared the serving line and sat down at a window table, they had a view of Kay's Chevy with the Dillard's bag still on the trunk.

But not for long. As they ate, they noticed a black-haired woman in a red gingham shirt stroll by their car, look quickly this way and that, and then hook the Dillard's bag without breaking stride. She quickly walked out of their line of vision.

Kay and Ellen shot each other a wide-eyed look of amazement. It all happened so fast that neither of them could think how to respond. "Can you imagine?" finally sputtered Ellen. "The nerve of that woman!"

Kay sympathized with Ellen, but inwardly a laugh was building as she thought about the grand surprise awaiting the red-gingham thief. Just when she thought she would have to giggle into her napkin, she noticed Ellen's eyes freeze in the direction of the serving line. Following her gaze, Kay recognized with a shock the black-haired woman with the Dillard's bag, _the_ Dillard's bag, hanging from her arm, brazenly pushing her tray toward the cashier.

Helplessly they watched the scene unfold. After clearing the register, the woman settled at a table across from theirs, put the bag on an empty chair and began to eat. After a few bites of baked whitefish and green beans, she casually lifted the bag into her lap to survey her treasure. Looking from side to side but not far enough to notice her rapt audience three tables over, she pulled out the tissue paper and peered into the bag. Her eyes widened, and she began to make a sort of gasping noise.

The noise grew. The bag slid from her lap as she sank to the floor, wheezing and clutching her upper chest. The beverage cart attendant quickly recognized a customer in trouble and sent the busboy to call 911, while she administered the Heimlich maneuver. A crowd quickly gathered that did not include Ellen and Kay, who remained riveted to their chairs for seven whole minutes until the ambulance arrived.

In a matter of minutes the curly-haired woman emerged from the crowd, still gasping, strapped on a gurney. Two well-trained EMS volunteers steered her to the waiting ambulance, while a third scooped up her belongings. The last they saw of the distressed cat-burglar, she disappeared behind the ambulance doors, the Dillard's bag perched on her stomach.

My friend Vivian's former brother-in-law swears this is a true story. And I've heard a couple of other versions, which makes me think that the basics must be true. Whenever it is passed around, people listening have had a similar reaction. After the laughter subsides, they say things like, "Justice prevails!" or "There _is_ a God!" This story, like many experiences in everyday life, seems to resonate and connect with some kind of meaning written in our hearts. There was a certain "poetic justice" (and certainly entertaining justice) for one overcome cat-snatcher who deserved that rude shock, we muse. Unfair episodes happen daily, and sometimes we long for revenge. We all seem to share this transcendent ideal of "justice."

Well, not all. Our children face a world that is losing confidence in shared ideals such as justice. A young man is killed for his Reeboks; a child whose day care center happened to be in a bombed federal building lies limp in a rescuer's arms. These assaults on our sense of justice are headline news. But the thinking that brushes aside our shared sense of justice begins in obscure places across our country, sometimes even in a classroom . . .

"With Liberty and the Need to Reduce Pain for All"

I can tell you about one class I visited in the fall of 1995. Dr. Phillip Johnson, professor of law at the University of California (Berkeley) and an articulate Christian author, was presenting a case to the University of Texas Law School students for the existence of "universal, transcultural standards" (such as justice and truth) as the basis of law.

But a UT constitutional law professor contested his ideas. "I hate to use words like *justice* and *morality*," the professor countered. "They just obfuscate [confuse] the debate." Imagine my surprise. I found out there is no standard of absolute justice behind our laws and inspiring our Constitution. I felt a little "obfuscated" myself.

The professor went on to explain that rights don't exist until governments grant them. In a "world of scarce resources" governments must determine "how to organize all these living organisms" so that "pain should be avoided or mitigated." In other words, there are no God-given inalienable rights to life, liberty, or anything. No ideals of justice or goodness. Just the need to reduce pain. And that is the only basis of law.

Oh.

So if somehow you could measure and prove that the majority of people experienced far less pain at the expense of a small minority experiencing some pain, then the professor's approach to law would justify, *excuse me, allow*, slave labor. When I put this to him as a question, he agreed—slavery would be allowed. (And my taxes go to support this man.)

This professor's worldview led him to some fairly astonishing conclusions. Here's a teacher of constitutional law who believes that justice and morality are beside the point. If the majority is well served by slavery, then so be it. He believes that only the material world is real. There is no supernatural Person or transcendent ideal to give us the meaning of justice or morality. His is a small view of the world that reduces everything to atoms, molecules, genes, numbers, economics, and chance. If larger numbers of people want legalized abortion or the "right" to die, then like slavery, so be it.

This is a view of the world that another agnostic, British author and journalist G. K. Chesterton, could not buy. Chesterton gazed deeply into the mysteries of the human spirit, of art, ecstasy, and beauty; at the soaring ideals of justice, virtue, and charity, and confessed, "I felt in my bones; first, this world does not explain itself. . . . The thing is magic, true or false. Second, I came to feel as if magic must have a meaning, and meaning must have someone to mean it. There was something personal in the world, as in a work of art; whatever it meant, it meant violently" (*Orthodoxy,* pp. 65-66).

Chesterton lived at the turn of the last century, but he wrestled with the secular worldview so many embrace today. Chesterton flirted with the first generation of Darwin enthusiasts, but rejected them. He sensed that life is a story with meaning, and that that story has an Author. Only in the Christian story did he find a worldview large enough to account for the expanse of life and the depth of meaning he observed.

This Christian view that life makes sense as a story implies several things, as Gene Veith explains in *Postmodern Times.* We understand that "life has a meaning, a plot complete with conflicts (the battle with sin), a turning point (accepting or rejecting Christ), and a final resolution with either a tragic ending (namely hell) or a comic ending (heaven)" (p. 130).

Talking about life as a story helps us understand what we may take for granted and what so many in our world have lost sight of. For over 2,000 years Christianity has been presented to the world as a story—"the greatest story ever told." And what we see in the cultural white water around us is that our world has lost its story, and with it, a strong sense of meaning, truth, and values like justice. We'll return to this idea later.

Now, as we begin to bring our Christian worldview into sharp

focus, it helps to review the basics of God's story—the biblical narrative that gives meaning to our lives and rock-solid content to our
beliefs. From the pages of *Orthodoxy*, Chesterton's spiritual biography,
I gleaned a wonderful phrase that fits well with the metaphor of this
book. Instead of just reviewing the basic truths of Christianity, or even
the beginning events of the Christian story in Genesis, let's launch out
with a figurative perspective from Chesterton's quote: "According to
Christianity, we are indeed the survivors of a wreck, the crew of a
golden ship that had gone down before the beginning of the world."

THE GOLDEN SHIP

In the beginning of His Grand Story, God created a great golden ship
with towering masts and pearlescent billowing sails that gleamed in
the sunlight. It was provisioned with a stunning array of exotic fruits
and other creature comforts for its breathtakingly scenic and adven-
turous voyage to Celebration Bay.

Now if I had written the story, I would have had the ship cruising
through lovely weather down a wide and deep river—no tricky cross-
currents or shifting sandbars. And the crew, a delightful married couple, would have spawned a number of other families, who would have
built new ships as needed, gradually merging into one grand flotilla of
glorious ships, flags fluttering, headed for the Bay.

And just like in Lake Wobegon, all "the women [would be] strong,
and the men [would be] good-looking." After storybook romances
they would marry and raise loving, deeply bonded families where the
children would be "all above average," love their school lessons, truly
appreciate the good life they lead, and never be bored. Each new day
would dawn with the promise of challenge without threat, bring interesting problems to solve without frustration, and offer new opportunities to explore and enjoy the journey without danger. No pain,
disaster, or heartache on the blue-skies-and-rainbows horizon.

I would have written a fairy tale. But not God. He had a sweeping
epic romance in mind. His golden vessel gets shipwrecked in the *third*
chapter. Instead of relying on Him to pilot them safely, that delightful couple, even though made in His image, grasped the rudder and
steered straight into tragedy—huge rocks of deceit, pride, and faith-

lessness. As a result, even the weather has grown ugly and the scenery and the river itself inhospitable. We _are_ the survivors of that shipwreck. We long for the beauty of our lost golden ship or the safe harbor of Celebration Bay. But we find ourselves headed downriver in life rafts that are hopefully adequate but often uncomfortable. Apart from God's grace, we would never make it.

As characters in God's Grand Story, we may question what the Author has done. Why write a story with so much pain and heartache? And at times we can begin to doubt God's heart, thinking of Him as only the brains behind the Story, boldly and powerfully directing the plot as He pleases.

But to think of God as only the Author of the Story misses the point. As Brent Curtis and John Eldredge have explained so beautifully in their book _The Sacred Romance,_ God is not just the Author. Through the Incarnation, God stepped right into His own story and in amazing love offered His own life in exchange for ours. Even the chapter on the Fall includes a promise of His coming (Genesis 3:15). Can there remain any doubt about God's heart?

From Genesis 3 on, the Bible tells us how God takes hopes, dreams, lives, and even nations after they are wrecked and smashed beyond imagining, and heals, restores, and redeems them into something new and deeply beautiful. Jesus' death and resurrection set the pattern for all of creation to follow.

Each of us as a fallen creature is determined to grasp the rudder and steer our own course. But our loving Father pursues us and woos us to acknowledge our sinful desire for control and put our faith in His Son's gracious sacrifice as the only acceptable payment for our sins. Then He is quick to forgive and restore. He helps us set a new course and grow to maturity in His Son. He provisions us with the riches of His Word, His Spirit, and "every spiritual blessing" we'll need to make it to Celebration Bay.

As we round the bend that is the Turn of the Twentieth Century, we see a river full of rapids, side channels, huge piles of boulders, and even some waterfalls. Our culture's confusion over truth and the loss of meaning loom as dangerous obstacles to our safe passage. Developing a Christian worldview and passing it on to our children is our strongest protection for the cultural white water ahead.

MISS SCARLETT IN A CHANGING WORLD

Most of us think of our lives in the context of God's Grand Story (without the nautical metaphor). We begin to pass the broad outlines of that story on to our children while they're still in diapers. We stake out where we came from, where we're going. We paint for them a picture of God and Jesus, and as they get older, we story-tell of God's "deep magic," as author C. S. Lewis called it in Narnia—the Fall, the Cross, Christ's atonement, His invitation to forgiveness and restored relationship with God.

Our children need our guidance; they need our navigational skills. In choosing my perspective, I certainly do not mean to undermine the role of fathers as family navigators. In fact many husbands are more immersed in cultural issues than their wives, but I wish to write as a mother to other wives and mothers.

When it comes to women trying to understand cultural issues, my sense of it is that women tend to care less about these ideas than men. As evidence, I offer the fact that you may find the editorial page in the business or sports section of the newspaper, but you will never find it in the Lifestyle section, the Fashion section, or next to the recipe of the week in the Food section. If you go to the women's section in a Christian bookstore, you will find plenty of Bible studies and books about the Bible (obviously), relationships and the home, but little on anything related to cultural issues or ideas. And I would not deny that God has given us a natural bent to be more focused on relationships and our homes.

But unless we live on an island or in a bunker with no TV or computer, these cultural ideas and issues *are* touching our homes and relationships—especially our children. And we know we are accountable to God to protect ourselves and our children from being pushed into the mold of the world's way of thinking (Romans 12:2). Some of these influences are so subtle that we are "half-jelled" before we realize it. Busy, disinterested, overwhelmed? Perhaps you can identify with one of the following profiles:

Profile #1: *The Miss Scarlett Approach*. "Cultural white water? Well, fiddle-dee-dee, I can't think about that today—I'll think about it tomorrow. I'm just too busy. Today I've got three different car pools, tennis lessons, four loads of laundry, company for dinner . . ."

Profile #2: *Go with the Flow.* "Sure, I read the papers." [shrug] "What can you do? Don't make waves, and don't blame me. I voted. I'm just not the radical type."

Profile #3: *I'm Mad, and I'm Not Going to Take It Anymore!* After reading Dr. Dobson's letter, I call for a tape, find out when the next Christian Coalition meeting is, fill out the AFA boycott card, attend the CWA Seminar on Educational Restructuring, sign up to counsel at the Crisis Pregnancy Center; mail checks to Chuck Colson, Rutherford Institute, Family Research Council, and Phyllis Schlafly; order the anti-evolution video from Institute of Creation Research and the American Heritage video from David Barton; renew my subscriptions to *World* and *Citizen* magazines, Ted Baehr's *Movie Guide,* Al Menconi's *Music Update;* read my daughter's science text and library book and conference with her teacher; write my senators and representative and tell them I'm praying for them; pray for them . . . *Red Alert, Red Alert, Overwhelm . . . too much . . . I can't keep up . . . Help, Lord! . . .*

Responding in a balanced way to the cultural pressures we feel is difficult. It is so easy to fall out of the boat on one side (uninformed, apathetic) or the other (overreactive, bitter).

You may not be drawn to cultural issues, but you *are* deeply involved with the training of your children. You may even spend considerably more time with your children than does your husband. You have so many opportunities to teach them a Christian worldview. You probably are already committed to the process. You can use this book as a study guide individually, in women's groups, or with your children to fill in some gaps. I hope it will help answer some questions now and in the future serve as a ready reference for dealing with Susie's teacher or Johnny's friends. (You want to go to *what* concert?)

Many of us cannot imagine life apart from God's Grand Story. We are sharing it with our children. And yet they are growing up among friends, teachers, sports and rock stars who are oblivious to the story. While we try to steer a fairly straight course from the shipwreck to Celebration Bay, we are surrounded by other rafts (and books and stories about rafting) that just drift aimlessly or head straight into harm's way. The river is full of life rafts almost capsizing from the shock waves of divorce, abuse, and neglect. Some rafts are trapped in whirlpools of deceit; others are tossed around and even punctured by dangerous ideas with the power to destroy lives.

We are witnessing America's moral and spiritual decline, but no one needs to hear the same old song with ten more verses of, "Ain't it awful?" We all know America is changing, but the deeper question is, why? Why are we seeing such moral and spiritual decline, and how can we protect our children from the fallout? Why is our culture caught in a crisis of meaning? Simplistic answers such as "godless evolution" or "those bums in _____" (Congress, Hollywood—fill in the blank) won't do. We must "understand the times" in a more probing way. The reason we are seeing moral and spiritual decline in our nation is because, in a nutshell, there has been a huge shift in our nation's most basic beliefs, a deep change in the way we think.

WHY IS THERE AIR?

The Bible has much to say about the way we think. What and how we think is determined by our deepest thoughts of all—beliefs that are so basic we may never really reason them out logically; we just take them for granted. Remember Bill Cosby's profound question, "Why is there air?" Cosby's attempt to explain something so basic, so fundamental, so obvious seemed funny and childlike: "Of course, you need air to blow up basketballs."

One of our deepest beliefs is how we define reality—we tend to take reality for granted. But what *is* real? Is only the material world that we see, hear, and feel real? Or is the material world an illusion? Is the only reality the spiritual world? Is reality some combination of the material and spiritual world? I have a friend who was very upset when her Rolex watch did not survive even the delicate cycle of her washing machine. But a Hindu or a Christian Scientist might respond differently to that material loss, because to them, all material things are illusion. Only the spiritual realm is real.

These most basic, taken-for-granted beliefs are our *presuppositions*. Now *presuppositions* is not a word we use every day at the grocery store or the Little League field. You won't even find it used in the Bible. ("How I long for your presuppositions and keep them with all my heart!") But it's a great word, because we all have them and live according to them, more or less—even if we rarely think about them. The truth is, the great change in our thinking as a nation has occurred in our presuppositions.

Your answers to the following questions are your presuppositions:

> ➤ What is real?

> ➤ Is God real?

> ➤ What is man?

> ➤ Is God involved in human affairs? That is, does He just let us do our own thing and watch us from a distance, or does He help us find parking spaces at the mall the day after Thanksgiving?

> ➤ How do we know what is true? Do we figure something is true because we saw, heard, touched it, or because we read it in our horoscope or in the Bible?

> ➤ How do we judge what is right or wrong? What standard do we use?

The list could go on, but I hope you understand we are talking about a person's basic sense of the way life works.

How do we form our presuppositions? When we are very young, we tend to absorb them from our family, friends, church, TV, etc. I doubt if your mother ever sat you down at a tender age to discuss whether matter is real or illusionary, but if you grew up in America, you probably absorbed the idea that the material world is real, much as a little Hindu child would come to believe that matter is illusion—*maya*. Most presuppositions are caught rather than taught. Consciously or unconsciously, our children have caught our presuppositions.

THE PUZZLE PIECES ON THE CARD TABLE OF YOUR MIND

It has been said that understanding our worldview is like assembling the edge and corner pieces of a jigsaw puzzle. We have all these pieces (our presuppositions, the basic ideas of God's Grand Story, assorted other biblical truths, facts, values, and logical reasons) lying around. But they tend to be disorganized—a corner with three edge pieces over here, twelve connected edge pieces over there, and lots of unconnected pieces mixed in with a number of extra pieces from Oprah, seventh grade science, Peter Jennings, Girl Scouts, Aunt Sally, and the grapevine.

When we confront cultural issues such as evolution, the "right" to die, or the question, "How do we know what is true?" it challenges us right where we keep our puzzle pieces. We try to pull some of the pieces together and come up with an answer. Sometimes we stare at presupposition pieces and wonder how we ever believed them. We toss pieces. We try to *make* pieces fit, knowing they don't. Sometimes we succeed, but it's pretty tough going.

The best way to understand our worldview is to work on figuring out what the pieces mean, deciding where they fit, and then connecting them. This is most certainly the task of a lifetime. And we will never find all the puzzle pieces. There are too many mysteries, paradoxes, and pieces only God knows about. (Plus, I think some of my pieces must have fallen on the floor.) But every piece we fit together helps us "understand the times" and "know what to do."

Here are some practical steps we can take to connect our pieces and make some progress:

> ➤ Know the basics of God's Grand Story. (See Focus Box #1.)

> ➤ Read through and respond thoughtfully to the Bible study for each chapter.

> ➤ As you read Scripture on your own, underline verses that relate to cultural issues in a certain color. Read other related books. Many excellent resources are recommended in Resource Boxes throughout this book. (My puzzle pieces started really coming together for the first time when I read some books by Christian apologist Francis Schaeffer.)

> ➤ Take time to examine your presuppositions thoughtfully. Don't just assume they are true. (See Focus Box #2.)

We can gently encourage our children to sort through their presuppositions, being sensitive to their intellectual maturity. It tends to happen anyway in the course of growing older, usually in the teens or twenties. Our children will naturally "take out" at least some of these presuppositions, examine them, and try to determine whether that is truly what they believe for themselves.

I personally experienced this most intensely in my late twenties, shortly after I was married. (I guess I was too busy having fun earlier.) I grew up in a Christian family with a great heritage. But I remember when I was in graduate school walking across the campus of the University of Texas at Dallas, it seemed as if the sprawling buildings full of Ph.D.'s from Oxford, Harvard, and Princeton represented a huge monolithic consensus that rejected my Christian beliefs. I would feel the weight of that rejection as I walked to classes, and I would quietly pray, "Lord, are these people wrong; am I wrong? Can I stand up to the sheer weight of opinion on the other side? Are You real? Is Your Word true? Is this huge campus built on a foundation of truth or of false beliefs?"

But the reality of years spent in close personal relationship with my Lord Jesus Christ could not be shaken. At that time in particular, I was going through the onset of rheumatoid arthritis and the loss of our dream to teach and minister in Latin America. On the one hand, the intellectual challenge to take a stand for Christ was enormous. But daily, on a personal level, God's grace was the only thing that kept me going in one of the toughest times of my life.

As I wrestled with the intellectual questions, I felt like the apostle Peter. When many of His disciples were deserting Jesus, He asked the remaining twelve, "'You do not want to leave too, do you?' Simon Peter answered him, 'Lord, to whom shall we go? You have the words of eternal life. We believe and *know* that you are the Holy One of God'" [italics mine] (John 6:67-69).

Now, years later, I watch my son as he faces his own struggles. As we see our children go through their own times of sifting and questioning their deepest beliefs, it can be pretty scary. We should understand that the sifting process is a natural part of growing up. We should not take offense at their questions or feel terribly threatened. In fact, we should encourage them to ask lots of questions and share that we have questions of our own. There is so much of God's Story that is mysterious and transcends our capacity to know or understand. We need to teach them the proper limits where reason ends and faith begins.

But we do our children a disservice if we dismiss their desire for reasons (where there *are* reasons) by saying, "Oh, you just have to have faith." We should realize that the more we teach our children—in both formal and informal settings—the reasons and the "whys" of our deepest beliefs, the better prepared they will be to hold them fast in the face of tremendous pressure.

But each one must decide for herself, because presuppositions are ultimately held by faith. They cannot be completely proved or disproved. Is matter an illusion? Is God real? Is the Bible true? Certainly our reason informs our faith, but in the end we must believe by faith that these things are true or real—and so must our children. I continually pray for my son Zach, now a teenager. I am scared that he will grow up and reject my values and beliefs. And I've told him I'm scared. It's not because of him, but because of the craziness out there and because of the statistics about Christian kids.

Once we get a worldview "frame" mostly put together, it gets easier to see how more and more pieces connect into the frame. When we are challenged with a new unfamiliar cultural issue piece tossed out by the media or a teacher, it's easier to figure out if the new piece fits our worldview, and if not, why not. Here's a challenge: read some cultural comments—or listen to someone with whom you think you don't agree. (The editorial page of the newspaper might be a good place to start.) Do you disagree? Why? Figuring out why you disagree will focus and strengthen your worldview. As your children get older, challenge them the same way.

A word to the impatient: if you just want ten reasons why *not* to cave in to Charles Darwin/Carl Sagan or a quick explanation of postmodernism, if you're ready to skip over this worldview stuff and get on to the practical part later on, then let me share my adaptation of a challenge from *Victory over Darkness* by Neil Anderson.

> We want a quick fix, a rule or instructions we can apply like a Band-Aid to make [navigating] easier. We don't have time to wade through the deep theological concepts of Scripture; we want a [focused worldview] and we want it now. Perhaps you have already discovered that a Band-Aid approach to ["understanding the times" and "knowing what we should do"] doesn't work worth a hoot. Why not? Because when you don't understand the doctrinal truths [that sustain your worldview, it will be out of focus and you will run into a rock] (pp. 53-54).

In America today, we all feel great cultural tension stemming from the change in the way we think. Even though the term "culture war" has become something of a cliché, it nevertheless addresses the reality of a conflict over control in our culture. As one editorialist has described it, our cultural struggle is about "power; it is about who determines the norms by which we live, and by which we define and govern ourselves. Who decides what is right and wrong, moral and immoral, beautiful and ugly, healthy and sick. Whose beliefs shall form the basis of law?" Our cultural conflict is a struggle between different worldviews—more specifically between deeply held presuppositions. All the differences over what is true, evolution, abortion, the "right" to die, media bias, and all the rest of it boils down to a heated disagreement over one crucial presupposition—the subject of the next chapter.

FOCUS YOUR WORLDVIEW #1: GOD'S GRAND STORY

Sprinkled throughout the book you will find boxes like this with suggested activities and creative ways to discuss these ideas with your children. All are intended for "as-you-walk-along-the-way" times or family night or devotional settings. They reflect the kinds of teaching strategies I have used in my home and teaching in and working with private Christian schools. I think they would also be helpful to moms who are home-schooling.

Suggestion: I produced some real family heirlooms as a child— some eight- to ten-page books, fully illustrated, telling the story of a rabbit in a garden and a mother horse with a little "clot" (colt). Instead of a wordless book with black-red-white-green-and-gold to tell the basics of God's Grand Story, take the elements listed below and let your kids expand them to tell the story in your own family's words. Have them suggest chapter titles. Let the writers in your family write it and the artists illustrate.

CHARACTERS

God the Father, Son, Holy Spirit—eternal, loving, righteous, all-powerful, all-knowing, never changing King of Kings and heroic Savior—*Adam and Eve, all their descendants, the angels, Satan*—a rebellious angel, Prince of Darkness

PLOT

Creation—it all begins perfectly: out of love God made Adam and Eve and prepared for them a beautiful paradise. Then . . .

Fall—Adam and Eve reject God and disobey Him; sin messes up God's creation.

God pursued a people for Himself—Noah, Abraham, Moses, and the nation of Israel

Israel and Judah finally reject God—they are destroyed and scattered by foreign armies. Only a few remain in Jerusalem.

Christ—enters the story as the hero to sacrifice His life.

Cross—Jesus took our punishment on Himself.

Resurrection—Christ broke the power of sin—opened the way to regain our lost love relationship with God.

Like the *disciples,* those who accept Christ as Savior become the church, His bride; but like *Judas* we may reject Him.

The Day of the Lord—those who trust Christ will live in love with Him forever; those who reject Him will suffer eternal punishment.

Suggestion: (older children) Write a book review of God's Grand Story as an *adventure* epic, a great *romance*—God pursuing and wooing us in love—or even as a *mystery.*

Suggestion: As an alternative, have your children role play this drama with costumes and dialogue.

FOCUS YOUR WORLDVIEW #2: DEAR GOD . . .

"Are you really invisible, or is that just a trick?"   —*Lucy*

"How did you know you were God?"   —*Charlene*

And from one wrestling with a Hindu puzzle piece:
"If-we-come-back-as-something-please-don't-let-me-be-Jennifer-Horton-because-I-hate-her."   —*Denise*

—*From Children's Letters to God*

Children are thinking about and questioning things that we just assumed a long time ago. Their questions are much more creative than mine below, but maybe these will prime the pump.

1. *What is real?* (Options: material world, spiritual world, or both?) *Is God real?* (Genesis 1:1; Colossians 1:15-17; Hebrews 11:1-3;

2 Corinthians 4:16-18; Romans 1:18-20; Acts 17:23-29; Jeremiah 10:3-10)

Suggestion: In a closed setting, such as a room in your house, ask your children, "What is real in this room?" Have them list what they can see, hear, touch, smell, taste. Challenge them to list things that are also unseen. (Air, cold viruses, radio and TV waves.) How do they know the unseen things are real? Probably by cause and effect. The unseen affects the seen.

Jesus said the same thing in John 3:8: "The wind blows wherever it pleases. You hear its sound [its effect on the seen], but you cannot tell where it comes from or where it is going. So it is with everyone born of the Spirit." By faith we *believe* God's Word to be true, but we also *see* the effect of the spiritual world (unseen) on the visible world.

What spiritual reality is also present in the room? (Holy Spirit, maybe guardian angels, spiritual interaction or warfare.) What difference has it made in the seen world inside your home lately? What difference have you made on the unseen world?

Suggestion: (High schoolers) From a copy of Francis Schaeffer's *Death in the City,* write a skit based on chapter 9, "The Universe and Two Chairs." To the Christian and materialist chairs you may want to add a New Age/Hindu chair (only the spiritual world is real). The spiritualists' lines could add some humor. Perform the skit as a play or reader's theater.

To quote Schaeffer:

> . . . supernatural is not a good word to describe the unseen portion. We must understand that the unseen portion of the universe is just as natural as the seen portion. Furthermore the seen and the unseen are not totally separated. When we do certain things, it makes a difference in the unseen world, and things in the unseen world make a difference in the seen world.
>
> —*Death in the City*, p. 130

The point is, we must not live our lives as though only half the universe were real.

2. *What is man?* (Genesis 1:27; Psalm 8:4-5; Romans 5:12; Hebrews 9:27) *How can he be forgiven?* (Romans 3:21-25; John 3:16)

Suggestion: (For high schoolers) Look up the word *paradox*. In what ways, do you think, is man's nature a paradox? To quote

Chesterton, a paradox is neither a compromise nor a balance between two extremes, but "both things at the top of their energy." "One can hardly think too little of one's self. One can hardly think too much of one's soul."

Contrast the biblical view of man's nature with Aristotle's view of human nature and moral virtue. From the Nicomachean Ethics, *Book of Virtues,* pp. 101-102.

3. *Is God involved in human affairs?* (Matthew 10:29-31; Psalm 139; Luke 12:27-31; Proverbs 21:1; Daniel 4:35)

Suggestion: Look up the definition of a Deist. Who were some famous Deists? If you were going to talk to Ben Franklin or Thomas Jefferson, list some of the greatest things God has done in our world that you might tell them about. List some of the smallest things God has done for you that still meant a great deal.

4. *How do we know what is true?* (Isaiah 45:19; John 3:31-32; 14:6; 17:17; 2 Corinthians 5:7)

Suggestion: Most children will think of scientific or sensory proof (what we see, smell, hear, touch, feel). What about mathematical proof? Legal or logical proof? Can your children give an example of each of the three kinds of proof? How is faith different from proof? Is faith less certain than proof? Why or why not?

Great resource on proof: *Evidence That Demands a Verdict* by Josh McDowell.

5. *How do we judge what is right and wrong?* (Hebrews 4:12-13; Proverbs 1:1-7; Psalm 119:9-11)

Suggestion: Give examples of how what's right keeps changing from time to time and place to place if we only rely on reason and experience. How is it different if we rely on God's revelation? What is the danger of revelation? (Jim Jones, David Koresh) How do we avoid the danger?

Suggestion: Play one of your favorite games, and toss out the rules, or for once, let everyone make up the rules as they go along! What happens? Talk about the benefits of rules.

THE HEART OF THE MATTER

2

*Who Makes
the Rules?*

ROCK MUSIC . . . DRUGS . . . FREE LOVE . . . ANTI-WAR DEMONSTRATIONS . . . "God is dead, and we did it for the kids." . . . For many of us the cultural revolution of the sixties is forever preserved in poignant images in the museum of our minds. I can remember looking out a classroom window watching our first "hippyfied" student body president of the University of Texas leading a sort of weird ring-around-the-rosy dance on the mall. I can remember the same mall packed with thousands of students listening to angry speeches against the government in the wake of Kent State and my parents' frantic phone calls: "Now, Lael, you stay away from those demonstrations. Did you hear me? Stay away!"

The year 1993 marked the twenty-fifth anniversary of the year 1968—by all accounts a watershed in American history. The "cruel war was raging" in Vietnam, and rebellious students took to the streets in America, France, Mexico City, Prague, Beijing, Tokyo, and Berlin. At the Democratic National Convention, more than 100 protesters were bloodied or beaten as thousands marched; it was also the year Dr. Martin Luther King and Bobby Kennedy were assassinated.

The following is a contrived "dialogue" of quotes between two people who both wrote retrospectives on that tumultuous year— Barbara Ehrenreich (*Time* magazine essayist) and Dr. James Dobson (from his May 1993 Focus on the Family monthly letter).

"It was the best of times."   —*Barbara Ehrenreich*

"What a distressing and significant period that was in our history."   —*James Dobson*

It was "a global breakthrough for the human spirit."   —*Ehrenreich*

And ever since then, "society (has flailed) about in search of what has been lost."   —*Dobson*

"'68 was one more awkward, stumbling half-step forward in . . . the 'long march' toward human freedom."   —*Ehrenreich*

"We took a wrong turn back there . . . departing from the biblical standard and substituting our own puny ideas for the wisdom of the ages."   —*Dobson*

"Hats off to '68 and . . . bras . . . !"   —*Ehrenreich*

"This backward look should make us feel better about our present circumstances. As crazy as our world seems . . . it could be worse."   —*Dobson*

"On this, the twenty-fifth anniversary of 1968, probably the only thing we can all agree on is that '68 marks the beginning of the 'culture wars,' which have divided America ever since."   —*Ehrenreich*

In our family "skit box" we keep a few relics of the sixties—my psychedelic fringed blouse and orange fishnet hose, my husband's peace sign shirt and love beads. When we pull them out and tell stories about growing up in the sixties, it must seem as foreign and distant to our son Zach as did our parents' stories of the Great Depression and World War II. (A sobering thought—I *feel so young!*) But I don't want to just tell Zach about rock concerts and war protests; I want to explain the beginnings of our culture wars and answer the question, "How did it get so crazy?" (See Focus Box #3.)

FROM THE FOUNDING FATHERS TO THE MAMAS AND PAPAS—
A BRIEF HISTORY

Our founders were not all Christians. But they shared enough pre-suppositions about who God is, what is true, and what is moral that they established a nation built largely on a biblical worldview. Most of them took seriously the truth of Psalm 33:12: "Blessed is the nation whose God is the Lord."

FOCUS YOUR WORLDVIEW #3: SIXTIES SHOW-AND-TELL

Our children enjoy that sense of immediate connection with the past that our storytelling gives them. Use a sixties show-and-tell night to create interest and then explain the changes that occurred in our cultural beliefs during the late sixties and early seventies.

➤ Pull out old clothes.

➤ Look at old pictures/photo albums.

➤ Play some old records (not just the "bubble gum" stuff, but songs with a message—"Revolution," "Fool on the Hill," "Four Dead in Ohio," etc.)

➤ Honestly storytell from your own experience; talk about how the cultural revolution did or did not affect you and why.

Our status as a Judeo-Christian nation was largely unchallenged until after World War II. Since then we have experienced increasing legal, moral, and cultural challenges to that status. Why? Several major trends have been factors.

First, our culture was already becoming increasingly secular. The influence of ideas from Charles Darwin, Sigmund Freud, Karl Marx, and others gathered momentum through the early years of the twentieth century, but the effect was for the most part limited to the intellectual elite and the universities.

Two world wars and a depression interrupted the cultivation of these intellectual seeds. As Christian sociologist Os Guinness writes

(*The American Hour,* p. 68), after World War II, "Due to the expansion of education (especially following the G. I. Bill in 1944), the wider dissemination of new ideas through the mass media, and the rising postwar status of academic (elites) . . . the intellectual revolution burst its dams and flooded into almost every sector of American life." The secular ideas finally bore fruit in the cultural revolution of the sixties, which completed our change from a Christian nation to a post-Christian nation.

The Baby Boom generation was the first to grow up with a youth culture all its own. For generations values had been transmitted from one generation to the next, from parents to children, aided by churches and schools. But the wildly popular mass media of TV and radio disrupted that pattern. Young people were exposed to new secular ideas and values that were in deep conflict with those of their own families and communities. Finding your "thrill on Blueberry Hill" had always been a common enough quest, but pursued in secret and fear of shameful exposure. Now it was celebrated on the Top 40.

Francis Schaeffer wrote that his generation (the Builders), more so than any that came before it, "knew the truth and yet turned away . . . not only from the biblical truth of the Reformation, but turned away from the total culture built on that truth" (*Death in the City,* p. 14). The Boomers' parents believed in the Christian story more in name than in substance, while they increasingly pursued the values of personal peace and affluence. Sensing no depth in their parents' "Christian" values, and wooed by secular voices coming from our culture's institutions (the media, schools, and courts), the Boomers chose a new course.

The acceptance of secular values finally reached a "critical mass." It was as if the majority of the generation of the sixties collectively passed through that sifting, questioning time and decided to reject completely what their parents had rejected in essence. They decided as a large and vocal group that they no longer shared belief in the Grand Story or the Author, nor did they want to maintain the outer traditions and trappings. They turned to new stories about the Ascent of Man or the Triumph of Certain Principles—Freedom, Peace, Love, or Democracy.

Additionally the vast increase in immigration from non-Christian countries after the war produced an increasingly diverse society.

Pluralism in America is now a *fact*. My doctors are Indian, our high school cum laudes are Asian, and all the guys at the Stop 'N Go speak Urdu or maybe Farsi.

While Pat Buchanan brought the issue of the culture war to national attention at the 1992 Republican Convention, he was certainly not the first to address it. Dr. James Dobson, in his book *Children at Risk,* warned of a "great civil war of values." Chuck Colson, writing in *Against the Night,* described the "new Barbarians" whose ideas pose a tremendous threat to civilization as we know it.

In America we haven't been drawn into cultural struggles until recently, because the support for abortion, homosexual "rights," condom distribution, etc., was powerless in the face of the Christian consensus. Things have changed. This conflict did not start because Christians and conservatives suddenly wanted more restrictions on abortions, homosexuals, and sex education. It started because supporters of these issues began to win court cases and cultural approval, and many Christians and conservatives found themselves on the defensive. To really understand how things have gotten so crazy and why laws and cultural approval have changed, we must focus in on our deep differences over one crucial presupposition: the source of moral authority.

WHO MAKES THE RULES?

In 1991 James Davison Hunter described the change that has taken place since the sixties in an insightful book called *Culture Wars*. Remember our presuppositions? One of the most crucial concerns is *who* determines what is morally right and wrong. Who makes the rules? You could say that in America the courts make the rules. But as we just pointed out, the courts have changed. They used to rule that abortion was wrong and school prayer was right. Why have they changed?

Because as a nation, as a culture, our presuppositions have changed. Especially our belief about who makes the rules has changed. As a nation we used to believe that there is a God who is real, who is independent of man, and who existed before human beings with unlimited power and wisdom. We believed that God makes the rules regarding right and wrong and that He communicated those rules to us through special revelation. Religious Americans have always disagreed on the approved list of that special revelation—whether it includes Old and New Testaments, the Torah, the pope, church tradition, the *Book of Mormon*, etc.

But these Scriptures and teachings contain a common view of a moral order—a transcendent, universal value system ordained by God. Millions of people in America still believe this. Hunter calls them the "orthodox" community—a better label, I think, than "Christian" or "conservative," since it includes orthodox Jews, Mormons, conservative Catholics, Fundamentalists, evangelical Protestants, and some who might be politically moderate or liberal on some issues. It would even include some classical humanists who subscribe to that moral order or at least to a transcendent ideal.

When I was growing up (and long before), the battle over the source of moral authority in our culture focused more on the differences between Protestants and Catholics. A core belief of the Reformation was *Sola Scriptura*. Only Scripture is the basis of moral authority—not Scripture and the pope, or Scripture and church tradition, but Scripture *alone*. Joel Belz has observed in *World* magazine: "What drives so many Protestant Evangelicals and Catholics together these days is the sheer mass of other people who reject authority of any kind." Now we link arms with conservative Catholics, Jews, and Mormons to protest abortion on demand, special homosexual rights, and condom distribution to our junior high students.

On the other side of the culture war, we often confront Reformed Jews, liberal Catholics, some mainline Protestants, and secular humanists banded together to support these practices. Hunter calls this group the "progressives." The cultural line in the sand—the great cultural divide is this: Progressives do not believe that moral truth is universal and final. They do not believe in special revelation from God that lays down what is morally right and wrong for all people for all time. They believe that the language and content of these ancient faiths is no longer completely relevant for modern times, that while faith can be important, it is at best a guide, and that ultimately *man makes the rules*.

"I would never seek to solve the ethical problems of the twentieth century by quoting a passage of Holy Scripture, and I read the Bible every day," says progressive Episcopal Bishop John Spong of Newark, New Jersey. "I wouldn't invest a book that was written between 1000 B.C. and A.D. 150 with that kind of moral authority" (*Time,* 11/15/93). Progressives reject universal transcendent moral truth given to us by an eternal God. They believe that what is true is *relative* to current circumstances and needs, and they believe that people can figure out what's true based on their own reason and experience.

This belief that man should make the rules is called *moral relativism*. Even though they may not know the label, this is what many of our children's teachers and friends believe. Truth may differ from time to time and place to place. Relative truth can be the advice of an "expert": "Sadism is all right in its place, but it should be directed to proper ends" (Sigmund Freud). Truth can be the result of a majority vote: How far should you go on the first date? Check out the *Glamour* magazine quiz. Is dating your daughter's boyfriend wrong? Tune into Sally Jesse Raphael. Or it can be determined by one individual trying to reason, "If everyone else made the same choice, would it be helpful?" This is the approach Chuck Colson confessed that he took to the Watergate cover-up before his conversion to Christ. If, as he firmly believed, the fate of our nation hinged on the reelection of Richard Nixon, and if they covered up the break-in, he would be reelected, then the highest good for the whole nation would be to cover up. Watergate was the result of relative morality at work.

There is another view of truth that flows out of relativism. Instead of worrying about what's best for everyone and what the majority thinks, each individual (or subject) determines what is true. Truth is *subjective*. Based on my own reasons, feelings, and experience, I determine what's morally right for me. And if you disagree with me, who are you to say that I'm wrong?

Woody Allen could be the poster boy for subjective truth. Allen deceived and betrayed his longtime companion Mia Farrow while carrying on an affair with her adopted daughter. In banner headlines under his picture in *Time*'s August 31, 1992, cover story, an unrepentant Woody justified his choice: "The Heart Wants What It Wants." This is a subjective view of what is true, right, and moral. I just follow my heart, not the Bible, and not what most people would say is moral. It just feels right. Like the people in Israel as described in the book of Judges, Allen "did that which was right in his own eyes." Well, when everyone behaves that way, the result can only be chaos. And the times of the judges were among the most chaotic in Israel's history.

THE DOG ATE MY HOMEWORK

We can show the differences between the orthodox and progressive views of right and wrong by looking at what each view says about lying. First the orthodox: God says lying is wrong. "You shall not give false testimony against your neighbor." There it is. Commandment Number 9. And in the New Testament: "Do not lie to each other" (Colossians. 3:9). This is *God's rule for living.*

Time magazine's October 5, 1992, cover story was titled "Lying— Everybody's Doin' It (Honest)." The article described the rising tide of deceit in our country. Americans are spinning increasing webs of lies to defend and protect themselves, to gain advantage, even intentionally to cause harm. We are awash in variations of "The dog ate my homework;" "The check is in the mail;" "This is a beauty of a deal— trust me;" "Read my lips—no new taxes." The *Stamford Advocate* (9/95) reported that at the University of Virginia, students were given diaries to report on their conversations. The percentage of lies amounted to 28 percent with friends, 48 percent with acquaintances, 77 percent with strangers, 46 percent with lovers, and 34 percent with their mothers. (With their *mothers?*)

Time magazine's analysis of this lying behavior is interesting. "Lies flourish in social uncertainty, when people *no longer understand, or agree on the rules* governing their behavior toward one another" [italics mine].

The key words here are *no longer.* This implies a change. We used to agree on the same rules. Now we don't. As a nation we used to believe that God makes the rules and that His Word was the source of moral authority. Francis Schaeffer put it this way: "The Bible is clear: there is a moral law of the universe. And that basic law is the character of God Himself. . . . When He reveals this character to us in [the Bible], we have the commands of God for men" (*Death in the City,* p. 94). Though a little difficult perhaps, this is crucial to understand.

God makes the rules based on His character and gave them to us in the Bible, and His rules are universal and final.

To modern ears this sounds so harsh, so . . . intolerant. It can sound that way to our children, too. That's why we need to give them *reasons* for our faith in the goodness and reasonableness of God's rules— they serve as boundaries on our rights and freedom so our decisions won't lead to chaos. Chaos is inevitable when humans make the rules, because human rules are based on human opinions. And human opinions are subject to everything from subtle error to incredible self-deception.

So if God's rules about lying are *no longer* accepted, then we get human progressive rules about lying. "Well, it's okay as long as it doesn't hurt anybody." "It's okay if it's socially helpful and gets the right policy in place or the best person elected." "It's okay because he is clueless about how much it takes to buy clothes. (Besides, I pay the bills.)"

But lying leads to chaos in our society. Skepticism increases, and trust breaks down. Voters become apathetic. Con-men and the unscrupulous rise to the top in business, and the work ethic is destroyed. Family intimacy becomes impossible in a vicious cycle of deceit and suspicion. Even a little child understands that one lie leads to another, and the consequences can be disastrous. God gives us His standard because it is *right,* and it protects us from such pain and destruction.

Observing the dangers of a subjective moral ethic, Pope John Paul II wrote a very strong encyclical, *Veritatis Splendor.* In it he explained the "splendor" of a value system based on God's absolute truth. As the pope correctly pointed out, if there is no absolute truth and every person is deciding what's true for himself, all that is left is raw power. The results are scary: loss of respect for authority, chaos, a continual struggle for power, and whoever has the money, image, and charisma to persuade people to follow his agenda will get the votes and gain control. No checks on that power by an appeal to an outside standard of "what's right" or "fair" will work, because people won't believe there is a standard. "All ways are my ways!" thunders the Queen of Hearts to Alice in Wonderland. "Now off with their heads!" (See Focus Box #4.)

Focus Your Worldview #4: Alice in No-Rules Land

In her own "passive-aggressive" way, Alice challenges the authority of reason and rules. She dreams of a "Wonderland" where the "books would be nothing but pictures" and "everything would be nonsense." "Be careful what you wish for, Alice," Anglican deacon, mathematician, and author Lewis Carroll seems to be saying in his tale of her adventure. Alice's story offers great insight into a world with no rules, where all do what they feel like doing.

Rent the video of *Alice in Wonderland*, and as you watch it, use the pause button to allow for a discussion of the following. Your family may see Alice in a whole new light.

➤ In the Caucus Race can you make out the lyrics the racers are singing?

➤ How does this approach affect the meaning of the race?

➤ In the book the race goes on for about half an hour, everyone running and resting as they like, until the Dodo bird calls out, "The race is over!" The racers crowd around, panting, "But who has won?" After a long pause he brightens and announces, "Everybody has won, and all must have prizes!" (Can you say, "outcome-based education?")

➤ In a world with no rules, how do the strong (the Walrus and the Carpenter) behave toward the weak (the oysters and later, the Carpenter)?

➤ The Cheshire cat offers some advice on finding the way through Wonderland. What is it?

➤ Wandering in the woods, Alice begins to have second thoughts about Wonderland: What seems nice at this point? What does she begin to conclude about "advice" and "reason"?

The final part of the movie makes an even stronger statement. Make a list of how life with no rules (manners) affects:

➤ a birthday tea party.

➤ fixing a broken pocket watch.

➤ the game of croquet.

➤ the trial.

Chaos often leads to tyranny, which is certainly what happens in Wonderland. In a place where "the way things are done" is no longer respected, what does the queen claim? And only if Alice gets big (more powerful), can she challenge the queen.

➤ If you had to choose three words to describe Alice during her trip to Wonderland, what would they be?

➤ In the end what did she have to do to survive?

➤ Summarize what you think Carroll, who wrote books about math and logic, was trying to say about life without reason or rules.

➤ Can you see any similarities with our world today?

Challenging authority is the hallmark of our relativistic times—glamorized in the media and played out daily in our schools and families. When our children seek our guidance, they need to see us in turn rely on the "splendor" of God's Word, open it up, and show them that this is where the answers to our questions about right and wrong can be found. They need to know that when they feel like risking consequences or following what their heart wants in disobedience, it's more than just a challenge to our opinions. It is sin against God. Whenever possible we need to deflect the conflict in the right direction—"your disagreement is with God, a God who is righteous and has designed life so that peace of conscience and joy in the moment are the result of right choices to seek and obey Him." The sad thing is that too many parents have no confidence that God's Word has the answers or that any absolute moral order even exists.

"Everything Is Negotiable"

A recent Barna poll asked the following question: "Do you agree or disagree with this statement: There is no such thing as absolute truth. People can define truth in different ways and still be correct." The answer: 28 percent of the public strongly agreed that there is no such thing as absolute truth. Another 38 percent somewhat agreed, meaning 66 percent of Americans do not believe in absolutes. Among those who identified themselves as Evangelicals, 53 percent agree that there is no such thing as absolute truth! (George Barna, *What Americans Believe*, pp. 83-85).

Concerned that this same drift toward a subjective and relative view of truth is happening among young people, even those from Christian churches and homes, a 1994 survey was commissioned by Josh McDowell and other national leaders of youth ministry. From over 3,700 responses the results show that even among our churched youth:

> ...57 percent...are likely to approve the view that there is no such thing as absolute truth; people may define truth in contradictory ways and still be correct.
>
> A mere 29 percent *disagreed* with the statement: When it comes to matters of morals and ethics, truth means different things to different people; no one can be absolutely positive they have the truth.
>
> ...45 percent of our churched youth could not disagree with the statement: Everything in life is negotiable.
>
> —McDowell, *Right from Wrong*, pp. 15-16

This is one area where the American educational system has done its job. Our students may have trouble dating the Civil War within fifty years of its occurrence or finding the USA on a world map, but they know an intolerant absolutist when they see one. Allan Bloom, a classical humanist and professor of philosophy, wrote a critically acclaimed book called *The Closing of the American Mind*. In it he soberly describes the state of mind in which most incoming freshmen enter his class.

> The danger [university students] have been taught to fear from absolutism is not error but intolerance. Relativism is necessary to openness; and this is the virtue, the only virtue, which all primary education for more than fifty years has dedicated itself to inculcating. Openness—and the relativism that makes it the only plausible stance in the face of various claims to truth and various ways of life

and kinds of human beings—is the great insight of our times. The true believer is the real danger. The study of history and culture teaches that all the world was mad in the past; men always thought that they were right, and that led to wars, persecutions, slavery, xenophobia, racism, and chauvinism. The point is not to correct the mistakes and really be right; rather it is not to think you are right at all. (pp. 25-26)

America has changed because too many of its citizens agree or tend to agree with these college freshmen. Homosexuality is not wrong. It's just another lifestyle. Premarital sex isn't wrong. Sex is pleasurable, and most kids are going to experiment. There is no right and wrong; just use a condom. Just deal with the consequences. *Man makes the rules.*

This is the *root* of our problems and our decline. It is not "the economy, stupid." It is not a lack of good schools, jobs, or enough jails. It's not even "Beavis and Butthead," or whatever the current excesses of TV happen to be. It is because we used to believe in absolutes—*God makes the rules.* Now we are divided between those who still believe that way (orthodox) and those who have embraced another presupposition: that truth is relative or subjective—*Man makes the rules* (progressive). And what the statistics show is that the progressive worldview is held by increasing numbers of evangelical Christians and *our children.*

In the May 1996 issue of his Prison Fellowship newsletter, Chuck Colson reports: "James Davison Hunter believes we are losing the culture war, and he's right. The reason is that we've poured immense effort into fighting social evils like crime, abortion, and pornography without understanding the deeper issues that move a culture." As you understand this crucial puzzle-piece about our source of moral truth and explain it to your children, you are making a difference in our cultural decline where it matters the very most.

THE CULTURE WAR IS NOT CHRISTIANS V. NON-CHRISTIANS

It is important to see the culture war for what it truly is. This is not Christians versus secular humanists. Secular humanists believe that people are completely independent of God and that Christianity is an obstacle to human progress. People must and will save themselves. But these humanists compose only 11 percent of the population. They exercise enormous influence because they are leaders in education, the courts, the media, and government. Secular humanists may lead the progressive community, but many people who defend abortion on demand, special homosexual rights, etc., count themselves as faithful Christians.

Our children need to understand that we are *not* saying that the struggle between orthodox and progressive factions is a battle between Christian and non-Christian. David Wilhelm, chairman of the Democratic National Committee, was invited to address an annual meeting of the Christian Coalition. When he asserted that there were many good Christians who defended a woman's right to choose, he was booed vehemently. We have to be careful here. I firmly believe the Bible speaks strongly to the issue of abortion (see chapter 8). But the last time I looked, the simple Gospel of Christ's atoning death and resurrection and our redemption from the power and penalty of sin said nothing about abortion. Christians can have blind spots.

I am a Southerner. Some of my great-great kinfolk owned slaves. I'm sure that among them were some who sought to love and serve the Lord as well. They may have believed the lie that slavery based on race was morally right. It doesn't mean they weren't Christians. We cannot dismiss generations of Southerners who loved the Lord as "not good Christians" because they owned slaves. We might say they were Christians who were deeply mistaken about slavery. Their worldview was not completely Christian.

As believers we have a personal relationship with Jesus Christ. We may be deceived or have a blind spot in many areas—pride, lack of compassion on the needy, materialism, even psychological dependence on ice cream. We may even have a faulty worldview, buying into the world's relative view of truth to some extent. But it does not mean that our confession of faith in the simple Gospel is void or that we are not children of God in the process of growing and maturing in our faith.

If, by God's grace, we know and understand His truth, we must not despise a sister or brother who does not. The problem with viewing this area of spiritual warfare as a culture war is that we forget who the real enemy is. We become emotional, and we savage other people.

The sword of the Spirit of truth is our best weapon. We need to wield it firmly but with love and grace.

Disagreements over doctrinal and moral issues are so difficult. If we assert that what we believe is true and moral, then we imply that those who disagree with us believe what is a lie and immoral. "Speaking the truth in love" (Ephesians 4:15) requires that we not compromise the truth *or* our love for those who disagree with us. We must, perhaps, go the extra mile to build relationships and show them that we love and value them as people, even if we disagree on tremendously important issues. We can show great respect for, and listen to, their views. We can identify with them as a fellow traveler with similar burdens and problems and make the distinction that *we* don't have all the answers, but we know the One who does. (See Focus Box #5.)

In all our agreements and disagreements, we as believers must remember that we have a higher priority than just winning. As God's children, we are called to reflect His truth and grace. In the strongest of terms Francis Schaeffer has declared that if we, as Christians do not have " . . . compassion for those of our kind, our orthodoxy is ugly and it stinks . . . (not only to an honest man, but)—orthodoxy without compassion stinks with God" (*Death in the City*, p. 123).

In a culture that no longer believes that truth is objective and knowable, people's beliefs are interpreted as an expression of their feelings, attitudes, and prejudices. You cannot "prove" homosexuality is wrong, so you must be "homophobic." You must have an "irrational fear" of homosexuals, abortionists, etc. And then you express your fear as "hate." You are judged guilty of hate-speech, hate-mongering, etc. A culture in revolt will not receive God's truth warmly. Jeremiah preached God's truth to his culture and went to the dungeon for his trouble. Discouraged, he told God, "I've neither lent nor borrowed, but everyone is cursing me" (Jeremiah 15:10). If we encounter the "hate-label," let's make sure we haven't earned it.

≈

FOCUS YOUR WORLDVIEW #5: SPEAKING THE TRUTH IN LOVE

We can teach our children how to show compassion as they defend their faith by example, critique of a bad example, or role playing.

Propose an interview situation with an unbeliever or someone of a different cultural or political stripe. Have them practice these suggestions for showing respect and compassion for those with whom they disagree.

1. Don't laugh at or mock the other's position.

2. Don't name-call, toss out labels, or do the famous teenage "eye roll."

3. Look for common ground. Tell a story to illustrate your point. People's lives are more interesting than bare logic or statistics.

4. Give the other person your full attention, listen well, don't interrupt.

GOOD RESOURCES

Rutherford Institute (especially *Religious Apartheid*) on violations of the free exercise of religion

Gianna's Story, an abortion survivor

Joni (Eareckson Tada) on quality of life, euthanasia issues.

5. Where there is no common ground or agreement, respectfully agree to disagree. Find out what they think about the Bible as a source of moral authority before you use it liberally in defense of your position. They may have a high view of Jesus but reject the Bible. If so, Bible Study #2 can be useful.

THE TRUTH AND AUTHORITY OF SCRIPTURE

While the culture war is not a struggle between Christians and non-Christians, neither is it a conflict between denominations. Usually we see disagreements *within* denominations over these issues: bishops split with bishops, laity splits with leadership. Those with a high view of Scripture divide with those who view Scripture to be less authoritative.

For example, like the Methodists and the Presbyterians, the Episcopal church is deeply divided over the ordination of gay clergy.

Observers have commented that for some, "prohibition against homosexual ordination seems an eternal truth, for others, a cultural prejudice" (*Houston Chronicle,* 5/16/96). In exasperation a local Episcopalian has exclaimed, "If we can't draw a doctrinal line somewhere, how are we different from the Rotary Club?" In a culture where hearts want some pretty strange things, even the notoriously inclusive Unitarians are struggling to be tolerant. The Spindletop Unitarian Church of Beaumont, Texas, is divided over whether some of its pagan members can dance around a fairy circle on its lawn, sprinkling glittery "fairy dust," and changing (metaphorically) into animals. Not even the Rotary would go for that.

The denominational debate shows clearly how biblical truth and authority relate to the question of who makes the rules. According to many mainline Protestant ministers, the Bible may say that homosexuality is wrong, but you shouldn't take it literally. Every substantive discussion I've personally had with homosexuals or those who justify homosexuality ends up in an attack on the truth and reliability of Scripture.

But they bring up a good question. If I believe that God is real and that He makes the rules and that He has given us those rules in the Bible, then shouldn't I take a very high view of Scripture? As believers, we should have no lower an opinion of Scripture than Jesus did. Our Lord believed in "every word" of it (Matthew 4).

Dr. Charles Ryrie, author of *What You Should Know About Inerrancy,* makes a clear and persuasive case from Jesus' teachings that Scripture is true for all people for all times. (See Bible Study #2.) Not only did Jesus endorse the authority of the words of Scripture but also their spelling. In Matthew 5:18, Jesus says, "I tell you the truth, until heaven and earth disappear, not the smallest letter (jot), nor the least stroke of a pen (tittle), will by any means disappear from the Law until everything is accomplished." A tittle (the stroke of the pen) makes the difference between an F and an E or a P and an R. Jesus defended every word and every letter of the Word.

"I am the God of Abraham, Isaac, and Jacob." Jesus used this verse from Exodus to teach about life after death. In Matthew 22 He used the present tense of the verb "I am" (not "I was") to convince the Sadducees that Abraham, Isaac, and Jacob were still living in heaven at the time God talked to Moses at the burning bush. Jesus rested His entire defense of the scriptural support for eternal life on the tense of one verb. Further, in John 10:35, Jesus straightforwardly said, "Scripture cannot be broken." Our Lord tells us that not just the ideas of Scripture are true, but the very words with their particular spellings and verb tenses are the source of authority for our lives.

If Jesus takes such a high view of the truth and reliability of Scripture, surely we can, too. Besides, it only makes sense that if God created us and made the rules for living right and joyful lives, He would insure that we received a trustworthy copy of that most important message. Not all the orthodox community believes that the Bible in its original manuscripts is error-free. But they do believe the Bible speaks with truth and authority on matters of faith and morals, and they are bound together by their high view of Scripture. (See Focus Box #6.)

THE MUSHY MIDDLE

Then there are the Marla Maples of this world. Marla believes the Bible but adds, "You can't always take [it] literally and be happy" (*World*, 3/6/93). Marla, like most Americans, may want to believe in God, that there is Someone in heaven watching over us and our loved ones. We like the security angle but reject the accountability. What the Bible has to say about dating a married man and having his child infringes on what makes Marla happy—so let's not believe it literally.

The truth is, many Americans don't have strong beliefs at all. Remember the poll? "There is no such thing as absolutes." While 28 percent strongly *agreed*, 16 percent strongly *disagreed*. That leaves 56 percent in the middle, which has led Greg Jesson of Focus on the Family's Community Impact Seminar to observe, "The moral majority does not exist. What we have is a moral polarity with most people in the mushy middle. . . . Never have so many people believed so little." Francis Schaeffer has described this majority as those with "both feet planted firmly in midair." Or many of those in the middle hold tenuously to beliefs that contradict one another, and they just ignore or live with the tension.

Eugene Peterson, professor at Regent University, described his congregation in "classic suburbia" this way: "They didn't read books.

They didn't discuss ideas. All spirit seemed to have leaked out of their lives and been replaced by a garage-sale clutter of clichés and stereotypes, securities and fashions. . . . It was a marshmallow culture, spongy and without substance. No hard ideas to push against. No fiery spirit to excite. Soggy suburbia" (*Under the Unpredictable Plant*).

And yet we've never been busier. It seems that the list of requirements to experience the American dream keeps getting longer. Most folks spend huge amounts of time and money pursuing comfort and happiness. As conservative humorist P. J. O'Rourke points out, this frantic pursuit of happiness is to be expected, because along with the right to life and liberty, the pursuit of happiness is one of our inalienable, God-given rights guaranteed to all Americans from day one.

> This is living! I gotta be me. Ain't we got fun! It's all there in the Declaration of Independence. We are the only nation in the world based on happiness. Search as you will the sacred creeds of other nations and peoples, read the Magna Carta, the *Communist Manifesto,* the Ten Commandments, the *Analects* of Confucius, Plato's *Republic,* the New Testament, or the U.N. Charter, and find me any happiness at all. America is the Happy Kingdom. And that is one good reason why we who live here can't bring ourselves to read . . . even the daily paper.
>
> —*A Parliament of Whores,* p. 9

So there you have it. Our nation is divided over the source of moral authority. Who makes the rules—God or man? We're not simply divided between Christians versus secular humanists or Christians versus nonbelievers, or some denominations versus others. What we see is a moral polarity between the orthodox and progressives with most people in the mushy middle.

I wonder how many in the mushy middle are women. As I noted in chapter 1, women tend to be less concerned about cultural issues than about their homes and families. But, as I pointed out, there *is* a connection. Most moms share my concern that the craziness of the youth culture and the peer group that has bought into it will seduce our children. And Josh McDowell's statistics certify that the threat is very real. (See Resource Box #1.)

Are we moms caught up in pursuing comfort and happiness? Are we too comfortable in "soggy suburbia?" Do we believe the absolutes of God's Word only when it makes us happy or comfortable? We all fall short in living according to our beliefs. The challenge to us is, do we know and believe God's Word to begin with?

Our priority will always be our relationship to Christ and sharing the Gospel through word and deed. But the marketplace of ideas in our school, our neighborhood, and our city needs our voice. We need to bring those ideas home to our dinner table and family devotions and sift them with our children.

It's easy to be complacent—too busy, like Miss Scarlett, or too indifferent—"don't make waves." The women of Isaiah's time were also complacent—indifferent to Israel's spiritual and cultural decline. Concerned with getting their sons to the rabbis' school and their daughter's dowry together.

Isaiah warned them, "You women who are so complacent, rise up and listen to me; you daughters who feel secure, hear what I have to say! In a little more than a year you who feel secure will tremble; the grape harvest will fail, and the harvest of fruit will not come. Tremble, you complacent women . . . mourn for all houses of merriment and for this city of revelry" (Isaiah 32:9-11, 13).

Our happy times are really pretty fragile. Sometimes we need to take stock and evaluate: what would we do differently if we knew that, unchecked, our spiritual and cultural decline would lead to a failed economy in a little more than a year? We still have a window of opportunity to disciple our children and to pray and work for repentance and revival. May God grant that we use it wisely.

RESOURCE BOX #1: RIGHT FROM WRONG

Explaining to young people (and sometimes their parents) that a relative or subjective view of truth doesn't square with God's Word is a good beginning. In order to make choices based on truth and not their feelings or experience, they may need to *learn* to do it. Josh McDowell has written the most wonderful materials for leading youth and their parents *out* of the mushy middle (or tendencies in that direction).

The book *Right from Wrong* is targeted at parents. McDowell wants to show people how to convince their children that God's

Word provides a standard for their choices and to help parents explain *why* His commands are true. The book discusses evidence for the belief that the greatest good for all of us is God's standard of righteousness. McDowell applies these truths to decisions about sex, honesty, family, love, justice, mercy, respect, and self-control— all front-burner concerns for our children and us.

Also available in the *Right from Wrong* series:

➤ *Truth Matters*. A video series or single tape to equip parents

➤ *Right from Wrong*. Audio tapes for parents

➤ *Right Choices*. Video series for youth (Our youth group has been really engaged by the creative drama sequences and high production values used.)

➤ *Truthslayer*. A *Right from Wrong* book for youth.

➤ Children's Church video series

➤ *103 Questions* book for children

➤ Workbooks for all age levels

FOCUS YOUR WORLDVIEW #6: WHY "I BELIEVE WHAT I BELIEVE BECAUSE I'VE EXPERIENCED WHAT I'VE EXPERIENCED" IS NOT A GOOD IDEA

This activity is for children old enough and strong enough in their faith to handle a little challenge and who have computer access to the Internet. It should be undertaken with parental guidance. Use one of the Internet search engines such as Yahoo (http://www.yahoo.com).

➤ Punch in the key words: *religious experience, conversion, testimony, Islam, Hindu, Voodoo,* or any other religion, or *near-death experiences.*

➤ Read a few testimonies of people from other faiths and other religious experience. If your search goes like ours has, you will find people with sincere religious experiences ranging from the Muslim woman who found a new depth of commitment to Allah when she finally consented to wear the *chador* (veil), to near-death experiences with "spirits of light" who assure people that all are headed for a realm of peace and harmony.

Discuss the following questions together:

➤ How are these experiences similar to experiences narrated in the Bible?

➤ How are they different?

➤ The following verses tell about people in Scripture who had or reported that they had religious experiences, but God's Word condemns them. Explain how and why. (Jeremiah 14:14; 23:25-28; 1 Samuel 28; Deuteronomy 18:10-13; Leviticus 20:27)

Scripture requires that we submit our religious experience to strong tests of reliability.

➤ Deuteronomy 18:21-22. What was the test for prophecy?

➤ Deuteronomy 13:1-5. Even if they experienced the truth of a prophecy, God told Israel they should not _____ a prophet if he says, "_____ _____," which is against God's Word.

Make sure your children get this main idea: We believe what we believe because God's Word says so. "Experience will influence and confirm what we understand Scripture to teach. But experience must never be placed above the Scriptures or on a higher level of importance. It is not even equally as important. [In Scripture] experience proved or confirmed the truth of the revelation, but our everyday experience did not and cannot establish spiritual truth" (Jack Arrington, sermon notes, "The Spirit of Truth").

JEREMIAH AND THE EGG HUNT

3

---

*What Happens As We Follow Our Heart
Instead of Our Conscience?*

PSST! HEY! HEARD ANY GOOD LAWYER JOKES LATELY? HOW ABOUT
... there was this CEO of a company who summoned his accountant,
his economist, and his lawyer to his office.

"Gentlemen," he addressed them, "I have an assignment for you. I
want each of you to work on this and get back to me tomorrow."

The accountant took out his pencil and note pad, the economist
his digital memo saver, and the lawyer checked his watch.

"Here it is," said the CEO. "What is 2 + 2?"

The accountant went back to his office and scattered a handful of
beans on his desk. No matter how he counted and rearranged them,
two beans plus two more beans equaled ...

The economist burned the midnight oil referencing an entire
computer bank of forecasts, indicators, charts, and graphs and com-
piling his statistical data.

The lawyer went out for drinks and to a movie.

The next day the three professionals assembled in the CEO's waiting room.

First the accountant was called. Frustrated and worried that he
didn't "get it," the accountant hesitated and then blurted out, "It's
four, sir, 2 + 2 = 4."

The CEO nodded and thanked him and then punched the inter-
com. "Next."

Loaded with color charts and graphs, the economist strode in and handed the CEO a bound report. "What I can confidently tell you, sir, is that I'm comfortable with a range of three to five."

"Thank you. Next!"

The lawyer walked softly in, closing the door behind him. His eyes scanned the room. In one smooth movement he closed the mini-blinds, visually checked under the lamp shade, and picked up the phone. Satisfied, he returned the receiver to the cradle. Then he leaned forward on both hands across the CEO's desk and said in a measured, low voice, "What do you *want* it to be?"

Actually that is one of the nicer lawyer jokes I've heard, one that raps the system—the way things are done—more than the person himself. And while we laugh, it's a little sad to think that our legal system is losing respect. If a strong view of truth, right, and wrong is a scarce commodity these days, then one of the first places to show the deficit will be a court of law.

Our children are growing up in a postmodern world that is rejecting the self-evident truths of America's foundation. As our nation is becoming increasingly secular and diverse, we are losing our shared vision of democracy, the basis of law and morality. Instead of our Constitution and laws standing like a rock and serving as a strong anchor to the truth, it seems the line has been cut, and the laws and even our Constitution have become something soft and pliable in the hands of activist judges and lawyers. "What do you *want* it to be?"

The Bible is like a yardstick. Throw out the yardstick, and how do you measure the cloth? Throw out the Bible, or any idea of transcendent universal standards, and how do you come up with a new basis for law and morality? How do you begin to rule on what is just and true? When man makes the rules instead of God, he makes them based on his own opinions, feelings, and experience. (This is increasingly true of our judges, as it is for the man on the street.) How do judges and people determine right and wrong once they reject God's truth? Primarily in just two ways.

TRYING TO BE "SOCIALLY HELPFUL"

We know what one constitutional law professor would say. Remember the professor from the University of Texas Law School? He is a logical descendant of Supreme Court Justice Oliver Wendell Holmes. Justice Holmes led the way in directing our courts' sense of justice away from the traditional morality of our Judeo-Christian heritage. Instead he emphasized that justice should be based on experience, and opinions should be written that seemed most socially and politically helpful.

The most helpful scheme the UT professor could come up with was for governments to "organize all these living organisms" so that "pain should be avoided or mitigated." That's the flip side of *utilitarianism*—making the moral choice that will provide "the greatest happiness for the greatest number of people." This is one of the main ways Americans determine right and wrong these days. And it fits neatly with our high national regard for happiness we discussed earlier. If the goal is happiness, then whatever produces it is useful; whatever obstructs it is useless. Law and moral choices should be a compassionate response to needs and circumstances. The end, or goal, of happiness justifies the socially helpful means, or choices made, to secure it.

So if your goal is the funding of a particular political group or program that will make a lot of people happy, then it may be socially helpful to lie to Congress. If there is a need to release a lot of unhappy spouses to find happiness in a new life, then no-fault divorce laws are socially helpful.

We can take our children to Scripture for a clear example of how utilitarianism can be a poor substitute for God's law. Satan tempted Jesus to embrace a utilitarian ethic. He tried to entice Jesus to prove he was Messiah in front of a big crowd at the temple (the "end"), by taking a flying leap off the pinnacle (the "means"). It must have looked really appealing to Jesus, too, or Satan wouldn't have used it as one of his big three temptations. "Come on, Jesus, just claim that Scripture about the angels protecting You; You'll make that temple crowd really happy!" What a dramatic shortcut around Calvary to claim an end that was rightfully His anyway.

Jesus responded with the absolutes of God's Word: "It is also written: 'Do not put the Lord your God to the test.'" Every end/goal we pursue should be measured by the absolute Word of God, and even if the goal measures up, the means to accomplish the end must measure up as well.

You see, there is a larger question here. Are lying to Congress and no-fault divorce laws really and truly socially helpful? Lying to Congress breaks down trust in the system and can personally land you in jail. We are realizing more and more that no-fault divorce leads to single-parent families and the feminization of poverty. Is that really the greatest good for the greatest number of people?

Josh McDowell makes an excellent case in *Right from Wrong* for teaching our children a "truth apologetic"—telling them not just *what* God's law is, but giving them an understanding of *why* it is really there for our protection. We can point out the consequences of replacing God's rules with human rules—we find *pain*, not happiness. This is a titanic moral rule of the universe, and one that our children need to learn early on. It is true for us as individuals as well as for families, communities, and nations. We can use our nation's departure from God's law and the resulting painful consequences as a kind of giant object lesson for our children. And in so doing, we can show them how God uses pain to steer us back to the path of blessing and obedience.

Our children need to understand the painful chain reaction that begins when society decides one of God's laws is no longer helpful. A good example is the sexual revolution of the sixties. God's standard has always been that sexual intimacy should be enjoyed only within the protection and commitment of marriage. Out of "compassion" and "understanding" of people's biological needs and loneliness, the centuries-old social stigma on sex outside marriage disappeared. Result: impoverished relationships and huge increases in crisis pregnancies and sexually transmitted diseases, including AIDS. Then, out of compassion for crisis pregnancies, the Supreme Court provided for abortion, virtually on demand, and out of compassion for teens-at-risk, condoms have been distributed. But now we have just suffered more painful consequences from these "compassionate" measures. Abortion has cheapened life and, some studies indicate, has led to increased child abuse. (See chapter 7.) Statistics indicate that condom distribution has encouraged more premarital sex and has not provided complete protection from pregnancies (15 percent failure rate) or HIV (31 percent failure rate).

So ask your children, what is more compassionate: God's rules or human rules? What is more socially helpful: absolute or relative morality? Are people happier now than before God's standard was abandoned by so many? The irony of utilitarianism is that the greatest good for the greatest number of people *is* God's moral law, not man's "compassionate" substitute. And we believe and obey, not just because it works, but because it is *right*.

THE SUPREMES ARE MARCHING ON

In trying to be socially helpful, the courts are ruling in baffling ways. Their findings seem more and more arbitrary, subject to individual will or judgment, unreasonable, or capricious. Increasingly, the decisions coming down from the Supreme Court have nothing to do with the Constitution and everything to do with the justices' own personal judgment. They determine what is socially helpful and then look through the Constitution to find some vague shred of support. I'll give you an example.

Probably the most radical decision the Supreme Court has handed down since *Roe v. Wade* hasn't even registered with most folks yet. In *Planned Parenthood v. Casey* the court ruled that each *individual* must determine "the concept of existence, of meaning, of the universe, and the mystery of human life." So if a woman determines that the baby she is carrying does not exist or has no meaning or human life, she can dispose of it. If you want to put a gun to your head or a lethal syringe to your arm or have a doctor help you die—well, whatever makes you happy.

One Catholic scholar has noted that *Casey* has given each person "a private franchise over matters of life and death." How does each person think or feel about what makes for meaningful life? "What do you *want* it to be?" The Supreme Court has written an ethic of subjective truth into laws that govern life and death. Former federal judge Robert Bork expresses the sentiments of many Americans incredulous at the *Casey* ruling: "One would think that grown men and women, purporting to practice an intelligent profession, would themselves choose to die with dignity right in the courtroom before writing sentences like that" (*Slouching Toward Gomorrah*).

Our children are growing up in a world where the courts no longer just interpret the laws, but they write new laws. The judiciary is an elite group that decides what is socially helpful to maximize our happiness and minimize our pain. Because courts have a progressive bent, progressive activists pursue their agendas there. These activists have met with great success in the nineties by making an end-run around the legislatures that are directly accountable to the people. In addition to *Casey*,

> ➤ two federal appeals courts have struck down laws forbidding doctors to "assist" terminally ill patients commit suicide.

> ➤ the Supreme Court has reversed Colorado's Amendment 2 prohibiting its legislature from giving special rights to homosexuals.

> ➤ a federal appeals court has overturned the law to protect children from pornography on the Internet.

> ➤ the issue of homosexual marriage is on the legal front burner.

There is no doubt that the courts exercise tremendous leadership in our cultural struggles. "Whatever is legal is moral" is a hard mindset to change. *Roe v. Wade*'s ruling on abortion was more progressive than the moral consensus in 1973, but now the majority has fallen in line with the court.

In many ways, though, the courts also reflect, perhaps even amplify attitudes and opinions taking hold at the grass-roots level. After all, how does one determine what is the greatest good for the greatest number of people?

VOTES NOT VERSES AND A FINGER IN THE WIND

What is the second way that judges and people determine right and wrong if man makes the rules? Well, we call a bunch of them up and ask, "What do you *think* about the moral questions of our day?" Or more and more you hear, "How do you *feel* about restrictions on abortion or condom distribution?" For those who believe that truth is subjective, then each individual responds solely according to her feelings. (Remember Woody Allen? "The heart wants what it wants." "What do you *want* it to be?") We now have law and morality determined by opinion polls.

Do you remember ever seeing opinion polls twenty years ago? Fifteen? I don't know at what point they really started multiplying, but it seems that today we are drowning in opinion polls. A "Charlie" cartoon makes the point. Staring blankly at a TV screen with fireworks on it, Charlie hears, "If you think these fireworks are nice, call 1-900-555-0876. If you don't think so, call 1-900-555-0877. There is a 95-cent charge for this call." Our children are growing up in a world where every article or debate on a moral issue is accompanied by an opinion poll. Since our culture is rejecting moral absolutes in favor of moral diversity, we give all the morally diverse people a vote and see what the majority agrees upon—at least for today. This results in morality by popular vote. The majority is always right. Right?

When I taught sophomore English at Trinity Christian Academy in Dallas, I included a unit on advertising propaganda. We focused on several devices used to persuade people to buy products. All these devices were manipulative and sought to break down people's resistance. We studied how one can use statistics, testimonials, and what was called the "Bandwagon" technique. "Everyone is buying this or doing that, so hop on the bandwagon and join the crowd. The crowd is always right. Right?"

Just ask any parents what they tell their teenager on Friday night. "Now, Susie, after the game a lot of your friends may want to pick up some six-packs and have car races once the traffic thins out a little. I want you to go along with the crowd. The herd instinct is a fine thing to follow." Hardly. What *do* we tell our kids? Don't succumb to the lure of peer pressure to do something you know is wrong. Take a stand. Don't jump on the bandwagon or go along with the majority, because the majority is often wrong.

Historically the majority believed in racial superiority, which resulted in slavery and the Holocaust. The majority may even get their view written into law, but that still doesn't make it right. What's legal is *not* necessarily moral, because what is morally right is finally a reflection of God's character. "Let God be true, and every man a liar" (Romans 3:4). God's truth plus even *one* person is a moral majority.

I collect pictures of the Lady Justice. In my Bible studies I show three images of justice that illustrate this change in the basis of law. One is a picture of a mural on the Supreme Court building in

Lausanne, Switzerland. In this mural the Lady Justice stands robed in white, towering over the judges and litigants at her feet. In her left hand she holds the scales of justice. In her right hand she holds a sword. But the sword is not raised or drawn. It rests point-down on a huge open book at her feet—a Bible. The message is clear: Justice rests on the foundation of God's Word. God's laws determine how justice is weighed and how the government's God-given sword will be directed.

This image stands in stark contrast to two other Lady Justices. One is pictured in a July 1989 *Time* editorial on abortion. She is also robed in white. She wields no sword, only the scales of justice in her left hand. In the two pans of her scale are two ballot boxes—one marked "yes," the other marked "no." The heavier box of ballots will tip the scales of justice.

Recently, *World* magazine ran a cartoon by Asay showing another Lady Justice surrounded by the Supremes—the six progressive justices happily replacing her scales with a weather vane while Rehnquist, Scalia, and Thomas stand mournfully to the side. Perhaps these are the images of justice that should be painted in our Supreme Court building—Lady Justice with ballot boxes or a weather vane. Not very noble images, especially compared with the one in Lausanne, but certainly accurate. They could be titled "The Majority Is Always Right," "Votes, Not Verses," or "The Answer Is Blowing in the Wind."

In an interview with *Christianity Today* editor Phillip Yancey, President Clinton acknowledged his belief that in a democracy public policy on moral issues should be determined by majority vote. He believes that a moral issue should only become a legal issue if "there is a consensus in the community that is sufficiently overwhelming to bring in the criminal law." (This sounded good in *Christianity Today,* [4/25/94], but when the consensus against partial-birth abortion *was* strong enough to bring in the criminal law, President Clinton seemed to forget his position.)

The president's stated position, which he seems to follow more often than not, echoed the opinion of his pollster Stan Greenberg. Mr. Greenberg has said that critics are wrong to "worry about poll-driven politics, when it is really a demonstration of respect for the views of the public."

JOE AND SALLY CITIZEN

Think about it. The president and his pollster thought that the founders' efforts to create a representative democracy should be deferred to the direct polling of Joe and Sally Citizen. The pollster calls and catches Sally on the way out the door to Little League practice, with Joe and two kids already in the car. Sally is asked to agree or disagree with some great moral question of our time. Sally hasn't read or thought much about it, but she saw it discussed on *Oprah*. Somehow *her* view on the matter should drive public policy more than her duly elected representative sworn to uphold the Constitution? By studying the matter, dialoguing with constituents, and carefully deliberating the matter, an elected representative should be able to make a much more informed decision than Sally. (Sometimes they disappoint.)

There is a sense in which public opinion in America is almost mystical, "an enlargement of what people think other people think" (Guinness). Polls are so prevalent and have become such a part of the landscape in politics, education, the news, and anywhere moral issues are discussed that we don't even stop to think about the bandwagon effect of the way they are used. But that is not to say majority approval is not important in America. (See Focus Box #7.)

Abraham Lincoln recognized that it is impossible to govern against popular consensus in a democracy such as ours. "Public opinion is everything. . . . With it nothing can fail; against it, nothing can succeed" (*Weekly Standard,* 12/25/95). And he was right. But he perceived that his responsibility as leader was to *shape* and *mold* that consensus, urging and persuading Americans to "do the right things." His vision was inspired by a universal standard of right, not a poll-driven picture of it.

≈

FOCUS YOUR WORLDVIEW #7: HEAVEN IS NOT A DEMOCRACY

In America the concept of majority rule is almost sacred, but our children need to understand the limitations of this concept from a biblical perspective. In a family get-together, give everybody one vote. Include the dog or cat if you need to make it more fun. Then pose two sets of questions, or send children out to poll the neighbors.

1. Questions of _personal preference_ such as: "Where shall we dine out this weekend?" or "What shall we get Grandma for Christmas?" (You can use the pets to create gridlock or break it.)

2. Questions of _moral choice_: Perhaps you can think of a question that would "lure" your children to vote against God's Word—something like "Should we keep some extra money for our vacation or give to God's work what we normally give?" or "Should Susie take a part in the school play if her character is just hinted to be intimate with her boyfriend?"

3. Then you could ask them to comment on the pitfalls of the majority vote:

   ➤ On _preferences_ it's okay, but on _moral_ questions, what would God say?

   ➤ Who breaks gridlock? Sometimes a leader must lead in order to take necessary action, especially in a marriage where only two people vote (one of the whys behind Ephesians 5).

   ➤ Secret ballot is important, but not always possible. In public voting, the bandwagon mentality sets in.

   ➤ In what ways is God more qualified to "vote" on moral issues than we are? (Isaiah 55:9)

   ➤ Remind children that heaven is _not_ a democracy. It's a monarchy.

4. Collect examples of opinion polls from the media. Categorize them as preference or moral choice. If moral choice, then look up Scriptures that either confirm or deny the majority view. You may want to keep a file on polls of significant moral issues and track the percentages over the years. You can readily see, even over just a few years, how opinions toward issues like abortion and homosexuality are changing.

HELP WANTED: LEADERSHIP OF CONSCIENCE

Conference speaker and author Steve Farrar tells about one confident mother's response to the question, "What do you do?"

"I raise leaders for the next generation. What do you do?" is her standard reply. Surely part of raising future leaders is to help them see through the "socially helpful" and bandwagon mentalities. You can help your children identify and discuss these false ways of making laws and moral choices and compare them to the truths of Scripture.

Whether it's choosing happiness and avoiding pain or making the choice applauded by the majority, this way of deciding cries out, "Trust your feelings. Follow your heart." In the hit movie *A Time to Kill,* the jury renders its verdict in response to the defense lawyer's appeal: "We have a duty under God to seek the truth, not with our eyes and not with our minds . . . but with our hearts."

But where are the leaders who inspire public opinion, who influence their peers, encouraging them not to follow their feelings, but to trust God and follow their conscience? Our children need to be inspired by people like Martin Luther. A monk charged with "heresy," he stood up against the false teachings of the pope and the entire Catholic church: "I am bound by the Scripture I have quoted, and my conscience is captive to the Word of God. I cannot and will not retract anything, since it is neither safe nor right to violate one's conscience. I cannot do otherwise, here I stand, may God help me. Amen."

This is the kind of leadership our children need to see—leadership of conscience held "captive to the Word of God." Consistently, graciously, faithfully, we need to live before them and lead according to conscience against the progressive cultural flow. When they or their friends choose not to follow their feelings or jump on the bandwagon, let's praise them to the skies. (By the way, the video *Martin Luther* is a great one to rent and watch together.)

And for an interesting contrast to the progressive mentality of many of our courts and politicians, rent *A Man for All Seasons.* Show your children a historical national leader, Henry VIII's lord chancellor, Sir Thomas More, who stood with the Catholic church against the king's desire for a divorce from his childless wife.

In one scene Cardinal Wolsey tries to explain how socially helpful

More's consent would be, how it would make everybody, especially the king, very happy, and how More is the only courtier not getting on the bandwagon. "Certain regrettable measures must be taken to insure that Henry VIII has an heir. Now explain to me," thunders Wolsey, "how you as chancellor of England can obstruct these measures for the sake of your private conscience!"

To which More eloquently responds, "Well, I think that when statesmen forsake their own private conscience for the sake of their public duties, they lead their country by a short route to chaos." Ultimately, for the sake of loyalty to his conscience and the church, he was beheaded.

Sir Thomas More's most famous written legacy is *Utopia*, his description of a peaceful society where everyone lives in justice and equality. In fact it was More who coined the word *utopia*.

If the progressives are right, if the basis of law and morality should be what is socially helpful ("Trust your feelings. Follow your heart"), then the more we pursue this course as a nation, the more we should head toward happiness and prosperity. And if, as Barbara Ehrenreich "argued" against Dr. Dobson, the cultural revolution of the sixties redirected us down a path toward the triumph of "the human spirit" and the goal of "human freedom," then why can't we take a walk in the park after dark anymore? Why can't I drive around, roll down my car windows, and enjoy the sights and sounds of Utopia? The Beatles sang, "I have to admit it's getting better, getting so much better all the time." Is it? (I wonder if John Lennon would have written those words knowing the fate that would befall him.) Instead it seems we are on a "short route to chaos."

SURVEYING THE CULTURAL WHITE WATER

I know, I promised no more choruses of, "Ain't it awful." How about just seven statistics and five "snapshots"?

Our moral and spiritual decline has picked up speed since the sixties. Bill Bennett's *Index of Leading Cultural Indicators* tells us that since 1960 the U.S. population has increased 41 percent, but total social spending has increased 500 percent to $787 billion. And what has happened to our problems on which we have lavished so much money? Some things are up:

- TV viewing from five to seven hours daily

- illegitimate births from 5 percent to 26 percent

- children on welfare from 3 1/2 percent to 12 percent

- teen suicide rate from 3 1/2 percent to 11 percent

- violent crime rate (per 100,000 population) from 16 percent to 76 percent

And some things are down:

- SAT scores from 975 to 899 (until they renormed the test)

- median prison sentence from 22 1/2 days to 8 days

I keep a file of news stories that illustrate this decline in graphic "snapshots." Here are some pictures that capture how hazardous our cultural white water has become:

- Houston, Texas. Homeowners protest a park or school being located in their neighborhood. They feel it will attract criminal activity and be a detriment to the neighborhood. (I remember when folks used to *like* parks in their neighborhoods.)

- Chicago, Illinois. Parents helping prepare a school Christmas party for the students started opening the presents and taking what they wanted. Over 200 children came to the party to find wrapping paper but no gifts. Many went home crying.

- South Portland, Maine. Rain forced organizers to move the yearly Easter Egg Hunt to a site with no taped-off waiting area to restrain the egg-hunters. Children and then parents started a stampede to gather eggs prematurely. In a second hunt for those shut out the first time, parents and older kids came back to scoop up candy as fast as it was hidden in the grass.

- Columbus, Georgia. Seven sixth graders are sentenced for trying to murder their teacher because she was too strict. They tried to poison her tea, trip her down some stairs, and brought a handgun and a knife to school.

➤ Orlando, Florida. Headline reads: "Boy, 9, Threatens to Kill Mother for Kid's Meal Toy." (At Burger King drive-through, with a pocket knife to her throat.)

The progressives hold that man makes the rules. God's Word is, at best, a guide; at worst, intolerant and divisive. They affirm that man, starting from his own reason, experience, and feelings, can solve all his problems. They promise utopia. But what do they deliver? As the old Christian consensus fades and the progressive worldview becomes the majority worldview, what is the reality?

William Bennett's statistics, elementary students plotting to kill their teacher, Christmas parties where parents steal the toys, and egg hunts where parents steal the eggs—the reality is _chaos_.

Most people think things are in a mess. Seventy-five percent surveyed in a _Wall Street Journal_ poll wanted a return to "traditional values."

Amidst all the evidence of cultural decline, however, I believe there is great hope for the future! Because, as the pain increases, people's hearts become open to the Gospel. Misguided public policies and people's lives are crashing into the wall of reality, and many are ready to admit failure and seek new solutions. This means we have a great open door to share the Gospel and to bring Christian influence to bear on our culture.

JUSTICE AND MERCY IN JEREMIAH

Jeremiah was a prophet who proclaimed God's pending judgment to Judah, a nation on the homestretch of moral and spiritual decline. He listed the Jews' sins against their God: greed, sexual immorality, lust for power, material comfort, and success. They sacrificed their children for the economic prosperity promised by idols. Their greatest sin was apostasy, turning their backs on the God of their fathers.

For their many sins, God was sending judgment, a terrible, savage army from the north—Babylon. But even after the army was well on its way, God told His people through Jeremiah, "Repent. Return to me, and I will deliver you" (Jeremiah 5). He would call off His avenging troops.

God's justice is always balanced by His tender mercy. But because of the "stubbornness of their evil hearts," they would not repent.

Later when Nebuchadnezzar laid siege to the city, again God in His mercy told the people, "If you will go outside the city walls and surrender, I will spare your lives." Inside the city, even God was fighting against them with plagues and poisonous snakes. But outside the gate there was mercy and life (Jeremiah 21).

And finally Jerusalem fell, her walls and buildings were destroyed, and families that remained were torn apart. Many of the best and brightest sons and daughters were marched off in chains to Babylon. God had told them (Deuteronomy 28:32) that their parents would "wear out [their] eyes watching for them day after day, powerless to lift a hand." Through his tears the weeping prophet once again told of God's wondrous grace and mercy. "When seventy years are completed for Babylon, I will come to you and fulfill my gracious promise to bring you back to this place" (Jeremiah 29:10).

We are not God's special covenant nation as Israel was (and is), and yet we are a nation founded on Christian principles. Our pattern of sin and apostasy is certainly similar to Israel's. Will God judge us as He judged Israel?

I agree with Pastor Erwin Lutzer, author of *Twelve Myths That Americans Believe,* who thinks that we are already seeing God's judgment on our land. There is no need to wait for some heavenly axe to fall. As Israel experienced the breakup and scattering of its families, so are we. Thousands of the children born this year will see their families split up, and they will have to live with that pain. Many parents miss sharing their lives with their children and spend many holidays and weekends waiting and watching for their turn.

God told the Israelis that their disobedience would bring "an anxious mind, eyes weary with longing, and a despairing heart" (Deuteronomy 28:65). Perhaps of all the dangers ahead, the greatest our children will face are a crisis of meaning and a loss of hope.

THERE IS NO STORY

"Hope is the thing with feathers," penned poet Emily Dickinson—the idea being that it floats, it flies. It is up, not under, as in "under the circumstances." Quite often the circumstances of a fallen world are so dark or overwhelming that we need hope of something better.

From the fall of Rome to the Renaissance, Western people centered their hope in a better life after this one—eternal life. They lived in a time we call the Age of Faith. People saw their lives completely within the context of the Christian Story, and they knew how the Story ended. So they had great hope. They looked _up_ to the Author and _forward_ to His kingdom.

Then beginning in the Renaissance and gaining great momentum in the Enlightenment, we saw the dawn of modern times—faith in reason and progress—in people's ability to do whatever they will—just give them until tomorrow, as Francis Schaeffer put it. Hope increasingly became something that was part of _this_ world, not the next.

Over the last century especially, people have lost faith in God's Story and produced their own alternatives. "There is no Author," they said. But intellectuals put forth a Story based on evolution called the Ascent of Man. Others looked at the history of Western civilization and talked about the Story of the Ascent of Western Democracy. In the sixties we celebrated _principles_—at Woodstock Richie Havens sang about Freedom while the Beatles sang, "All We Need Is Love." There was still a reason to keep looking _forward_, if not _up_.

But now other intellectuals are tearing those Stories and principles down. Most biologists are saying that people are not special, just a little more clever about propagating their genes (which are really responsible for all their thoughts or behavior, success or failure); and hard-core multiculturalists claim that Western democracy is no crowning achievement either. They revise history to correct the impression that our cultural values are any better than the Hutus' or the Tutsis', the Shiite Muslims' or the Somalis'. They point out that our history of racism, greed, and oppression of blacks, women, and gays invalidates our claim to "Western ascendancy." "All cultural value systems are equal!" they insist. And on our college campuses the Darwinian biologists are claiming the sciences, while the multiculturalists influence or dominate the humanities.

The secular voice that we grew up with cried out, "There is no Author, and there may be no Story, but we still have certain principles and ideals, and life makes sense as we make progress toward achieving those ideals." John Eldredge, Director of Public Policy Research and Seminars for Focus on the Family, has correctly observed that the secular voice our children are growing up with is more honest. It cries, "That's ridiculous. If you don't have an Author, you have no Story. And if there's no larger Story to live in, then nothing makes sense."

The human race is not ascending, just surviving. History is not the Story of the West ascending; it is all the equal cultures and nations just surviving. Faith in reason is crumbling as each person turns to his own experience and feelings. And hope? There is nothing to look *up* for or *forward* to. The "thing with feathers" is a roadkill beside our post-modern highway, humming with technological excellence, but going . . . well, no one seems to know where we are going. That's why our current age is being called postmodern. It is *after* the collapse of modern belief in reason and progress. No one knows what comes next. (See Focus Box #8.)

Reflecting on this crisis of hope and meaning, Sven Birkerts, a book reviewer for the *New York Times*, has written:

> The understanding and assumptions that were formerly operative in society no longer feel valid. Things have shifted; they keep shifting. We all feel a desire for connection, for meaning, but we don't seem to know what to connect with what, and we are utterly at sea about our place as individuals in the world at large. The maps no longer describe the terrain we inhabit. There is no clear path to the future. We trust that the species will blunder on, but we don't know where to.
>
> —*The Gutenberg Elegies,* p. 20

Nowhere is the loss of hope and meaning and lack of connection to a Story larger than ourselves felt more keenly than by our children's generation. The first time I set foot in our public high school on the day of freshman orientation, I encountered a rather nice-looking young man sporting a T-shirt that read, "I used to be depressed. But that was before I gave up all hope." This from a generation enjoying more affluence and freedom than any other in history.

MTV knows our children are identifying with its message. In its national survey of young people aged sixteen to twenty-nine, "the word selected as 'least' describing their generation was 'lucky,' while 'angry' and 'stressed out' appeared among the 'best' descriptions of this age group." Film critic Michael Medved cited this survey in a 1995 address to Hillsdale College's Shavano Institute for National Leadership. He warned: "This depressed and nihilistic attitude toward life could be the biggest threat to America today . . . if [our children] believe that discipline and hard work are pointless, that life is meaningless and unfair, and that the outlook for the future is grim."

One young woman quoted in Gene Veith's book *Postmodern Times* expressed her emptiness of meaning and hope this way: "I belong to the Blank Generation. I have no beliefs. I belong to no community, tradition, or anything like that. I'm lost in this vast, vast world. I belong nowhere. I have absolutely no identity" (p. 72).

If you listen to your children's music and hear lyrics such as "I declare I don't care no more, I'm burning up and out and growing bored" (Green Day), if your children or their friends are identifying with that music, then you can see how the postmodern loss of meaning and hope is touching your family, your school, your community. If your children are younger, you know what is coming.

Returning to the Story analogy, Focus on the Family's John Eldredge hears today's secular voice saying that if there is no Author and if there is no Story, then there is no content or meaning to life. So "go live in your own small story. . . . We all need a story to live in, so go find one; just don't pretend it's true." Each of us must write our own little story and try and make it as interesting as we can. I know kids who live in the football story, the cheerleading story, the alternative rock story, the girlfriend or boyfriend story. So do you. And we know . . . small stories end badly.

We have a great treasure to pass on to our children—the heritage of God's Story. And as we navigate our way past life rafts that have crashed or capsized in the postmodern turbulence, we have a wonderful message of comfort to give others. No matter how bad the white water gets, no matter how concerned we are about the river ahead, God is in control. And He reassures us, "Never will I leave you; never will I forsake you," and "In all things God works for the good of those who love him" (Hebrews 13:5; Romans 8:28). "For I know the plans I have for you . . . plans to prosper you and not to harm you, plans to give you a hope and a future" (Jeremiah 29:11).

I love the following quote, which I've adapted a little from renowned British author and journalist Malcolm Muggeridge: Behind the debris of chaos and pain and loss of meaning and hope and sad little stories "stands the gigantic figure of one Person *because* of whom, *by* whom, *in* whom, and *through* whom alone mankind may still have hope. The person of *Jesus Christ*" (*The End of Christendom*). The more we see of the end of human stories and promises, the more beautiful God's Story looks, and the more brightly His promise of a hope and a future shines in the deepening darkness.

≈

FOCUS YOUR WORLDVIEW #8:
A POSTMODERN SCRAPBOOK

What if you had been born in the Middle Ages but had seen some of the great changes brought in by the Renaissance during your lifetime? Or what if you had been personally swept up in the Reformation? What would you have seen if you had been around to witness the Enlightenment, the beginnings of modern times? (Maybe you grew up in the fifties and early sixties like me and *did* witness the cultural revolution of the sixties—the beginnings of postmodern times.)

Our children are growing up in the beginning of a new age of civilization. Modern times—characterized by faith in man's progress and human reason—are passing into postmodern times— a loss of faith in progress and especially in reason. Some historians give the pivotal date as November 1989—the fall of the Berlin Wall—the collapse of Marxist communism, the ultimate attempt of people to devise their own social order, rejecting faith completely and relying on reason alone. What will our children see as they watch this new age unfold?

Perhaps they would like to assemble a scrapbook recording this change for generations to come. (Wouldn't it be interesting to have a family scrapbook contrasting the fifties with the sixties?) Find examples of the contrasting characteristics of modern and post-modern times listed below. Sources could be any printed media, computer printouts from the Internet, pictures, descriptions of TV, movies, events, conversations—the possibilities are endless. If a scrapbook sounds like more time than you want to give, perhaps your children would like to journal their thoughts about the changes. Or maybe a bulletin board or even a few noteworthy items on the refrigerator door would be more your speed. Actually, each entry would make for an interesting discussion as you talk about examples together. (Thanks to Gene Veith's excellent book, *Postmodern Times: A Christian Guide to Contemporary Thought and Culture*, for most of what follows.)

As you read the chart, you may feel that modernism compares quite favorably with postmodernism, but remember that any worldview based on a rejection of Jesus Christ is fatally flawed. On the other hand, not all these characteristics of postmodernism are negative; some are a refreshing change from modernism. (I really like the Energizer Bunny busting in on what seems to be a soap ad with what is *really* a battery ad.) But if one had to summarize postmodern advice for living, it would be something to the effect: Accept the meaninglessness. Live life on the surface. Concentrate on your own small story—your own little world. Make it look good and be as interesting as possible. Play the game. Use your image, language, and choices to assert as much power as you can. Postmodern password: *whatever*—the ultimate in tolerance.

MODERN TIMES	POSTMODERN TIMES
- Confidence in reason, the intellect. We can solve all our problems apart from God	- No confidence in reason, "A breakdown in belief," intellect replaced by will ("Just do it."); no confidence in solving our problems
- Thinking systematically—no holes, gaps, or embracing opposing ideas	- Believing what you like to believe regardless of holes, gaps, contradictions
- Progress (meaning) achieved in pursuit of ideals—Peace, Love, Freedom, Equality, Democracy, etc.	- There are no ideals. Everyone creates her own meaning, and each one's sense of meaning or purpose is equally valid. Just don't pretend your idea of what's meaningful is true for everybody.

MODERN TIMES	POSTMODERN TIMES
- Standing up for what is right	- Tolerance, pluralism
- Values order, structure, hierarchy	- Accepts chaos, anarchy, fragmentation
- Interest in meaning, depth, substance	- Interest in surfaces, combinations and collections of images, style over substance
- Sustained attention and inquiry	- Need for "instant impact" and gratification
- Accumulates valuable objects, experiences	- Accumulates status that objects and experience may bring
- Deep impact of symbols, actions, etc., that are holy or profane	- Both the holy and profane are trivialized by satire, endless repetition, etc.
- Emphasizes truth, achievement	- Emphasis on impression, image, charisma, style (especially fashion)
- Commends honesty, consistency	- Affirms irony, satire, saying one thing today and saying or doing another tomorrow (whatever works)
- Values being true to oneself	- Values role playing; "We really are different people at home, at work, at church."
- Prizes originality	- Prizes reproducibility, recycling
- Values the norm, the type	- Values the aberration, the mutant
- Art: Judged by level of skill, appreciated as a finished work	- Art: Significance found in shock and outrage to audience (instant impact); appreciated as a process or performance

MODERN TIMES	POSTMODERN TIMES
- Architecture: Emphasizes unity, simplicity, sleek lines, neutral colors, glass	- Architecture: Emphasis on past styles (sometimes in clashing combinations), splashes of color, decorative detail, inside structural framework (beams, ductwork) appears on the outside—distinction blurs
- Literature/Media: Makes sharp distinction between fiction and reality	- Literature/Media. Distinction blurs: TV docudramas, infotainment programs, unhistorical history movies, magical realism, (highly realistic stories with elements of complete fantasy mixed in, i.e., Groundhog Day, Field of Dreams, many commercials)
- Education: Individual student learns lesson, does homework; emphasizes language: reading, writing	- Education: Group work, projects; emphasis on image (computer, VCR), and experience (interactive games, field trips, etc.)

All the adjacent postmodern particulars flow out of a postmodern worldview. For the read-more-about-it crowd, compare the postmodern presuppositions below with the biblical worldview presuppositions in Focus Box #2.

➤ *What is real?* Reality is what you (or your culture) make it. Earth is a "vast universe of multiple realities." "Different groups construct different stories." You can't even perceive or talk about "reality"— all you see is your point of view; all you can say is what your language allows you to understand and express.

➤ *What is man?* You are molded by your culture, your language. Your identity depends on the cultural group you are a part of (women, minorities, gays, etc.). (Result—segmentation and tribalization of society.)

➤ *Is God real? Is He involved in human affairs?* It depends on your point of view. Whatever.

➤ *How do we know what is true?* What I like, want, and choose is true for me. Whatever works is true. Beyond that, truth does not exist.

➤ *How do we judge what is right and wrong?* "What I like, what I want, and what I choose is not only true for me, but right for me." There are no rules—God's or man's. Sin doesn't exist, so there's no need to be forgiven. Cultures may make rules, but the rules are only preferences and opinions as to what works in that culture. There is no ultimate reality of goodness or fairness. There is only power. When you communicate, you are just trying to exert your power over another person or group.

WORLDVIEWS

CHRISTIAN	MODERN	POSTMODERN
- There is an Author.	- There is no Author, but there are ideals.	- There is no Author and no ideals. Nothing.
- We live in a Grand Story, the triumph of God's plan for the ages.	- We live in a Grand Story— the triumph of reason, evolution; the progress of the human spirit.	- There is no Grand Story.
- Hope	- Progress (false hope)	- There is no hope.

≈

THE FLAME
PASSES ON

4

*Leading Our Children Toward
What They Must Find for Themselves*

IF OUR CHILDREN ARE TO THRIVE AND SUCCESSFULLY NAVIGATE the postmodern rapids ahead, they need *hope*. This hope must be based on faith in God's tender love for them and confidence in the truth of His Word. But the cultural deck is stacked against parents who want to teach their children the truths of God's Story and a Christian worldview. Growing up in the late sixties and early seventies, many of this generation declared independence by wearing love beads and psychedelic prints and listening to Led Zeppelin. Being countercultural was hip. Today in our ethically relative, pleasure-seeking culture, we have to *teach* our kids to be countercultural. And it is no easy task, even for those making a great effort.

As I am writing, it is back-to-school time. I talked on the phone yesterday morning with my friend Patty whose son had just announced his homecoming plans to her—and they needed some "modification." We lamented together that there was no verse in Proverbs that plainly says, "My son, thou shalt not go out with seven other couples after the homecoming dance to a lake house and spend the night and jet ski the next day when we know not the parents who will be chaperoning."

Then at lunch I talked to Mollie, another friend, whose pretty freshman daughter is plunging into the social world of high school and attracting a lot of attention. (Does running an errand with a guy in a car qualify as a date? What if they stop at Burger King?)

Then yesterday evening I talked to an old friend whose husband is an elder at their church. They have raised two very godly daughters, but their third daughter is currently reaping the results of some wrong decisions. She naively rejected her parents' teaching and the biblical principles they tried to pass on to her. As a consequence, she is pregnant and unmarried. The baby is biracial.

Still discouraged after talking to her, I watched the 10:00 news to find out that an elder from a neighboring sister church and his wife had been murdered by their twenty-five-year-old son, who then committed suicide.

There is no magic formula for raising godly children. There are no guarantees. Many Christians would like to take Proverbs and *make* it a guarantee: We train them right; they trust God. But Proverbs is a book of general principles, not iron-clad promises. It *is* generally true that if we train our children up in the way they should go, when they are old, they will not depart from it. But it's not a personal promise, as the two elders' families mentioned above could attest.

Our *desire* is to have a godly child. But that is something over which we ultimately have no control. Our *goal* is to be godly parents. That is an outcome over which we *do* have control and need to make daily choices to pursue.

Raising worldproofed kids is something of a desire *and* a goal. Ultimately that outcome depends on our child's choices. But we can do much by way of nurturing his heart and mind with the truth and teaching of a Christian worldview.

Before we go any further, I would like to offer what I call the "Dobson Disclaimer." Dr. James Dobson has written the following words of wisdom: "One who teaches God's Word in this area is also a student and fellow traveler. God's words are true and trustworthy. He does not need me to validate His Word." This book does not come with a money-back guarantee that teaching these principles will produce worldproofed kids.

Jack and I are still definitely in process with Zach. In fact, in these teen years you could say it's just now getting interesting! We're ordinary, imperfect human beings. We must look to Jesus Christ and the Scriptures for wisdom. And we have to remind ourselves constantly of the fact (already mentioned) that we cannot trust Christ *for* our son. We cannot yield to the Holy Spirit *for* him, nor can we make him love

God with all his heart—just as Moses could not make the children of Israel walk with God. Even Adam and Eve, who had the most perfect parent of all, chose to rebel and believe Satan's lies.

The safest passage through cultural white water is reliance on the truth of God's Word. I've tried to make the case in these first three chapters that those who depend on their own feelings or reason or experience, or even their faith as a supplementary guide, will wind up on the rocks. That even though the progressive view of truth is the main cultural message our children hear about truth and the source of moral authority, they will suffer the consequences if they use this view as a map. Before we consider what God's Word has to say about particular cultural issues, I want to wrap our discussion of truth with a careful consideration of the context, setting, and strategy for passing God's truth on to our children.

THE POWER OF OUR LIVES TOUCHING THEIRS

"Okay, lunch break's over. Everybody back in the raft. Now! . . . I mean business. . . . Come on, move it! . . . etc., etc., . . . Where is everybody?!" Sometimes we find it hard to win a hearing with our children. Whether we will be heard or not depends perhaps most on the context of our advice, namely a good relationship and a good example. Entire books have been written on this subject, by many wonderful and gifted authors. It is not the purpose of this book to pursue such fundamental and vitally important subjects in depth, but to acknowledge their role in this discussion.

God's Word teaches that a good relationship with my child is based on unconditional love, good discipline, and communication. It's worth noting that the only time I can show unconditional love to Zach is when he is not meeting my conditions. Sometimes that's very difficult for me, because he really knows how to push my buttons—"Look at this bathroom!" Unconditional love and good discipline, Dobson has said, are like the lights on each side of the runway needed to land an airplane at night. They serve as healthy nurturing boundaries so our children don't crash in the dark.

Cultivating good family communication is the heart of good family relationships and something we have to consciously pursue. The challenges of a busy schedule and the lure of the media will gradually intrude into our family life and, if we're not careful, squeeze out communication like a kudzu vine taking over an undeveloped lot. In his book *Winning Your Kids Back from the Media,* Calvin College communications professor Quentin Schultz discusses our profound need for family communication to fulfill our basic desires for identity and intimacy.

Schultz encourages Christian parents to use dinnertimes and other family times for storytelling—sharing what happened in our day and how we feel about it, and inviting our children to do the same as we really listen. "When a child has a problem," he writes, "we need to listen to the story that gives rise to the problem before we offer a solution." Beyond storytelling and listening, good family communication requires empathy, "putting ourselves in the shoes of the storyteller" and "suspending judgment until the story is fully told" (pp. 30-31). Questions about how our children feel will lead to deeper communication. When we invite them to open up to us, but give them quick, thoughtless responses in return, we're taking one step forward but two steps back.

In our quest for communication and relationship with our children, we adults must take the initiative and find a way into their world. We can't expect a child to find his way into ours. As we show our children unconditional love, good discipline, and a desire to really communicate with them, we create the moral authority we need to teach them about God and His truth.

Our moral authority is also established as we set a good example. We need to teach forgiveness by example. We need to model commitment—to know God's Word, to love God as our Father, and to love others sacrificially, beginning with our own family. Jack and I need to model what a godly marriage looks like. We need to live our lives so that our children clearly see that our source of security and significance is Jesus Christ—not plenty of good times, friends, or money.

As Jack and I have discussed this, we realize that we are continually teaching Zach by example—by the way we drive, by the way Jack carefully keeps the game laws when they are out hunting (especially when many disregard them), by visiting the sick and the poor, by pointing out that the sales clerk undercharged us, by turning in lost valuables, by asking forgiveness when we lose our temper, by serving in our church and in our schools and community, by talking to the theater manager or the video store owner when we have concerns about what they are offering, and by the routine faithfulness of carrying our responsibilities with a spirit of joy and contentment.

In the introduction to his *Book of Virtues,* Bill Bennett states, "It has been said that there is nothing more influential, more determinant in a child's life than the moral power of a quiet example" (p. 11). God's design for a family is so crucial. Children need two parental relationships: one with their own sex and one with the opposite sex. They also need two examples.

Perhaps your home is hurting because a father is missing. You can take comfort in God's promise that He will be a father to the fatherless. Certainly the church needs to come alongside single parents and help in practical ways. But while we reach out to broken families, we do not change God's design for the family.

Relationship and example are the indispensable foundation upon which our children's spiritual and moral education rests. But they need more. God calls us to teach our children His truths—about Him, about ourselves, about life. These are the main puzzle pieces that will frame and focus their worldview—the map that will direct our life raft through the tumbling rapids ahead.

LINKS IN THE CHAIN

Again and again in Scripture we are told to teach God's revealed Word to our children, precept upon precept (Deuteronomy 6:6-7). We are also told to teach our children *and grandchildren* "the things your eyes have seen" (Deuteronomy 4:9). In other words we are to share with them our own spiritual lives—our struggles, our victories, our failures, and God's gracious forgiveness. We need to share our rejoicing over God's provision and those times when His truth triumphs. (See Resource Box #2.)

In this marvelous age of computers it's easy to summon up every verse in the Bible that contains the words *teach* and *children*. When we do that, we find that in all of Scripture we are directly commanded to teach our children three things:

1. *To love the Lord*—to develop a relationship with our Creator to whom we are to be committed above all others, to whom we are devoted with all our heart, soul, and mind. And here's the challenge: do our children see us loving God out of duty, or delight? Which of these two motivations do we prefer from our husbands? It's hard to teach love motivated by delight. This is our toughest assignment! It helps when our children see their lives in the context of God's Grand Story—how they are being pursued and "romanced" by the Hero of that story who loves them dearly. Do they see us responding in delight to God's loving pursuit? John Piper's book *Desiring God* provides a deeply insightful discussion of this topic. Also *The Sacred Romance* mentioned earlier.

2. *To fear the Lord*—to understand who He is and what He is like (Creator, Judge, Savior, Holy, Omniscient, Infinite, and so on) and who we are in relation to Him. This involves teaching our children the basics of a Christian worldview, discussed in chapters 1 and 2. We teach that God is the source of universal, transcendent truth, against which our reason, experience, and feelings are finite and error-prone, and that our proper response to Him is reverence, worship, and submission. It is the relationship between the potter and the clay (Isaiah 29) that prompts us to be in awe of God's righteous power, to lay our brokenness and failure at His feet, and to long for God to fill us up and make us whole. Friend and pastor Bob Livesay has said that the fear of the Lord is "a wholesome dread of displeasing God."

3. *To keep His commandments*. This assignment is a little more straightforward. But it requires that we know God's Word ourselves. That's why it is important that we study it and really learn it. (When a teachable moment presents itself is not the time to go looking up chapter and verses.) Especially as they get older, our children's motivation to keep God's commandments comes not just from knowing *what* God commands, but from understanding *why* God commands it—developing that "truth apologetic," as Josh McDowell calls it.

When we teach our children right and wrong based on God's commands, we summon up a great moral authority far beyond ourselves. This should give us confidence. Imagine the insecurity a parent must feel when her child challenges her authority, and she has no support for her claim to know what is right beyond her own opinions and feelings.

We have grown up in a society that delegates most of the teaching of children to specialists and professionals. As a professional teacher, I can appreciate the advantages of a professional's or specialist's help in this information age. However, we must not look to preschool, public school, private school, or Sunday school to assume the job of educating our children. These professionals and specialists may assist us, but ultimately *we parents will stand before God and give an account of our children's spiritual and moral instruction.* What are some effective strategies for teaching this curriculum? Scripture tells us to use two types of opportunities, both unplanned and planned.

RESOURCE BOX #2: "LEAD ON, OH KINKY TURTLE"

It requires a supreme effort to take what one radio commentator calls "young skulls full of mush" and teach them to love and serve the Lord, *and* get the words to the hymns right (it's "King eternal"). Here are some of my favorite sources of advice and encouragement for the spiritual nurturing of children.

You and Your Child: A Biblical Guide for Nurturing Confident Children from Infancy to Independence, Charles R. Swindoll, Nelson, 1990. General parenting with a couple of chapters that focus on spiritual nurturing. Comes with Study Guide.

Building a Christian Family: A Guide for Parents, Kenneth and Elizabeth Gangel, Moody Press, 1987. A good general resource on Christian parenting, with chapters on distinctives of a Christian home and family worship.

Raising Kids God's Way: A Biblical Guide for Christian Parents, Kathi Hudson, Crossway, 1995. General parenting with chapters on family nights, goal-setting as a family, nurturing your children in prayer, wisdom, decision-making, with good suggestions for incorporating material with applicable Scripture into family nights.

Making God's Word Stick: A How-to-Really-Do-It, Five-Star Road Map for Anyone Investing Time in Making God's Word Stick in the Hearts of Children at Home, Church, or School, Emmett Cooper and Steve Wamberg, Nelson, 1996. Fun, creative, practice-proven tips to inspire you "as you walk by the way" or sit down for family devotions.

Guiding Your Teen to a Faith That Lasts: A Blueprint for Building a Relationship with God, Kevin Huggins and Phil Landrum, Discovery House Press, 1994. Profoundly insightful, very readable, full of practical suggestions. Huggins is also the author of *Parenting Adolescents*, a wonderful resource, especially for dealing with troubled teens.

Intimate Family Moments: Lessons from Galilee, Drawing Your Family Closer to God and One Another, Dr. David and Teresa Ferguson, Dr. Paul and Vicky Warren and Terri Ferguson, Victor, 1995. Suggestions for family time—very practical, creative, and fun; Bible drama for each section developed from Scripture passage; separate suggested activity sections for preschoolers, grade schoolers, middle and high schoolers. Activities also designed to prompt storytelling and build intimacy in family relationships. Also suggestions for family outreach.

"WHEN YOU [DRIVE] ALONG THE ROAD"

Impressing God's commands on our children's hearts is the subject of Deuteronomy 6:4-9. The recommended method is this: "Talk about them when you sit at home and when you walk [drive] along the road, when you lie down and when you get up." We are to develop a habit of teaching as we go about life.

When little Mary breaks the rules, we often will take a few minutes to review the rule, maybe even talk about how the rule relates to God's commands, deal with apologies, forgiveness, restoration of the relationships involved, and the consequences of disobedience.

We also have opportunities when our children come to us with "big questions" such as: "When the world stops, where will I be?" These subjects usually come up seemingly "out of the blue" while we're cooking or driving or doing laundry. Children like to probe the big questions that are on their minds when they are feeling secure and in a familiar setting. From the time they are old enough to string sentences together, some of their questions can be very profound. I love the little booklet *Children's Letters to God,* mentioned in chapter 1. Think of the opportunities that present themselves when children ask questions such as: "Instead of letting people die and having to make new ones, why don't You just keep the ones You got now?" or "What does it mean You are a jealous God? I thought You had everything."

Robert Coles, a secular psychiatrist and professor at Harvard, is one of the leading researchers on early childhood development. In his book *The Spiritual Life of Children,* he observes that children spend a significant amount of time in reflection and wonder about God, guilt, moral successes and failures—such questions as "What are we?" and "Where are we going?" Coles determines that a child's spiritual inter-action and reflection starts very early on, and by age three is really growing. Dr. James Dobson concurs with Coles's findings: a child is most receptive to spiritual training in the first six years.

Coles and Dobson encourage parents to listen to their children closely to know when to take the time to answer the big questions that usually begin with phrases like: "What do you think about . . . ," "How can it be . . . ," "Do you think it's good when . . . ," "How can you tell if . . ." However, Coles's conventional wisdom, recommending that parents let kids pick the time and place for spiritual training, does not agree with Scripture. The command in Deuteronomy 6:6-7 is for *us* as parents to talk about God's Word as we go. That means we don't always wait for our children to ask. We need to look prayerfully for opportunities to relate God's Word to what we see, hear, or do as we're going about life.

Of course, balance is needed. We can over-saturate our children with efforts to create "teachable moments." We need to be sensitive to God's leading and what our children are open to and seem interested in. We should also pursue conversations about their other interests (and make sure they have other interests)—reading, music, sports, raising animals, or whatever.

In a newsletter to his supporters, Al Menconi (who teaches and writes about a Christian perspective on popular music) confesses his overstepping in this area. He talks about being on vacation and trying to make it a learning experience for his two daughters as they were "driving along the road." "It wasn't working. It seemed like every time I had something 'teachable' to say, I could tell they were turning me off. If you're a parent, you know the feeling. They look at you, but they're not really *looking* at you."

He gave up and decided to just enjoy their company. "Wouldn't you know it, when I quit trying to force 'teaching,' opportunities of deep learning presented (themselves). As we listened to Christian music together, we began to discuss the values presented. We had some great conversations about important issues." (But notice, this dad still had a hand in encouraging these discussions by choosing to listen to his girls' choice of music on _his_ vacation.)

Many parents believe that not only should parents let their children initiate these informal times of discussion, but that they should not try to set aside any prearranged time for such interchanges. Again this advice from Coles and others disagrees with Scripture.

Teaching our children spiritual and moral truth as we lie down and as we rise up could mean an informal "as we do these things" kind of approach, or it could be more formal—something we prearrange. Certainly there were other instances of prearranged teaching time when Israelite parents were commanded to teach their children. The Jewish feasts were such a time. The rituals the family performed were given by God to be object lessons in assisting Jewish parents to teach things about Israel's needs and God's provision to the next generation.

FAMILY DEVOTIONS—BLIND SPOT OR BLESSING?

Say the words "family devotions," and different people conjure up different images. For many of Jack's seminary professors' families, such as the Howard Hendrickses, I'm sure these times were interesting, deeply informative, and fun. While growing up, I glimpsed one family having devotions. They were kneeling around a small bench on a hard wooden floor for a _long_ time. It did not look interesting, and it certainly did not look like fun. I remember feeling glad _we_ didn't do that. Having said that, I don't think family devotions or "quality time" or whatever you call it needs to be entertaining. But it's important to note that young children especially need to feel generally positive about these times. As they grow older, they are more apt to remember the way they felt rather than the specifics of what was taught.

For many the words "family devotions" conjure up a vague responsibility that they never understand or consider seriously. For those new in their faith, the words have no association at all—zero. For others, it has one major association—guilt. They have started and fizzled too many times to count. They mean well, but the TV, school, and sports schedules continue to win the battle. No matter what you call a formal, prearranged time of instruction—family devotions, after dinnertime, special bedtime—for many it remains a blind spot in their role as Christian parents.

Blind spots are funny. We can have it all together and be doing something well or looking pretty good. But a blind spot can significantly detract from all these good intentions. Let me illustrate. I was invited to a large wedding in Dallas awhile back. The groom was the son of one of our elders and dear friends. Since my husband couldn't make the trip, I went alone. I took a new outfit I had recently purchased. Scurrying so as not to be late for dinner, I pulled on my new suit jacket at the last minute and ran out the door to meet the groom's aunt and uncle at their hotel. After a lovely dinner we drove to the church. I was headed into a back pew in this huge, beautifully decorated church, but the family insisted that I walk all the way down to the front and sit with them.

The wedding was beautiful. The bride worked with the Dallas Symphony, so the sanctuary was filled with beautiful voices and the accompaniment of a string quartet, brass ensemble, harp, and the mighty pipe organ. When they pledged, "I do," it was not the last time I would shed tears that evening.

Downstairs at the reception I floated around for a while and finally landed at a table with my plate full of goodies. I introduced myself to some of my tablemates who turned out to be with the Dallas Symphony. After a while, one of them sitting next to me leaned over and whispered, "May I tell you something?"

Red alert! I could see genuine nervousness in her eyes. "Yes, of course," I responded.

"Did you know that the price tag is still on your jacket?"

"No."

How could that be? I thought. My friend and I had spent about fifteen minutes pulling at least twenty tags off this outfit. It must have been a small one we overlooked. "Where is it? Is it very big?"

"It's under your arm, and—yes, it's pretty big. Would you like me to try and pull it off?"

"Please!"

So this poor lady tugged and pulled and struggled to get not one, but *two* tags off. Finally, just as I thought she was going to put her foot on my hip for leverage, the tags tore off the stubborn nylon cord, which still stuck straight out.

I sat in stunned silence. I could not fathom how my friend and I had missed two white tags, both about two inches wide and four inches long on that dark plum suit. I'm sure the people on the back row could read "Loehmann's Back Room" in large print (and probably the size!).

Then in slow motion, I relived the entire evening, picturing these huge tags fluttering in the breeze—flashes of waiters collapsing in laughter in the hotel kitchen, of wedding guests wondering if the groom had the sort of friends who would wear something once and then take it back to the store—flashes of having felt pretty and "together" for a special evening, but like the rich man who wanted bigger barns, the hand in my mind's eye wrote "F-O-O-L" across my image of the evening.

A blind spot can significantly detract from our best intentions. A lack of effort to pursue a planned family time of moral and spiritual training will hinder us from fulfilling God's command to teach our children to love, fear, and serve Him. To properly address this blind spot, we have to understand how seriously it detracts and catch a vision for how much eternal benefit can be gained from this investment of our time and resources.

A planned family time is worth doing and worth doing right. If we can spend great gobs of time and money training our children in sports, music, dance, gymnastics, horseback riding, and so on; or helping with their homework; or sending them to tutors or private schools, we can put a balanced effort into planned times of spiritual training.

No one requires the extracurricular activities we love to provide. The state requires compulsory education in certain academic subjects. But the Lord requires that we teach His commands to our children. When we finally stand before Him to give an account of our lives, He will not ask us if Johnny played first string on the football team or if Susie was first-chair clarinet. He will ask us if we taught our children to "love Him, fear Him, and keep His commands."

Below are some specific strategies for planning a family time; most are taken from Carolyn Williford's very practical book *Devotions for Families That Can't Sit Still*.

1. *Plan Ahead.* Everybody, including Dad, needs to schedule this time into their weekly activities.

2. *Set Realistic Goals.* Plan not to watch TV during this special time. It seems like the older kids get, the busier families become. Several times a week may be realistic for younger families; those with older kids may have to scale back or combine with mealtimes or bedtimes. If bedtime works best, move it up to allow plenty of time for discussion.

3. *Keep the Devotions Short and Relevant.* Be creative. Cruise the Christian bookstore or church library. Use the best material you can find, afford, or borrow. Choose topics that relate to seasons, holidays, current struggles (friendship, sportsmanship). Focus on application of Scripture to life. (See Resource Box #3.)

4. *Stretch Out the Time with Fun.* Use activities occasionally or special videos and discussion. Some devotions may be more worshipful; some may focus on application, and some may be more recreational. Williford's book gives many examples, such as writing parables, constructing a building block temple, celebrating with New Year's blessings, and many more.

5. *The Importance of Prayer.* Always spend time together before God's throne of grace. We take requests from each family member and also pray through our Christmas card stack, two or three cards at a time—a wonderful idea that the Dobsons passed along. (And while we're on the subject, let me encourage you to pray individually for your children as you walk by the way or have your own devotions. One friend of mine walks her children to the bus stop and then prays for their day as she walks back home. Pray that your children will grow to love, fear, and serve the Lord and that their future spouse will, too. And during those times when they seem to be straying off course, nag less and pray more! Scripture promises that it's much more effective.)

Beyond these basic strategies, what's best is what really encourages your family and serves to bring them together before God and teach them His truth.

RESOURCE BOX #3: MAGNIFICENT MEDIA AND MATERIALS FOR FAMILY DEVOTIONS

GREAT BOOKS

Dangerous Journey—a "Spielbergian" version of *Pilgrim's Progress* with wonderful illustrations.

The Family Book of Christian Values, Stuart and Jill Briscoe—similar to *Book of Virtues* format with sections on personal, spiritual, and relational values.

More Than Conquerors—a collection of Christian biographies including Abraham Lincoln, George Washington Carver, Corrie ten Boom, and Tom Landry.

The Chronicles of Narnia, C. S. Lewis.

The Bible in Pictures for Little Eyes, by Ken Taylor—includes a picture, a short story, and two or three questions with each story, by the author of *The Living Bible*, a biblical paraphrase. An excellent starter for little ones.

GREAT VIDEOS

Focus on the Family Series: *McGee and Me, Adventures in Odyssey, The Story Keepers* and, with even better production values and content, *The Last Chance Detectives* for preteens.

Institute of Creation Research or Ken Ham—excellent resources on this important topic.

Veggie Tales—fun combination of silliness and seriousness for preschoolers. Available in Christian bookstores.

The Chronicles of Narnia—wonderful video versions of Lewis's magnificent stories.

Animated Stories from the Bible and *American Hero Classics,* from a former Disney animator and director. High quality combination of animation art and faithful retelling of Bible stories. Call 1-800-447-5958 for information.

A View from the Zoo, featuring Gary Richmond and kids' narration. Teaches values through exploring animal design and behavior. Available 9/97 from Keynote Communications, 1-800-962-7664.

In the Spirit of 1776 and other historical Christian Heritage videos by David Barton.

GREAT TAPES

Listen to lyrics of contemporary Christian music, discuss; try out some Christian comedians such as Mark Lowery.

AND MORE

Walk Thru the Bible, *Family Walk,* a monthly topical family devotional guide. Subscription information 1-800-877-5604.

CURRENT EVENTS

Use parts of the Bible Studies at the end of this book combined with a hot news item to spark discussion. Today's current events reporting on the stunning consequences of following the progressive worldview provide almost daily material for fitting puzzle pieces into children's Christian worldview frameworks. Especially good with older children who are more difficult to hook. After I read the newspaper or a news magazine, I'll leave an article of interest on the dinner table. "Did you see this?" often jump-starts our dinner conversation.

≈

MY SON, LISTEN TO PROVERBS

Above all, the best resource is God's precious Word. It is so rich, revealing the scope and sweep of who God is and how He loves us—resplendent with beautiful imagery and stocked with profound answers to our biggest questions, with real examples of others who have shared our struggles to overcome the power of sin. The best of the best for training our children is the book of Proverbs. The desired goals or outcomes for this curriculum are set forth mostly in the book's introduction (Proverbs 1:2-4). According to Solomon, successful students of this curriculum should be able to:

➤ achieve wisdom (skillful living).

➤ achieve a disciplined life.

➤ understand words of insight.

➤ do what is right and just and fair.

Successful completion should also:

➤ save you lots of heartache (Proverbs 2:12, 16).

➤ prolong your life and bring you prosperity (Proverbs 3:2).

Wouldn't you love your children to successfully complete a course like that? Wouldn't you love for this to be taught in school?

Ah, but that is not how this course was designed to be taught. Proverbs 4:1-4 describes the teacher qualifications and prescribed classroom. "When I was a boy in my father's house, still tender . . . he taught me and said, 'Lay hold of my words with all your heart; keep my commands and you will live.'" Now the teacher is passing this on to his son. "Listen, my sons, to a father's instruction; pay attention and gain understanding. I give you sound learning, so do not forsake my teaching."

Classroom: home when children are still at a tender age.

Teacher qualification: Father (parent) with sound learning who knows the commands of the Lord.

We are to start when they are young, and we are to teach them this in our home. Every home should be a "home school" teaching this curriculum.

The world's wisest dad is taking the _initiative_ to teach his simple, naive son how to grow up to be wise. Proverbs has wonderful passages on sex education (chapter 5), drinking to excess (chapter 23), the pursuit of riches (chapter 23), and the choosing of friends (chapter 22)— all vital subjects for discussion with our children. We all need to return periodically to this core curriculum.

To Your Children's Children

The Christian rock group Whiteheart has written an inspiring song titled "The Flame Passes On," describing how our "faith is a fire"—a torch passed from "mothers to sons, fathers to daughters." We must be found faithful in this and trust the outcome to a loving God. (So many times I expect the kind of mature Christlike behavior out of Zach that I didn't demonstrate until I was thirty.)

We never know how our children will respond to our efforts to pass our faith and our values on to them. They may take it to heart later rather than sooner. Even if they turn away, it could be that "eventually a growing emptiness creates a hunger for the Christian principles that once guided us, the fellowship that church involvement provided us, the family devotions that once united us," writes Alma Barkman, author of *Rise and Shine* (excerpted in *Women's Devotional New Testament,* p. 238). "I believe the Holy Spirit uses our childhood memories to whet our appetite for the things of God. As we obediently search out His will and obey it, we in turn are establishing a Christian tradition for our children."

As I look back in my life on some of the "roads not taken," I realize it was my Christian heritage that weighed in back where the roads forked. In my mid-twenties I was trying to choose my life partner. On the same weekend in November one fellow I was dating told me he loved me, and the other fellow I was dating asked me to marry him.

Both were intelligent, tall, handsome, witty, and charming. The first fellow was quite successful already. Our times together were spent at country clubs, elegant parties, and lovely dinners. The second fellow was scrimping by in seminary, and our time together was spent over a bucket of chicken on a study date—he writing papers and I preparing lecture notes for the high school classes I taught.

The first fellow and I did not share the same spiritual heritage or level of commitment, but the second one and I did. In fact, his level of commitment was greater than mine at the time and required a great deal of sacrifice. He wanted to teach and train Christians on the mission field.

The lap of luxury looked much more appealing than a vow of poverty. But the difference that made all the difference was that spiritual heritage passed down from my grandmother to my mother, and from my parents to me. When it came down to making a decision, *I could not walk into the future and not share my past.* After trusting Christ, it was the biggest and best decision I ever made.

We still get the bucket of chicken, and many nights are study nights—Jack working on his sermons and me working on my lecture notes for the classes I teach. But the blessings flowing from that decision are a source of profound and continuing joy. I think of them when I catch snatches of a father-son post-breakfast discussion over a Bible study together or every time I pass Zach's door at night and hear him and his dad talking about life and God and "stuff."

The flame passes on. (Lord willing!)

PERSONAL
VALUE

---

*Now, let's see—who deserves
to ride in our life raft?*

MOM, WHERE DID I COME FROM?

5

_The Top Ten Reasons to Believe
the "Fact" of Evolution_

PERHAPS IT HAS HAPPENED TO YOU. RIGHT IN THE MIDDLE OF rinsing the spaghetti, your six-year-old needs to know about the great mysteries of life. So it was with my friend Mary, whose son Mikey came in and asked, "Mom, where did I come from?"

At first Mary thought it might be time for another chapter in the "Birds and Bees" saga. But then she thought, no, maybe a statement on creation versus evolution was the answer he was after. Sensing her need for clarification, Mikey explained, "You know, like Grandpa is from Michigan. Where am I from?"

Alas, not every such episode ends so easily. Most of us probably feel better able to explain the "facts of life" than to counter the "facts" of evolution. And there's no getting around it in our culture—_Ranger Rick, National Geographic_ specials, trips to the museum, science class, and, what is the deal with kids and dinosaurs? Our children's tremendous fascination with these monsters of antiquity have netted Spielberg millions of dollars and us parents countless challenges to our ability to mesh science with Scripture—an area where most of us feel moderately-to-totally inadequate.

Given the overwhelming consensus on evolution, we moms who believe in creation may feel that we must take an absolute leap of faith and leave our brains on the cliff. We are told that belief in creation is based on _faith_, not _facts_, scriptural text instead of scientific evidence, and that because our approach is unreasonable, we should give up all hope of winning a hearing for creation outside our family and church.

The purpose of this chapter is to show how belief in evolution and creation are both *faith* positions and to help you show your children that creation is the *more reasonable* of the two.

THE TWO POSITIONS ON THE TABLE: AN OVERVIEW OF CHANCE AND DESIGN

Let's reflect on the way evolution has become such a dominant theory of origins. Darwinian evolution was born out of a worldview based on certain presuppositions. There are basically only two ways to answer these questions: "Where did I come from?" "How did the universe in general, and humans in particular, come to exist?"

We can answer beginning from the presupposition that *man* is independent of God and must depend on his own limited reason and experience. According to this worldview, the *only* source of truth about origins is scientific facts and data—fossils, rock layers, radio waves, and so on. (The problem with this is that we have to interpret what the facts and data mean.)

We can also answer the question of origins starting from God and His Word—from the God who was present at the beginning and gave us an eyewitness account: "By faith we understand that the universe was formed at God's command, so that what is seen was not made out of what was visible" (Hebrews 11:3).

Depending on our presuppositions and worldview, we will find two different explanations of our origin. The Darwinian theory of evolution says that the universe is the product of matter + time + chance; that this matter over millions of years produced a "warm pond" from which some lucky kind of life spontaneously appeared. This life then mutated—underwent a random genetic change (you know, those genetic "mistakes" that cause breast cancer and sickle cell anemia). Those life forms that somehow changed in a helpful way were naturally selected to survive. Life forms that left fewer offspring died out and became extinct (survival of the fittest). Man evolved from lower life forms. Some progressives will give God credit for nudging the process along, but Darwin himself asserted that this process was purely natural, not supernatural—that the mutations were random and incremental (tiny), and the whole process moved along slowly over millions of years. The dominant scientific community is squarely behind the "fact" of evolution.

Beginning from God and His Word, however, we find a totally different explanation for the origin of the universe. God spoke and created light and matter out of *nothing*. He created the heavens and the earth. He did so with meaning and purpose according to His plan. He created the animals and living creatures "after their *kind*" (a designation not necessarily as specific as "species"). And then God created man as a unique spiritual being in His own image. These are the "nonnegotiables" from Scripture. Many aspects of *how* He did this are matters of interpretation. But Scripture is very clear on these points in both Old and New Testaments. God was and is in control of creation.

We could illustrate these two theories of origins this way.

INTELLIGENT DESIGN	DARWINIAN EVOLUTION
MAN:	MAN:
made in God's image	*evolved from lower forms of life*
UNIVERSE:	UNIVERSE:
result of God's command	*result of matter + time + chance*
TRUTH ABOUT MATERIAL WORLD:	TRUTH ABOUT MATERIAL WORLD:
facts, observation in harmony with Scripture	*facts, observations + man's interpretation*
MORAL TRUTH:	MORAL TRUTH:
revealed by the Creator	*not revealed by nature; therefore, relative, subjective*
FOUNDATION:	FOUNDATION:
God, His Word	*man, his reason, experience, feelings*

Well, there are the two views on the table. Which one is more reasonable? We needn't jump off a cliff or deposit our brains elsewhere to find out. Let's carefully examine the Top Ten Reasons to Believe in the "Fact" of Evolution. Great credit for the following discussion goes to law professor Dr. Phillip E. Johnson (first introduced to you in chapter 1 at the UT Law School) whose *Darwin on Trial* helped make the issues clear to my unscientific, nontechno-jargon mind.

REASON #10—ASSUME THAT "WE ARE LIVING
IN A MATERIAL WORLD AND [WE ARE ALL] MATERIAL GIRL[S]."

Belief in Darwinian evolution assumes that Madonna was right! We live in a natural, material, closed system where nothing outside the system (especially anything supernatural) has any influence or control over the world around us. *"All the history of life, and man in particular, is the result of a 'purposeless and natural process that did not have him in mind,'"* explains evolutionary scientist George Gaylord Simpson (*Darwin on Trial*).

According to the National Academy of Sciences, science is based on naturalism (the assertion that only the natural world is real). Since science claims to be based on the study of nature (facts, data), it alone would offer the true knowledge of reality. So, by this neatly crafted definition, supernatural creation is unscientific and does not address the real world around us. Scientists confidently conclude that evolution is the *only* explanation of origins because no other possible alternatives exist!

This may seem abstract and not worth the effort it takes to understand it, but it is *very* important to justify a practical issue. If all science education must be based on the "fact" that only the natural world is real, then what we have are classrooms where any criticism of evolution or presentations of any evidence of intelligent design are taboo.

In 1982 a federal court ruled that the Arkansas legislature's statute requiring "balanced treatment to creation-science and to evolution-science" was unconstitutional. The court said the statute would break down the wall of separation between church and state. This ruling was based primarily on testimony by Michael Ruse, a Darwinist philosopher of science and leading advocate of the "fact-faith" dichotomy. Let me explain.

Science, Ruse testified, is based on "facts," observations and analysis of the natural world. On the other hand, belief in creation is based on "faith" in things that are unseen, unprovable, and supernatural. The judge agreed that only "fact," not articles of "faith," should be taught in a public school.

Is it possible that God commanded and it was so? Yes, that is our *faith* position.

Is it possible that God does not exist and that we are all the result of matter + time + chance? Many people also believe this, but they cannot *prove* it. Unlike Dorothy in Oz, who could pull back the curtain and prove the wizard did not exist, you cannot scientifically prove that God does not exist. This is also a faith position, born out of a certain worldview. The person who chooses to believe evolution does so based on his presuppositions. His beliefs about reality and God determine how he handles the "evidence."

Both are faith positions. At the heart of the matter there is no "fact-faith" dichotomy.

The exciting thing is that even Ruse himself is coming to this conclusion. Ten years later he admitted to the American Association for the Advancement of Science, "the science side has certain metaphysical [intangible or unprovable] assumptions built into doing science, which—it may not be a good thing to admit in a court of law but I think that in all honesty—we should recognize" (Foundation for Thought and Ethics newsletter, April 1993).

REASON #9—ASSUME THAT "NOTHING TIMES
NOBODY EQUALS EVERYTHING."

This quote from author and pastor Erwin Lutzer summarizes what it takes to believe in the creation of the universe when you deny the reality of the supernatural. You either have to believe that matter and energy are eternal—they always have existed—or you have to believe, as some scientists do, that suddenly a cold, dark, incredibly dense pocket of matter just appeared. Scientists are completely clueless as to what caused the matter to exist or appear in the first place. There are no ideas even on the table. Whether it always existed or appeared suddenly, scientists have detected the echoes of a huge explosion that sent matter flying out and expanding throughout the universe. This is what they call the "Big Bang theory."

Many of those eager to harmonize science and the Bible enjoyed announcing the discovery of these "Big Bang" shock waves with reference to Genesis 1:3: "And God said, 'Let there be light.'" I can just imagine from Genesis 1 that God did get creation going with a bang—a Big Bang. But there are problems in assuming that the scientists' Big Bang theory is completely true. Everyone who has watched a space movie knows that space junk (and sabotaged astronauts) float through space forever unless they encounter some other object or some gravitational force. However, according to the Big Bang theory, you must *assume* that some of the matter exploding out into an empty universe, for no apparent reason, slowed down here and there, coalesced, and began to form galaxies, stars, and planets.

The more scientists peer through the Hubble space telescope, the more they are coming up with data that really does seem to have come from "outer space," such as:

➤ The universe seems to be about two billion years younger than some of the stars in it (*Time*, 3/6/95).

➤ They can't find the "dark matter" that they assumed was keeping galaxies together. Without it, galaxies should be flying apart. They point the Hubble to where they expect to find dim red stars doing the job, only to find "large open dark regions with distant galaxies shining through. . . ." "Something is wrong with our theories," says Filippenko, an astronomer at the University of California, Berkeley. "We may have to consider some new, perhaps wild ideas" (*Houston Chronicle*, 11/94).

How about Colossians 1:16-17? "For by [Christ] all things were created: things in heaven and on earth . . . and in him all things hold together."

From a biblical perspective the Big Bang theory also has a problem with sequence. According to accepted theory, the order of appearance was 1) energy, 2) galaxies, 3) stars, 4) planets. As the planet cooled off, life evolved—single cell to multicell, plants then animals. According to Genesis 1, the sequence is 1) heavens and earth, 2) light—1st day,

3) sky—2nd day, 4) oceans and dry ground, 5) plants and trees—3rd day, 6) sun, moon, and stars—4th day, and on to living creatures and finally, man and woman—definitely a different setup altogether.

REASON #8—ASSUME THE EARTH'S ROCK LAYERS WERE LAID DOWN SLOWLY, INCH BY INCH, OVER AEONS OF TIME, AND NOT QUICKLY BY CATASTROPHE (AS HAPPENED AT MT. ST. HELENS).

Perhaps you've had the privilege to visit the Grand Canyon. If so, you know it is "drop-jaw" awesome—almost unreal in its expanse and beauty. As with the memorial of stones the Israelites built after they crossed the Jordan, our children may stand before it and naturally ask, "What do these stones mean, Mom?" If Dad is along, we can pass on this one—"Go ask your father."

The signs on the edge of the canyon explaining its origin resonate with astronomer Carl Sagan's cadence: "It took millions and millions of years. . . ." This again *assumes* what geology textbooks call uniformity—one millimeter of sediment laid down in a year, building up the canyon wall, then the river eroding it slowly over aeons of time.

Creation scientists like Ken Ham (Answers in Genesis ministry) raise some strong questions about these assumptions. "Is it possible that the rock layers were laid down quickly by giant catastrophes?" (Catastrophe theories are steadily gaining popularity. They are being offered as solutions to questions such as, "Why did the dinosaurs become extinct?" or "How did the woolly mammoth quick-freeze in Siberia?")

We can tell our children about one recent catastrophe, the explosion of Mt. St. Helens, which has yielded some interesting scientific data:

Fact: 600 feet of sediment have been laid down in a couple of years.

Fact: 25 feet of sediment were laid down in twenty-four hours.

Fact: A mud flow from a volcano carved out a canyon 1/40 the size of the Grand Canyon.

Ken Ham postulates, "Suppose people look at the river at the bottom of that canyon. They might wonder if it took millions of years to carve it out. No, a mud flow did it in one day. How do we know? We got it on video!" (ICR, *Back to Genesis*, Video Series).

So when children ask, "What do these stones mean?" parents may need help to answer the question. The Institute of Creation Research, headquartered near San Diego, California, has some excellent resources exposing the false assumptions behind the "fact" of evolution. These scientists think there is much more to Genesis 7:11-12 than meets the eye. In the words, "The springs of the great deep burst forth, and the floodgates of the heavens were opened. And rain fell on the earth forty days and forty nights," they see massive changes in the earth's crust, even the shifting of continents.

Excellent resources are also available from other scientists and thinking people who believe in an old earth but still deny the basic premises of Darwinian evolution—Hugh Ross, William Bradley, Dean Kenyon, and Phillip Johnson have all written materials to help us answer, "What do these stones mean?"

RESOURCE BOX # 4: BETTER REASONS FOR BELIEVING
THE FACT OF CREATION AND INTELLIGENT DESIGN

Of Pandas and People, by Percival Davis and Dean Kenyon. Textbook format for secondary/college students. Very readable, well illustrated. Written in two sections: general overview and in-depth follow-up material. Available from Foundation for Thought and Ethics, P. O. Box 830721, Richardson, TX, 75083-0721, or 972-661-1661. Also available from Baker & Taylor, book distributors.

Defeating Darwinism by Opening Minds, by Phillip E. Johnson, InterVarsity Press, 1997. This easy-to-understand explanation of the creation/evolution debate is meant especially for bright high schoolers, their parents, and teachers.

Darwin on Trial, by Phillip E. Johnson, InterVarsity Press. A more scholarly page-turner, great for thinking Christians with nagging questions on this subject.

Access Research Network. If you surf the web, you will find many items by and about Professor Johnson, including videotapes, at http://www.arn.org/arn.

Institute for Creation Research. A whole catalog of materials;

Dinosaurs by Design by Dr. Duane Gish. Great for younger readers. For general audiences, the *Back to Genesis* videotape series, especially the one on *Mt. St. Helens*. 800-628-7640.

Ken Ham's ministry, Answers in Genesis. Great books on Genesis for younger readers, *A Is for Adam* and *D Is for Dinosaurs*. For general audiences, *The Lie*. Available at Christian bookstores or 606-727-2222.

Creation Facts of Life, by Gary Parker, Master Books, Colorado Springs, CO, 1994. Dr. Allen Gillen, local biology teacher, used this as his text to teach a Sunday school class on creation versus evolution in our church. Three major sections discuss evidence of creation, problems with Darwin's theories, and the fossil evidence. For general audiences.

———————————————————— ≈ ————————————————————

REASON #7—**ASSUME** THAT EVEN THOUGH NATURE LEFT
TO ITSELF TENDS TOWARD DISORGANIZATION (WITNESS YOUR YARD
OR POOL AFTER YOUR VACATION), THERE IS SOME LAW
OUT THERE THAT MAKES NATURE DO THE OPPOSITE. WE
JUST HAVEN'T DISCOVERED IT YET.

The more we learn about genes and DNA, the more we realize how incredibly complex living organisms are. Scientists are staring this complexity in the face and trying to make it square with the "famously depressing second law of thermodynamics"—"the tendency of things to become more chaotic" (*Time*, 12/25/92). How do you evolve so much complexity and organization out of a universe that is constantly becoming more chaotic and disorganized?

A few scientists look at the "self-organization" capabilities of crystals and snowflakes, and by faith claim that similar undiscovered capabilities could possibly explain the appearance of life in Darwin's "warm pond."

Dean Kenyon is a professor of biology at San Francisco State who has been working for years at simulating life's origins, i. e., getting molecules to self-organize. In 1969 he coauthored an influential text entitled *Biochemical Predestination*.

But years of lab experiments trying to produce complex organic molecules (like the amino acids that make up DNA) yielded no proof of self-organization. By the late seventies his views began to change. The years of producing unfruitful biological goop in the lab, taken together with the virtually zero mathematical probability that chance alone would produce the complex molecules needed to build life, convinced him to adopt a different view of origins—intelligent design.

Although he arrived at this conclusion through scientific research, he was asked to check *his* brain at the door and *not* teach his views to his students. The limits placed on Kenyon's academic freedom produced a firestorm of controversy within academia. While his faculty senate and the American Association of University Professors defended him, the chairman of his biology department insisted that Kenyon not be allowed to teach about the problems in the evolutionary view or evidence for intelligent design. The chairman subsequently reversed himself, and Kenyon now enjoys the academic freedom he is due.

Many observers have called Kenyon's ordeal a Scopes Monkey Trial for the nineties—only the roles were completely reversed. The evolutionists are now in power and intolerant of any other theory of origins being taught in the classroom, even when backed by scientific experts and evidence.

Persevering in spite of the opposition, Kenyon has continued his efforts to impact the discussions of origins with the results of his research. Collaborating with the Foundation for Thought and Ethics, he has helped author a textbook for secondary and college students. *Of Pandas and People* is a tremendous resource for our children once they encounter the big guns of high school and college texts and teachers. Your children's teachers may demand that they defend their beliefs with more than Bible verses. *Pandas* provides a wealth of scholarly research and offers an alternative interpretation of fossils, genetic research, and the like, pointing to intelligent design. And the book is winning a following! Over 900 copies were ordered by teachers and curriculum supervisors in the first year, and several hundred of these immediately adopted the book for use in their lesson plan preparation. Public schools in over a dozen states have placed volume orders. (See Resource Box # 4 for more information.)

REASON #6—ASSUME THAT EVEN THOUGH PROTEINS ARE
NEEDED TO MAKE DNA AND THAT DNA IS NEEDED TO MAKE
PROTEINS, SOMEHOW ONE OF THEM POPPED UP FIRST WITHOUT
THE OTHER OR THEY BOTH POPPED UP TOGETHER.

One of the greatest problems with evolution boils down to the
chicken and the egg controversy. Not only do scientists have no idea
as to how DNA self-organized to get life going, but they also must
assume that proteins self-organized alongside the DNA against all
odds. But remember, evolution is based on *facts*, not *faith!*

REASON #5—ASSUME THAT SINCE A WHITE-PEPPERED MOTH CAN
BECOME A DARK-PEPPERED MOTH, A FROG CAN BECOME A PRINCE
(GIVEN MILLIONS AND MILLIONS OF YEARS).

I remember staring in great dismay at the infamous dark-peppered
moth in my tenth grade biology text. There he was, parked on a sooty
tree trunk in England—living proof of the theory of evolution.
During the Industrial Revolution and in times of great pollution, this
darker moth was camouflaged to survive attacks from bird predators.
Almost the entire population shifted from its previous light wing color
to dark wing color. When tree trunks became lighter after pollution
was reduced, the moth population again adapted to its environment,
and most surviving moths were light.

This, asserted the authors of my text, obviously proved the "fact"
of evolution: mutation of wing color, natural selection of the best
camouflaged moths, and survival of the fittest. Surely then, given
enough mutations and enough time, all life forms could have evolved
from simpler life forms that existed millions of years ago. Right?

I will be the first to acknowledge that random genetic mutations
can produce important, observable evolutionary changes. Scientific
data has proven this possibility to any reasonable person. One has
only to think of bacteria becoming resistant to antibiotics or all the
creative attempts to re-configure the fruit fly—fewer bristles, smaller
wings, etc.

But this whole line of evidence only proves a kind of *microevolution*—changes within the "kind" (as designated in Genesis 1). None

of the examples offered by scientists show one *kind* of life form changing to another *kind*.

But, of course, there is the fossil record. What about all the transitional forms from one kind to another in the rock layer (arms to wings, back-bending knees to forward-bending knees, etc.)? Answer: You won't find them. One of the most striking characteristics of the fossil record is the virtual absence of transitional forms. Nearly all the animal life forms appear suddenly in the Precambrian rock layers. This irritating fact has been known by scientists for some time and is now becoming more commonly known, thanks to books like *Pandas* and *Darwin on Trial*.

The fossil record is not characterized by an abundance of transitional forms. Instead it is characterized by sudden appearance, stasis (a long period of survival with little adaptive change), and then extinction. According to Darwin himself, the slow process of small genetic mutations, natural selection, and survival of the fittest must have left an "inconceivably great" number of transitional forms in the fossil record. A precious few possibilities exist, but most are considered to be weird little creatures, the duck-billed platypuses of their time. (See Focus Box #9.)

FOCUS YOUR WORLDVIEW #9: DARWIN'S JUST SO STORIES

How did Darwinian evolution produce a frog from a fish? Or a bird from a reptile?

To look at *Time* magazine, a school textbook, or a museum display, you would think that several intermediate forms of animals link the fish to the frog or the reptile to the bird. The first intermediate animals look more like fish or reptiles. Next you see a creature that is half fish/half frog or half reptile/half bird. The final intermediate forms look more like frogs or birds, which then fully develop into the new kinds of animals.

So how did the fish begin to "walk" on its fins enough to crawl out of the pond? (If you've seen the Far Side fish baseball team staring determinedly from underwater at the baseball that landed just a couple of feet on shore, you have Gary Larson's best guess.)

As we've seen, there is no fossil evidence for all those transitional forms. Many *evolutionists* are asking honest questions: "What good is half a leg or half a wing?" (Or half an eye?) They are concluding that the intermediate creatures never existed. The fish who gradually started walking and breathing on shore never existed. The reptile who gradually exchanged its scales for feathers is complete fiction. And Darwin's little stories of how one *kind* of animal gradually developed the wing or the trunk or the hump and became another *kind* of animal fantasies. They have more in common with Rudyard Kipling's *Just So Stories* than modern science.

Settle in with your children and read some of Kipling's delightful stories: "How the Camel Got His Hump," "How the Rhinoceros Got His Skin," and how the crocodile did a number on "The Elephant Child"['s] nose.

Then discuss with your children the fact that one of the world's most famous biologists, a strong believer in evolution, has declared that many people have tried to sell the idea of intermediary creatures changing from one kind to another. Here's what the biologist, Stephen Gould, actually said: "These tales in the Just So Stories tradition of evolutionary natural history do not prove anything" (*Natural History*, 6/7/77).

What part have museums and textbook publishers played in this sales job? This discussion would be even more effective with a copy of your child's science textbook showing intermediary forms in front of you. Or take a field trip to your local natural history museum.

You can tell your children as they gaze at the series of fish/frogs or reptile/birds or monkey/men, "Remember, those are just as real as the humpless camel and the short-nosed elephant in Kipling's stories. Leading scientists say so."

————————————————— ≈ —————————————————

Many scientists *assume* that great numbers of transitional forms are out there (we just haven't found many of them yet). Several well-respected scientists in a more candid moment have acknowledged that "the extreme rarity of transitional forms in the fossil record is the trade secret of paleontology" (study of fossils). "The fossil record does not convincingly document a single transition from one species to another." "We paleontologists have said that the history of life supports [the story of gradual adaptive change] all the while knowing that it does not" (*Darwin on Trial*).

When my friend Sue, a chemistry teacher and a new Christian, heard of the confessions of these eminent scientists, she became angry. She realized that in order to teach her the "fact" of evolution in college, and in order for her to pass that "fact" on to her high school students, crucial data had been suppressed by an educational system committed to protecting their faith in evolution rather than to an honest pursuit of truth. She felt betrayed.

While there is proof that a population of moths can change from light to dark (microevolution), there is no proof that a frog can become a prince, or even a reptile or a bird (macroevolution). It seems that while there may be great variations within a kind, there are certain limits as to how much a gene can mutate. As Phillip Johnson points out, dog breeders have produced everything from a Saint Bernard to a Chihuahua, but they still come up with playful little creatures that love bones and hate cats. Intelligently designed selective breeding can only produce variation within a kind. How can unintelligent, random breeding change one kind to another? Some scientists have suggested the following option.

REASON #4—ASSUME THAT A REPTILE LAID FOUR EGGS. THREE HATCHED TO BE REPTILES, BUT ONE HATCHED TO BE A BIRD.

Largely rejected by the scientific community, this hypothesis accomplishes something: it shows how desperate science is to explain the origin of life by natural causes alone. In a more serious effort to account for all the diversity in living things, some scientists see the only possible vehicle as some degree of macroevolution (significant numbers of simultaneous mutations). Never mind that virtually all macro-mutations observed in the lab are harmful.

But how else can you explain the evolution of a complex organ like the eye? Eyes need corneas, lenses, lids, retinas, tear ducts, optic nerve, etc. What advantage is any one of these developments without the others? What advantage is an eyelid or an optic nerve by itself? What creature needs tear ducts and a wet snoot without eyeballs to see?

Some scientists have pointed out that if all these mutations can be granted simultaneously and fully formed, it would be nothing short of a miracle. Indeed! Mathematicians have even argued that the number of small micro-mutations needed to evolve an eye would take much more time than what was available. Darwinists have responded that the "fact" is that the eye *has* evolved. So the problem must be with the mathematician's math. (See Focus Box #10.)

≈

FOCUS YOUR WORLDVIEW #10: A DAY AT THE DESIGNER'S FASHION SHOW

Every season top fashion designers show their clothing at gala fashion shows. God's exquisite designs are all around us, but one of His finest collections is now showing at your local zoo. On your next trip prepare your children to look at the animals through the eyes of a fashion critic or designer. What has the Master Designer been up to?

We see some of God's finest design work in his creatures. In addition to the eye, we have the ear ("Does he who implanted the ear not hear? Does he who formed the eye not see?" Psalm 94:9) and many other organs and systems.

Some of the animals at your local zoo are outstanding examples of design packages that, according to evolution, would have required many (too many) simultaneous mutations. Any one of these genetic changes would have been useless by itself.

As you tour the zoo, point out the design packages:

1. The giraffe: long legs *and* neck (legs only—how does he drink or eat grass?), strong heart and high blood pressure to get blood up to head *and* special sensors along the neck to monitor blood pressure. If the giraffe's head goes down, arteries constrict, and blood pressure drops. Otherwise, every time the giraffe takes a drink, the high blood pressure would pump too much blood to his head, and he would pass out in the pond (*Pandas*).

2. The woodpecker: extra-strong beak for pecking, extra-strong neck muscles, extra shock absorbers around skull, extra-long tongue to reach in and get insects, special groove around brain to hold extra-long tongue. What would happen without a place to store his tongue? What would happen if he pecked really hard with no shock absorbers around his brain? With no long tongue to reach down into holes and lap up lunch? With no special feet and claws to cling

to the tree? No special tail to brace himself? (*Creation Facts of Life,* Gary Parker.)

3. Most birds: digestive system designed for rapid elimination of waste (quick weight loss. Warning: don't stand under a mulberry tree in spring.), unique respiratory system with more air sacs, a rapidly beating heart in order to flap its wings fast, and larger eyes to see its food from the air ("A Theory for the Birds"). How did a half reptile/half bird develop: feathers from scales, muscle control of feathers, hollow bones, and so on? If any one or two of these design features did not appear, what would happen? Remind your children that flight had to have evolved three different times—for birds, bats, and insects.

4. The bat: in addition to evolving the ability to fly, they also had to have simultaneously mutated and developed their echo location package—high-frequency squeaker (beeper) transmitter, system to receive the echoes of their squeaks, system to transport signals to the brain and interpret them, and coordinate the information with swooping and scooping up their food (*Answers in Genesis*).

5. The kangaroo: ingenious undercarriage of bone, muscles, and tail that helps it bounce along. It would be useless half formed and helps only when fully operational at high speeds. What baby animal could hang on to the back of such a bouncy mom? None. The kangaroo's design package includes a pouch and God-given instinct in the baby to crawl up from the birth canal to the pouch and find a teat (*Does God Exist?*, Alan Hayward, p. 90. Also *Answers in Genesis*).

6. The camel: designed for desert living. What would happen to this ship of the desert without any one feature of his design package? No layer of fat under the skin to keep the heat in, but a camel-hair coat that serves as a reflector shield to keep the heat out. (Fat is efficiently stored in its hump.) A body thermostat that can cool down to 93° at night and heat up to 105° in the day. Urine much more concentrated, using less water. Can lose a quarter of its weight through water evaporation without suffering harm (Hayward, pp. 91-92).

7. Bighorn sheep rams: like the woodpecker who uses his head, the rams frequently butt heads and are in danger of their brains turning to jello. Their package features a double skull plate below the

horns with a shock-absorbing cushion in between (*Answers in Genesis*).

Check out these unique design features.

8. The wombat: also has a pouch, but it opens toward its tail. What advantage is this for a burrowing creature?

9. The bear: all have the same kind of teeth, yet some eat only meat, a couple are vegetarians, and many eat anything.

10. The wolf: according to evolution animals cannot interbreed and produce offspring outside their species. But in the dog *kind* many different *species* commonly breed and produce offspring. Wolves with dogs and coyotes; dogs with foxes, dingoes, and jackals.

We also see design packages that do not promote the "survival of the fittest":

The peacock: long, cumbersome tail feathers make the peacock easy prey. According to evolution, why would peahens be attracted to such a harmful characteristic? How do evolutionists explain the success of so many drab-colored birds?

On their cars some people like extra chrome, tail fins, sleek lines, fancy lights, etc. What are your favorite design options as you look around the zoo?

What design characteristics from God's creatures do we enjoy in our clothing or home decoration (for example, color schemes, patterns, etc.)?

REASON #3—**ASSUME** THAT THE MOST RECENTLY DISCOVERED MISSING LINK REALLY IS THE MISSING LINK.

Consider the inconsistencies in the current status ascribed to Neanderthal Man in a *Time* cover story from March 1994, "How Man Began": "Neanderthal is a subspecies of Homo sapiens (modern humans). . . . Neanderthal is a separate species which met a dead end. . . . Neanderthal genes survive today because they interbred with Homo sapiens. . . . Neanderthals evolved into early Europeans."

Large numbers of entire Neanderthal skeletons have been found in Europe, but the abundance of ancient bones has not yielded a unified interpretation of their lineage. On the other hand, when 40 percent of one skeleton was unearthed in Africa in 1974, it was dubbed Lucy, *the* missing link. The researchers *know* it walked upright because its knee was constructed so that it could straighten its leg.

"Poppycock," says leading primate expert Solly Zuckerman. After years of biometric testing of primates like Lucy, Zuckerman says that the claim that these fossils are human ancestors is "flimsy" and "unacceptable." His premise, according to Johnson, is that there is such great variation among ape fossils that any one of them could have a few characteristics that could be interpreted as prehuman, but they don't hold up to rigorous testing.

It seems that anthropologists, desperate to come up with Darwin's equivalent to Adam and Eve, are quick to seize on bone and fossil fragments and engage in a lot of grand pronouncements based on puny evidence. Museum directors, *Time* magazine artists, and *Nova* TV producers are swept up in the excitement. Invariably the next ancient tooth discovery means that huge parts of the exhibits, illustrations, and TV shows must be updated and corrected. Like Orwell's Ministry of Truth in *1984* constantly rewriting history, anthropologists' theories of the origins of man are constantly in flux.

Recently research by geneticists has been raining on the anthropologists' parade. The March 1994 *Time* reported that there are two major views of human origins: scientists claiming that fossils show that humans evolved simultaneously around the world from different prehuman groups that migrated out of Africa, and other scientists arguing that chromosomal studies indicate that all Homo sapien women descended from one "African Eve."

A mere fifteen months later, genetic research validated the chromosomal study indicating that "all men descended from *a common ancestor* who lived about 270,000 years ago" (*Science*, 5/95). (While people disagree over the date, at least they got the Adam part right.) But if the current theories are in such incredible flux, what are they teaching our children?

In a seminar at the University of Chicago, one scientist asked his peers, "Can you tell me anything you *know* about evolution, any one thing . . . that is true?" After a long silence one person said, "I do know one thing—it ought not to be taught in high school" (*Darwin on Trial*).

Time's story, "How Man Began," is rife with the language of uncertainty—"may have," "may be," "most scientists believe," "almost surely," "goes the theory"—the language of faith. The article concludes with this statement: "The only certainty in this data-poor, imagination-rich, endlessly fascinating field is that there are plenty of surprises yet to come"—more or less.

REASON #2—ASSUME THAT EVEN THOUGH THE EARTH
SEEMS CALIBRATED TO SUPPORT LIFE AND THE COMPLEXITY
OF LIFE SEEMS TO INDICATE INTELLIGENT DESIGN, IT JUST
ISN'T SO. (UNLESS "ALIENS DID IT!")

Fact: If the earth were closer to the sun, we would burn up, or further away, we would freeze.

Fact: If the force of gravity were any stronger, stars would burn out faster, and the cosmos would be pulled together and collapse on itself; if gravity were any weaker, our solar system and galaxy would fly apart.

Fact: Every atom is made up of negatively charged electrons and positively charged protons that are balanced precisely. If the electron carried more charge than the proton, the universe would never have come together, because all the negatively charged atoms would have repelled one another.

Quote: "One intriguing observation that has bubbled up from physics is that the universe seems calibrated for life's existence" (*Time*, 12/28/92).

Quote: "For this is what the Lord says—he who created the heavens, he is God; he who fashioned and made the earth, he founded it; he did not create it to be empty, but *formed it to be inhabited*—he says: 'I am the Lord, and there is no other'" [italics mine] (Isaiah 45:18). Note: The *Planet Earth* video mentioned in Resource Box #5, chapter 7, illustrates the truth of these quotes extraordinarily well.

The deeper scientists delve into the mysteries of the universe, the more baffling things become. The great physicist Richard Feynman has cautioned his students, "I think I can safely say that nobody understands quantum mechanics. Do not keep saying to yourself . . .

'But how can it be like that?' . . . Nobody knows how it can be like that" (*Time*, 12/29/92).

Faced with the complexity of the universe and living organisms and the growing case for intelligent design, some notable scientists are beginning to offer a novel solution to the question of the origins of life: *"Aliens did it!"*

Suppose that a superior extraterrestrial civilization sent some bacteria to earth in a spaceship. Suppose these E.T.s were in danger of extinction, so they launched a life form that could survive the voyage, the crash, and evolve in the severely unstable environment of ancient earth. This theory has been proposed by Francis Crick, not a B-list Hollywood screenwriter, but the co-discoverer of the organization of DNA.

Or suppose our planet is a zoo for extraterrestrial beings. Suppose they planted the seeds of evolution and are just watching their experiment. Every once in a while they fiddle with it, causing what some people call "miracles." This fanciful speculation comes from famous Oxford evolutionary biologist William Hamilton, who labels it "a kind of hypothesis that's very, very hard to dismiss" (*Time*, 12/28/92).

Why would eminent scientists who recognize the fingerprint of intelligent design prefer to think that aliens did it rather than God? Why do they "suppress the truth and exchange it for a lie"?

"For although they knew God, they neither glorified him as God nor gave thanks to him, but their thinking became futile and their foolish hearts were darkened" (Romans 1:21). According to Scripture, our worldview determines the extent of our reasoning capability. If we reject God and believe only in a material world where science is the only sure path to knowledge of that world, then our reasoning will lead us to some pretty futile speculations.

The issue is also one of *control*. To "glorify and thank God" assumes we acknowledge that He is who He says He is and that He has done what He says He's done. We acknowledge Him as creator and judge, and we are accountable to Him for our actions. Aliens don't require so much.

Julian Huxley, an honest evolutionist, once admitted, "The reason we accepted Darwinism, even without proof, is because we didn't want God to interfere with our sexual mores" (Lutzer, *Twelve Myths Americans Believe*, p. 42).

REASON #1—ASSUME THAT PEOPLE WHO BELIEVE IN CREATION
AND REJECT EVOLUTION ARE "IGNORANT, STUPID, OR INSANE."

This accusation from Oxford zoologist Richard Dawkins is a quin-
tessential example of the "censorship of fashion." It is the attitude that
"reasonable people wince" at those naive enough to believe the
"myth" of creation. Our children are subjected to it in public school
classrooms. We encounter it in the marketplace or when we read the
newspaper. Another prime example was written up in a newspaper
column by Donald Kaul (*Houston Chronicle*, 10/93).

Kaul's column was responding to a Gallup poll that showed that
over 50 percent of Americans believe in the biblical account of creation, 35 percent believe that they are the result of a long evolutionary process in which God had a hand, and only 11 percent believe that
humans evolved from simpler life forms by natural causes and chance.

Kaul's attitude was one of discouragement and exasperation at the
"failure of our compulsory educational system" to eradicate such an
absurd belief from school children who, after having been taught a
steady diet of evolution for fifty years, still can't get it right!

In Western Europe and America, we have a wonderful tradition: a
great conversation about what constitutes a good idea. Ideas are discussed on the merit of evidence and logical arguments proceeding
from that evidence. Name-calling and ridicule are reserved as the last
and best defense of those who cannot win an argument on its merit.

It exasperates the academic and cultural elite that they cannot get
belief in evolution to trickle down to the masses. So some are reduced
to taking cheap shots and hurling insults. "There aren't forty scientists
in the world that believe in creation!" bellowed an ACLU lawyer at a
Houston debate on church/state separation.

Actually, the majority of people who believe in creation are in
excellent company, historically speaking. They agree with great men
of science such as Newton, Galileo, Kepler, Pascal, Pasteur, and the list
goes on. Additionally, over 1,000 scientists are members of the
Institute of Creation Research, with terminal degrees from schools
such as Harvard, Berkeley, Penn State, and UCLA. In ignorance, Kaul
dismisses them as pseudo-academics—"maybe they went to college."

No wonder the scientists and cultural elite are frustrated. The majority of the populace rejects their views, and in the halls of academia the armor-clad "fact" of evolution is sporting more and more chinks. Even the *New York Times* has reported that a few scientists "are beginning to question the bravado with which science piles assumption on top of assumption, climbing toward the heavens on great theoretical towers."

Phillip Johnson's book *Darwin on Trial* made big waves. Universities all over the nation are inviting him to speak and are reopening the debate. Emboldened by excellent resources such as *Pandas*, the collapse of the "fact/faith dichotomy," and a 1987 Supreme Court ruling allowing a "variety of scientific theories about the origins of humankind" in public schools, school boards across the country are also allowing the debate to be reopened.

Of course the scientific/educational community is not taking these developments kindly. They were outraged when a group of scientists who believe in evolution *and* the Bible sent out a booklet to thousands of science teachers, encouraging them to discuss some of the problems with evolution. Responding in the *Science Teacher* journal, they condemned the booklet as "an attempt to replace science with a system of pseudoscience."

The progressive scientific/educational establishment is committed to a worldview of naturalism (Reason #10). Evolution is the result of chance and random, natural causes. God did not create us. He did not even lend a hand. To even hint that He did is "unscientific," to say the least, even "stupid or insane." Darwinists strive to offer a Science Story to replace God's Grand Story. They already feel a little touchy because they know their first chapter starts with a big gaping hole. They have no explanation for how the heavens and the earth started off. If chapter 2—Darwin's theories about the origin of life—is called into question, it makes a bad situation much worse. People get pretty hostile when you challenge the presuppositions upon which their whole worldview is built.

We are told that everyone must *assume* that the "fact" of evolution is true. The academic and cultural elite will not have it otherwise—even though the experts realize there is hardly anything about it they can *know* with certainty. Belief in Darwinian evolution is clearly a faith position that smiles and shrugs at "evolution's admitted inconsistencies."

A MORE REASONABLE FAITH

Ours, too, is a faith position. "By faith we understand that the universe was formed at God's command, so that what is seen was not made out of what was visible" (Hebrews 11:3). But our faith is not a denial of our reason. The evidence increasingly points to the intelligent design of the universe and ourselves. To quote Greg Jesson from Focus on the Family's Community Impact Seminar: "Reality is the wall you hit when you are wrong." Modern secular thought is slamming into the wall of reality with increasing frequency. Marxism's political promise of economic equality has collapsed, and its murderous oppression has been exposed. Freudian psychology's definition of who we are has fallen into academic disrepute, and now Darwin's theory of how we came to be may be falling on hard times. What else could have been expected from a worldview that was wrong to start with? Darwin was only looking at half the picture. There *is* a spiritual dimension to the universe.

Many believers have given up thinking that the truth about creation could ever win a hearing in the marketplace of ideas. For the longest time the two sides of the evolution debate have been firmly entrenched, and the discussion has been reduced to a tired exchange: "Creation!" "Evolution!" "Young earth!" "Old earth!" The encouraging thing is that the debate is being reframed: "Intelligent design!" "Chance!" And overwhelmed by the complexities that modern research is revealing, some of the troops from the other side are jumping out of the trenches and bolting toward the truth.

But if we never gain big concessions from the academic-cultural elite or in a court of law, we can teach our children God's truth with confidence. Let's return to our worldview-as-puzzle example. If our presuppositions about truth, reality, right and wrong, God, and salvation are the anchoring corner pieces in our worldview frame, then our core beliefs about creation and our identity as great but fallen creatures made in God's image are connected groups of key side pieces. With them in place, our children can see how the puzzle pieces of animal "rights," abortion, and the "right" to die do not fit in, as we'll see in the chapters that follow.

More importantly, helping our children establish their core beliefs in creation strengthens their commitment to their faith and world-view as a whole. As they contrast God's Grand Story with the Science Story, they can see that only God's Story offers sufficient answers to "Where did I come from?" and "How did all this begin?" And they can see that the Science Story with its gaps at the beginning has absolutely no chapters that really give hope and meaning to our lives—nothing to explain "Why are we here?" The Science Story offers no chapters on how or why to be just, compassionate, honest, or loving. It holds out only one value and one goal: survival. Its final chapter, "How does all this end?" is much like chapters 1 and 2—with a random accident. Nobody likes it.

By contrast, Christianity answers all these questions. Creation is the magnificent beginning to God's Grand Story, in which our lives play a significant part. And when Satan's lies threaten our sense of value and worth—"You're only an animal! A cog in the wheel! An insignificant speck in the universe! A 'Boy-Toy'!" "A miserable fail-ure!" "An unwanted child!"—we can respond with conviction: "No, I am a dearly loved child of the King, uniquely created in the image of the One who said, 'It is I who made the earth and created mankind upon it. My own hands stretched out the heavens; I marshaled their starry hosts.... I, the Lord, speak the truth; I declare what is right.... I have made you ... and I will sustain you'" (Isaiah 45:12, 19; 46:4).

ANIMAL "RIGHTS" VERSUS EVE'S LEATHER DRESS

6

*Unblurring the Line Between
Human and Animal Life*

CHRIS P. CARROT CAME TO OUR TOWN LAST MONTH. THE *Houston Chronicle* pictured the seven-foot-tall, smiley-faced carrot creature in a school yard surrounded by adoring children, giving hugs and brandishing his sign: "Eat Your Veggies, Not Your Friends."

Children love animals. Parents who finally give in to pleas for puppies, kittens, hamsters, horses, and gerbils know it. Storytellers from Aesop to Disney know it. Purveyors of petting zoos and pony rides know it. And People for the Ethical Treatment of Animals (PETA) know it.

"Kids are so in tune with animals that they understand what we're advocating," states Kathy Savory, PETA spokeswoman. The big orange veg is taking PETA's campaign against using animals for food, clothing, experiments, or entertainment to the nation's school children. But schools in Texas denied the request for in-class appearances. As the *Houston Chronicle* reported, this is cattle country, and, as one principal put it, "I don't have time to talk about a carrot."

But, we might wonder, who is inside this Trojan carrot waiting to be invited into your child's classroom? Is it one of the PETA activists who paraded in the buff around the White House wrapped in a discreetly positioned sign that read, "I'd Rather Go Naked Than Wear Fur"? Or is it one of the early risers who launched his boat into prime duck hunting areas on opening day to noisily scare off the unsuspecting ducks? It could be someone who pickets medical experimentation facilities with signs condemning the lab-coated "torturers" inside because "There Are

No Lesser Animals" and "Animals Have Rights Too." Or maybe it's one of PETA's Hollywood celebrities campaigning for animal "rights" by day, and by night exchanging the carrot suit for tux and red ribbon to attend a fund-raiser for AIDS research, as in AIDS *medical experimental* research on animals. (What's wrong with this picture?)

ANIMAL "RIGHTS," OR, CAN THE WORM TAKE THE EARLY BIRD TO COURT?

Actually animal "rights" activists are in some ways the most logically consistent of Darwinian evolutionists. If we are all just animals, then how come some animals have more "rights" than others? Are you a "speciesist"? Are you "prejudiced" against other species for no good reason? If animals have rights, then why are you wearing fur or leather or eating meat? (Well, as comic "Father" Guido Sarducci has pointed out, "We a-really only mind a-killing animals that are cute and-a smart. If they are-a dumb and-a ugly, like-a chicken or-a fish, well, then it's-a okay.")

But, seriously, PETA's crusade raises an interesting question: Where do animals get rights? From nature? No. The example of nature is the food chain. Just think of your basic *National Geographic* special: The big fish and the bird—neither of which consider for one moment the rights of the little fish or the worm. Nature shows us the survival of the fittest. The little fish and the worm do not shake their fists at the big fish and the bird, demanding, "Hey, you can't eat me. I've got my rights!" And even if they did, the big fish and the bird would say, "Oh, for cryin' out loud. I'm hungry, and I'm bigger than you." GULP! Most animal groups are not democracies where animals enjoy their "rights," but brutal dictatorships dominated by the strongest male or the "queen bee."

So are animals "endowed by their Creator with certain inalienable rights" such as "life, liberty, and the pursuit of happiness"? Well, what did the Creator say? We can take our children to Scripture for a clear understanding of the relationship He intended between people and animals.

➤ Genesis 1:28; Psalm 8:6-8: God has made people the rulers over animals.

➤ Genesis 1:29; 9:1-3: At first people were given plants for food, but after the flood, God amended our diets to include animals.

➤ Genesis 3:21: God was the first to kill an animal and use its skin to provide clothing for Adam and Eve.

➤ Genesis 4:3-5; Hebrews 9:22, 24-28: God has always required the shedding of blood for forgiveness of sin. The Old Testament prescribed animal sacrifice for this purpose.

➤ Genesis 2:20; 7:2-4; Proverbs 12:10: Human rule over the animals is balanced by responsibility to be a good steward of them.

➤ Genesis 1:27; 9:5-6: Human life is different from animal life not in degree but in kind. We are moral and spiritual beings like God, in whose image we were created. Human life is sacred. If you take an innocent human life, you must forfeit your own.

➤ Luke 12:24; Romans 5:6-8: God places great value on human life—much, much more than on animals. We are so precious to Him that He sent His Son so that we might have forgiveness of sin and eternal life.

Ignoring the example of nature and Scripture, animal "rights" activists build their case on the assertion that animals have *feelings*. "Activists say lobsters have feelings too," reads a *New York Times*, (12/96) headline in my file. This approach should come as no surprise in a culture where stock in feelings has been soaring since the sixties. In the *Times* article no less a celebrity than Mary Tyler Moore pleads for sensitivity: "Like humans (lobsters) flirt with one another and have even been seen walking 'claw in claw'! And like humans, lobsters feel pain."

PETA is now pressing for a ban on fishing. "Fish are animals. Lobsters are animals. Crabs are animals. Just because they don't scream doesn't mean they don't suffer," insists PETA fish campaign coordinator Tracy Reiman, often accompanied by six-foot mascot Gill, the Fish (*Houston Chronicle*, 3/30/96).

And when animals do suffer, many activists show their true colors. Responding to the malicious torching of a Miami puppy, they immediately raised a $10,000 reward for the dog's killer. ("When a serial murderer—still being sought—started burning and killing homeless

Miami *women*," the *Miami Herald,* [4/96] reported, "he had slain three before a cash reward was offered.") One local activist charged, "It is a heinous crime on an individual who is absolutely innocent—whether the individual is four-legged or two-legged, black or white, male or female." Of course she was referring to the *dog's* murder.

The scientific community is at a loss to measure animals' feelings. When asked, scientists assert that animals cannot feel as we feel because their central nervous systems are so inferior. But the clear teaching of Scripture shows us how God values animals (and their feelings). God is not indifferent to animals' suffering. "A righteous man cares for the needs of his animal" (Proverbs 12:10). But human feelings are immeasurably more important to God.

Jesus was moved with compassion when He met a demon-possessed man in the region of the Gerasenes (Mark 5:1-20). This pitiable creature was naked and homeless and lived among the tombs crying out and cutting himself with stones. You may recall that the legion of demons Jesus cast out of the man were permitted to enter a large herd of pigs. Obviously Jesus cared much more for the feelings and well-being of that one poor man than the 2,000 pigs who took a dive in the lake and drowned.

On the Sunday evening after my husband, Jack, made that point so well in his sermon, we headed for our small group meeting at Patty's house. Patty is almost as tenderhearted toward animals as the lady in chapter 1 who scooped up the cat. She made her statement on a small sign stuck in the middle of her front-door wreath. "I still feel sorry for the pigs." But she grills pork chops and tosses a football around with her guys. Scripture gives our lives a balance.

WE ARE RULERS *AND* STEWARDS

The biblical view of human life is so different from the Darwinian view. Man and woman are not the result of matter + time + chance. We have great value, great dignity, and significance and are created for a special relationship with the Creator. Animals are a different *kind* of creature altogether, far less valuable to God.

Our children may love animals, and they may "understand what the PETAs are advocating," but we can clearly show them from

Scripture that the PETAs' worldview is contrary to God's truth. We are appointed to rule over animals, and we may use them for food, clothing, experimentation, and entertainment without guilt, as long as we are good stewards over them.

This has some very practical applications for our children. It tells us that the way we treat our own animals is a measure of our character. When Johnny takes good care of his puppy, it pleases God. We can also point out to our children that being a good steward of animals is a biblical concept. It is not a concept inherent in Darwinian evolution. On this point, animal "rights" activists who think we are all animals are illogical and inconsistent evolutionists. Survival of the fittest teaches that the strong ravage the weak. When PETA campaigns for good stewardship of animals, it is taking a page right out of Genesis 2, which is completely contrary to their evolutionary worldview. (See Focus Box #11.)

God's Word also raises questions about the wanton destruction of animals for selfish pleasure. Recently in Houston several adolescent boys sneaked into a prize quarter horse's corral, cornered the animal, and then bludgeoned the poor horse to death with clubs and sticks. We can discuss this with our children and ask, "What difference is there between that behavior, which landed those kids in jail, and in dropping bricks on frogs or going 'varmint hunting,' not for predators or nuisance animals, but just for the 'sport' of killing?"

≈

FOCUS YOUR WORLDVIEW #11:
BLESS THE BEASTS AND THE CHILDREN.

Jonah sat under a vine fervently hoping God would blast Israel's enemies in Nineveh, the Assyrian capital. But Nineveh repented, and Jonah pouted. God rebuked Jonah, telling him that "Nineveh has more than 120,000 (children) and many cattle as well. Should I not be concerned about that great city?" (Jonah 4:11). God concerned about destroying cows? Yes.

Our children can learn much about the stewardship of God's creation through the responsibility of caring for animals. They can also become students of animal behavior and observe the similarities and differences between animals and humans.

If your children are not already taking care of a family pet, perhaps they could be assigned that responsibility for a period of time. Perhaps you would like to add a pet to the household and regularly give feedback on their stewardship of and kindness to their pet. Or have the children keep a journal of observations of the animal.

➤ Does it have a personality? Does it seem to be happy or sad?

➤ Does it understand verbal commands? How large is its vocabulary?

➤ Does it try to communicate? How?

➤ Does it seem to act "guilty" (whether it has behaved badly or whether you just scold it for no reason)?

➤ Does it make "moral" choices, or choices out of fear of punishment?

➤ Does it show any creative tendencies? Spiritual tendencies?

➤ Does it seem to show any emotions?

Note: The idea that animals have no thoughts or feelings is a result of modern behavioral psychology. Its demise should not threaten us.

Watch for stories on animals in the newspaper or on TV. Use them to spark discussions with children about the subjects in this chapter. For example, when the female gorilla Binti Jua at the Brookfield Zoo in Illinois rescued a small child who had fallen into the gorilla enclosure, the public's response was overwhelming. "If this animal that's supposed to be below us can be this way, why can't we?" "You are a wonderful example to all humankind to show that no matter who or what you are, you should always help one another." "Many Go Ape over Binti's Heroics as Basic Human Craving Fulfilled" (news headline).

Binti's rescue of the child has been trumpeted as heroism by "some 3,500 news organizations; she has received more than 200 fan letters; the zoo has been deluged with marketing ideas" (*Life*, 11/96).

Was her action a moral choice, a conscious or intuitive response of retrieving, or the result of her parental training by zookeepers (rewarding her with grapes, raisins, and praise for picking up and carrying a little primate)? What do you think?

Another example: *Life* (11/96) shows in-utero photographs of the similarities between developing animals and humans and suggests, "Prenatal pictures of different species provide new insight into what it means to be one of us. . . . Their miraculous transformations provide a glimpse of how our earliest ancestors made us what we are today."

Instead of "weird creatures reveal[ing] a shared ancient history," could they not just as easily reveal a shared ancient Designer? If the specifications for *traveling* in the real world mean that the chassis for Ford trucks and Cadillacs look similar in the beginning, might not the specs for *living* in the real world also require a common fundamental design? What do you think?

DIFFERENT IN KIND, NOT JUST DEGREE

I use a cartoon in my classes that shows a woman loaded with shopping bags and packages, explaining to her frowning husband, "I shop because it is what distinguishes us from the animal kingdom." While true, of course, her statement does not quite reflect the depth and complexity of our differences.

The Bible tells us clearly where to draw the line between man and animals and why. Ever since Darwin assumed that we evolved from lower animals, many scientists and philosophers after him have tried to establish that man is a higher being than animals because he can reason, use tools and language, and act morally.

However, current animal research is revealing that animals are much more capable than previously thought. In a cover story, "Can Animals Think?" *Time* magazine (3/22/93) reports on sea lions who equate different symbols in games of logic and a parrot who can correctly say how many blue socks lie in the clutter on his tray. The chimp "Amy," who used sign language in the movie *Congo*, was modeled after real chimps such as Kanzi, who can communicate at the level of a two-and-a-half-year-old toddler with a keyboard of 256 abstract symbols. Other chimps can *make* tools out of bamboo stalks and flint rocks and plan for their future use.

It is small wonder, then, that scientists such as astronomer Carl Sagan claim that humans are different from animals only in *degree*, and not *kind*. "If we insist on absolute rather than relative differences, we do not discover any distinguishing characteristics of our species," noted Sagan. Best known for his PBS series, *Cosmos*, Sagan enjoyed his role as science's most popular PR man for Darwinian evolution. In his book *Shadows of Forgotten Ancestors,* Sagan even made a case for animals' "moral grounding and courageous resistance to evil." He described experiments done on macaques (monkeys) who were unwilling to pull a chain to receive a treat because to do so would send an electrical shock to a fellow macaque whose agony could be seen through a one-way mirror.

Of course, Sagan saw what he wanted to see, an ethical animal. But the poor beast could have acted out of confusion or fear. How was he sure the chain would always shock the other monkey and not himself, especially when he had once been in the shock capsule on the other side? How did he know the mirror was one-way? How did he know the other macaque would not get free and attack him, or attack him later?

To impute ethical behavior to animals is wishful thinking. My dog may look guilty when she has chewed up the doormat, but she may just be fearful of my response. She does not like to be scolded. I will grant her some primitive feelings, but not ethics.

Why? Because righteousness is part of God's character, and I am made in God's image. My dog is not. I am a moral being. God has written His law in my heart (Romans 2:15). My dog has no conscience. If she ponders whether to munch on the mat or not, she may "fear" she will be scolded, but she is not paralyzed by moral guilt, her "thoughts now accusing, now even defending" her. Fear of punishment is not the same as knowing and choosing right from wrong. We will never see our dog turn herself in out of remorse or lead us to the place where she chewed up the rug, as my son thoughtfully observed. Carl Sagan never found an ethical animal because animals, not being created in God's image, have no moral capacity.

In a "cosmic" twist of irony, Sagan found himself depending for his life upon the benefits of medical research on animals. In a *Parade* article (3/10/96) he admitted that he had been diagnosed with a rare blood disorder that put him on "death's doorstep." For a couple of years he was spared because of experimental medication developed through animal research.

Aware of this glaring inconsistency as an animal-rights champion, Sagan wrote, "I have tried to show how closely related we are to other animals, how cruel it is to gratuitously inflict pain on them, and how morally bankrupt it is to slaughter them, say, to manufacture lipstick." This was a whitewash of his views printed three and a half years earlier in *Parade* (9/20/92), which condemned everyone who would "bend (animals) to his will, make them work for us, wear them, eat them—without any disquieting tinges of guilt."

In the heart of every consistent evolutionist lies a deep tension, because his view of the world is basically in conflict with the way God created it. "And it is this tension which works on your behalf as you speak to him," stated Francis Schaeffer. "A man may try to bury this tension, and you have to help him find it, but somewhere there is a point of inconsistency. He stands in a position which he cannot pursue to the end" (*The God Who Is There,* pp. 133-134).

Carl Sagan stared his point of tension in the face every morning of his last two years as he woke up to look anew at his reflection in the mirror. "I remain very conflicted on this issue," he confessed. "I would not be alive today if not for research on animals." Perhaps Sagan carried his conflict to the grave—or perhaps God used it in some way to prepare him to meet the One in whose image he was created.

WHY ANIMALS NEVER COMMIT SUICIDE

In many behaviors, such as language, reasoning, tool-making, etc., science may find genius chimps who differ from us in degree. But we are a different *kind* of being, a moral and spiritual being made in God's image. And until the invention of the modern secular humanist, we have all worshiped a spirit or spirits whom we have loved or feared. Only man has been created with what the famous French scientist Blaise Pascal has described as a sort of God-shaped vacuum in his soul. Pascal put it this way: "There once was in man a true happiness of which now remain to him only the mark and empty trace, which he in vain tries to fill from his surroundings. . . . But these are all inadequate, because the infinite abyss can only be filled by an infinite and immutable object, that is to say, only by God himself" (*Pensees,* p. 113).

Animal researchers will never find a spiritual animal. They will never discover an ape colony worshiping a sacred tree or sacrificing a virgin ape to the volcano's spirit. (However, Sagan's macaques might get together and form a twelve-step therapy group.)

Furthermore, animals will never despair over their own significance. Sam Storms, pastor and friend, in his book *To Love Mercy* contrasts animals and humans: "Nary an animal on this earth has lost a minute's sleep worrying about whether or not its life is worth living. They just live. But when you and I 'just live,' we die. When life is reduced to mere existence, we shrivel up inside, wither away, and perish. If our *being* doesn't matter, why *be* at all? Perhaps I'm uninformed, but I've never heard of an animal committing suicide" (pp. 48-49). (Except for the macaque who dropped out of the twelve-step group.)

So why is human life sacred while animal life is not? Or as "politically radical vegetarian lesbian defender of wildlife" pop singer k. d. lang laments in the *New York Times,* "How can you place human life above every other form of life?" If we start from God's truth, we can. We are created in God's image, and that is the difference that makes *all* the difference.

Carl Sagan and many of the PETAs deny God and deny that man is a spiritual being, and they want to believe that animals are moral. They are left with no unique differences between people and animals. They have no rationale for believing that people are significant unless they try to elevate the significance of animals and talk about animal "rights." Theologian R. C. Sproul has addressed their dilemma, observing that you cannot believe that human beings evolved from chaos and are destined for oblivion, yet somehow attain great significance in between. It is no coincidence that the more people deny their sin and their need for God, the more like animals they become.

Man, starting from himself, asks,

Q: How did man come to exist?

A: Evolution. Man is the result of matter + time + chance.

Result: No image of God, no sacredness, no dignity or significance.

Man, starting from himself, asks,

Q: How are we different from animals?

A: We are not unique, only different in degree of intelligence, creativity, other behaviors.

Result: Devaluation of human life—the common thread running from evolution, to animal "rights," to abortion.

If our children's worldview is framed by a clear understanding of the inestimable worth of human life, then they will be able to keep clear in their own minds the distinction God makes between the value of human and animal life. They may still encounter criticism from classmates and a youth culture that is becoming increasingly politically correct, but they will know why the animal "rights" puzzle piece does not fit a Christian worldview. And in their own proper use and stewardship of animals they needn't be "conflicted."

As with the evidence for intelligent design, they can be assured that their faith position on creation makes for a much more sensible approach to animals than the inconsistencies and extreme tactics on the other side. They can spot the Trojan in the carrot. Then with boosted confidence in God's Word, they can begin to sort out how the really difficult pieces of abortion and the "right to die" relate to the framework of their Christian worldview.

Abortion Kills Children, But Jesus Heals and Forgives

7

Teaching Our Children to Value
"the Least of These"

OFTEN WHEN WE ADDRESS THE SUBJECT OF ABORTION, WE hammer away at the evil of it and then stick on sort of a P.S. about God's compassion. But that is where I would like to begin our discussion.

The first time we participated in the Life Chain abortion protest about three years ago, I remember lining up to get my sign. I wanted to make a strong statement in this long curbside line of silent protest across from the mall. Something like, "Abortion Kills Children" or "Adoption, not Abortion." Instead, I got "Jesus Heals and Forgives."

Oh, well, I thought, *this is important, too.* And then I joined the line for two hours and meditated on the truth of my sign. I thought about my brief nightmare of possibly being pregnant while on toxic drugs for rheumatoid arthritis, about the fear of not being able to carry and care for that child, and of no insurance for R. A. or pregnancy. I remembered how hard it was to trust God in my pain and fear even when I had known Him intimately for a long time. I didn't change my mind about abortion, but God softened my heart on the subject.

That time of reflection impressed me always to address this concern with the compassion it deserves. It is a hard, painful, fearful situation for anyone who confronts a crisis pregnancy, and she needs compassion, not harshness. Angry shouts and aggressive, condemning protest is unproductive. Extreme behavior is marginalized in our society, but an eloquent, compassionate appeal for life silences even presidents.

I think of Mother Teresa's moving appeal at the presidential prayer breakfast in 1994, "Please don't kill the child. I want the child. Please give me the child." She received a standing ovation and silenced all the pro-choice critics. Those, it seems, are the words that echo God's heart. Our God who heals and forgives even when we break His law. Our God who knows our moral frailty. Who knows all our wanderings and keeps all our tears in His bottle (Psalm 56).

If we take a stand against abortion, it will make others angry. But the mothers of hundreds of babies saved from abortion this year at our local crisis pregnancy centers were not persuaded by angry protest or smug self-righteousness. They found listening ears, open hearts, and practical help. They were won by the love of God in action.

May our children always see the compassion of Christ first and foremost as we teach them about this issue and deal with its consequences in our nation and our homes. And, if you have had an abortion, or if someone in your family confesses that choice to you, then remember, "Jesus heals and forgives." We have all sinned, and all sin needs to be dealt with in repentance before the throne of grace where we will "receive mercy and find grace to help us in our time of need" (Hebrews 4:16). Chuck Swindoll's little book *Sanctity of Life* speaks at length of God's standard on abortion, but it also ministers greatly to women who have broken that standard.

How a Baby Came to Be a Nonperson

Children tend to love babies even more than they love animals. So as we give them age-appropriate teaching on abortion, they are naturally amazed and horrified to find out that people kill babies in the womb. As they get older and begin to understand the complexities of sex and family relationships, they need more information.

Dr. Linda Flower has researched the history of abortion in American Medical Association records and reported that just before the Civil War, English microbiologists using the newly invented microscope discovered the process of fertilization. After the war the ethics committee convinced legislatures in every state that all human life should be protected from conception. Abortion became punishable as a felony in all states until 1967.

Then court fights chipped away at the rights of the unborn until

1973. In *Roe v. Wade* a seven-man majority on the Supreme Court struck down laws prohibiting or restricting abortions in all fifty states. Like the Dred Scott decision of 1857 where a seven-man majority declared that Negroes "had no rights which the white man was bound to respect," the court declared that unborn children, like the Negroes of 1857, were nonpersons.

The justices were moved by the case of Norma McCorvey ("Jane Roe"), a carnival barker pregnant with her third child. She had given the other two up for adoption, but this time she decided she wanted an abortion. She was shocked to find it was illegal. In the blackest of ironies the *Roe v. Wade* decision was based on an appeal for "compassion": This poor woman was the victim of rape. She should *not* have to carry an unwanted child. Texas lawyer Sarah Weddington had been looking for just such a compassionate appeal to challenge state abortion laws. In a blacker irony still, the rape story was a lie. McCorvey confessed years later that the pregnancy was the result of a casual affair.

Another black twist in this tragedy of "compassion"—by the end of McCorvey's trial she was six months pregnant and still hopeful she could get an abortion. Only when her lawyers told her it was much too late for that did she fully understand her situation. They had their ammunition for a Supreme Court appeal and moved on. She was left to work through her profound disappointment, have the baby alone, and put it up for adoption. Two years later she picked up a paper and read the headlines—"Compassion" had won. Abortion was legal.

In the past twenty-three years over 33 million unborn children have been aborted. The rate is currently about 1,500,000 per year. Abortion may be "safe and legal," but it is by no means "rare." Summarizing his view of the Court's 1973 decision, columnist Paul Greenberg has reflected, "In a society that has lost its moral bearings, strange and terrible decisions can be made and can come to seem quite ordinary, even praiseworthy."

Malcolm Muggeridge has observed that King Herod killed thousands of babies to protect his lifestyle, but he went down in history as a villain and a murderer. Satan's greatest coup has to be that over a million and a half babies die from abortion every year, and this is done in the name of *compassion*—the "Humanitarian Holocaust."

We know Satan's triumphant-looking march to the abortion clinics will not end in victory for him. In fact, God has a lovely way of raining on Satan's earthly parade no matter how "grand." Perhaps you've heard about God's true compassion reaching out to Norma Jean McCorvey. Even in such a sad life used for such destructive purposes, God has worked things "together for good." Christian families and pro-life workers reached out to her. One of the children invited her to church. Norma found the arms of a loving and forgiving God and has trusted Christ for salvation. Celebrating her baptism, *World* magazine ran the headline, "Roe Wades."

DOES GOD SEE A BABY AS A NONPERSON?

The population in general, and Christians in particular, disagree over abortion right along progressive/orthodox lines. A pro-choice university professor wrote in the *Houston Chronicle* (8/30/92), "There are a lot of church-going Americans who prefer to believe in a loving and compassionate God and who are disturbed by the 'biblical correctness' of the fundamentalists." Not all orthodox are fundamentalists, but they do take a high view of Scripture. So what does Scripture say?

I would encourage you to take your children to the following verses so they can read for themselves what God thinks about the unborn child.

➤ Genesis 21:1-2; 29:31; 30:22-23; 1 Samuel 1:5-6, 19-20: God opens and closes the womb and permits and prohibits conception. (A friend of mine who pursued in vitro fertilization told me that her doctor could even manipulate the sperm into the nucleus of the egg, but that did not guarantee fertilization. Sometimes the chromosomes would begin to unravel and recombine, and sometimes they just sat there!)

➤ Job 10:8-12: God shapes us and molds us like clay.

➤ Psalm 22:9-10; 51:5: David sees Himself as being accountable to God from his mother's womb; he also traces his sinfulness or moral nature to the moment of his conception.

➤ Psalm 139:13-16: God creates our inmost being and weaves

and knits us together in our mother's womb. God sees our unformed body and ordains all our days in His book before we're born.

➤ Genesis 25:23: God knew Jacob and Esau in the womb and told their mother that they would both become leaders of nations. God loved and blessed Jacob over Esau before he was born.

➤ Jeremiah 1:5: God knew Jeremiah and set him apart as a prophet before he was born.

➤ Luke 1:41, 44: While still in the womb, John responded to Jesus' arrival. The Christmas story itself is the story of a crisis pregnancy of sorts and includes the celebration of the coming Messiah by an unborn babe!

➤ Proverbs 24:11-12: We are told to rescue innocent lives headed for slaughter. Taken together with the verses describing how we are made in God's image, Scripture pleads for life, for the "personhood" of the unborn child.

As Chuck Swindoll writes in *Sanctity of Life,* "it is God's way of saying, 'Life is so important no one has the right to murder it. Don't end it. Let it live. Because all humanity represents My handiwork; it is Mine to do with as I please. My image is, in mysterious ways, stamped into human life'" (p. 17).

I wish God had come right out and said, "Abortion is wrong." I wish He had said that slavery is wrong, but He didn't. He did say homosexuality is "detestable" and "perverted." But in our relativistic society the progressives in many churches try to explain the verses away. Theologians disagree on when the unborn child is infused with soul and spirit. The Bible is not clear on this point, but if God grants the conception of a human life, forms him, knits him together, knows him, blesses him, and calls him before he's born, then the weight of biblical evidence is on the sanctity of that life. Where are any verses to infer otherwise or that defend a mother killing an unborn child?

Additionally, as every good hunter knows, even if we (like the theologians) claim uncertainty, let's not shoot if we can't tell if there's an animal or a human in the bushes. Let's err on the side of protection.

When, as a nation, we reject God's Word as our moral authority, as the basis of law, we are left with no image of God, no involvement of God with the unborn child, no fashioning, blessing, or calling of God on the babe to be born. Once again we are left with utilitarianism. In ruling on abortion, the courts have tried to determine "what would be socially helpful."

DRAWING THE LINE ON ABORTION

As it turns out, the most helpful solution is judged to be abortion on demand. For the sake of the woman's "right to privacy" spelled out *nowhere* in the Constitution, in *Roe v. Wade* the justices separated the unborn child's life from its personhood and its "right to life" clearly laid out in the Declaration of Independence. It's ironic that so many choose to focus on the Declaration's other phrase—the right to the "pursuit of happiness" (a familiar theme), but they ignore that unborn child's right "to life."

The state affords protection to the unborn child on the basis of function. What can it do?

Q: Can it successfully pass through the birth canal?

A: After it is born, the state recognizes it as a person—with rights, protected.

Q: Can it survive outside the womb if its umbilical cord is cut? (The court calls this viability.)

A: Justices afford a viable fetus some protection in the last trimester *if* the mother's health is not affected adversely. The definition of mother's health though is very broad. Thus it is socially helpful to allow almost all abortions that the mother wants. The father has no legal say.

The *Roe v. Wade* decision has many detractors from the legal, religious, and medical communities. Let's look at a couple of the "common-sense" objections that your children can easily understand.

Now when doctors are dealing with a patient near death, the criterion for determining if she's still alive are the presence of a heart-beat and brain waves. The baby has a heartbeat after about three weeks and brain waves after forty-three days (five and a half weeks). Most babies are aborted later, in the seventh week, soon after the mother finds out she is pregnant. Unfortunately, drawing the line at heartbeat or brain waves is not socially helpful when dealing with all the women who want abortions. So the Court has developed different criteria to define and protect a life, depending on whether you're dying or being born. This is totally inconsistent.

Joining the Court in the "inconsistent" category is Carl Sagan's view on when the unborn child becomes human enough to be protected. His popular opinions reached millions, but they often make for a solid con-trast against Scripture and common sense. He wrote in *Parade* magazine (4/22/90), "We must decide what distinguishes a human being from other animals and when, during gestation, the uniquely human quali-ties—whatever they are—emerge." Early on the fetus resembles some-thing fishlike, then something "reptilian," and then "piglike," and eventually it "resembles a primate's" (face). But when does it begin to look truly human? The article justified taking a life that is subhuman. As we have already seen, Sagan didn't make much distinction between animals and humans, so his own quest for distinction seems hopeless.

Besides, as every seventh grader knows, the study of genetics clearly identifies a human embryo as human life from the moment of conception. To argue that a human embryo is subhuman or only potential life is to say that "the nature of any bodily being is deter-mined by what it looks like at maturity or some other point in its development. But the very opposite is true," writes Professor Leo Kelly in the *Houston Post*: "What it looks like at any given point in its development is determined by the kind it is to start with. . . . At con-ception a human being is as immature as possible, but he or she is an immature being of the same kind as the parents. It could not be oth-erwise. An expectant mother does not wait with baited breath for three, six, or nine months to learn whether her child is human or of some other species!"

The Supreme Court's attempt to draw the line at viability (rather than heartbeat or brain waves) and Sagan's suggestion that we wait until it looks more human both center on development. What can the fetus *do?* Does it look human? I believe that a biblical ethic ascribes value to a person based on who she *is*. To ascribe value based on looks or ability to do something disagrees with common sense, and it is not an ethic that reflects the heart of God.

God loves us because of who we *are*—His unique creation made in His image. He loves the unlovely, the poor, and the weak. An ethic that assigns value based on looks or ability is dangerous for the poor, the elderly, the handicapped, and the very young. All ethics should be judged on how they treat "the least of these" especially.

A WOMAN'S RIGHT TO "REPRODUCTIVE FREEDOM"

The pro-choice activists have never concerned themselves with the right to life of the unborn child. They have focused instead exclusively on the rights of the mother. The feminists who led the charge have viewed access to abortion as a great leveling force between men and women. If a woman should be able to do whatever a man can do, then a woman should not have to tolerate the limitations on her freedom imposed by a pregnancy if she doesn't want to.

"I have always seen the abortion issue as being ever so much larger than abortion itself," says Gloria Feldt, president of Planned Parenthood. "It's a question of whether women should be equal partners to men" (*New York Times*, 4/96). From a feminist perspective, equality is the end—abortion is the socially useful means.

(I talked to a Brownie troop at Zach's Christian school once about the role of women. I asked them, "Do you think that a woman should be able to do whatever a man can do?" Most nodded their heads in emphatic agreement. Yikes! I'm hoping they were thinking doctor, lawyer, or scientist. I tried to explain the difference between equality of worth and difference of roles, especially in regard to nurturing children. [More on that later.] We need to be careful what goals we encourage our daughters to pursue. The path to full equality of the sexes leads straight through an abortion clinic.)

Pro-choice forces campaign for the "right to reproductive freedom." They even succeeded in including this language in the platform of the U. N. Fourth Conference on Women in Beijing on women's rights (September 1995). Kate Michelman, president of the

National Abortion and Reproductive Rights Action League (NARAL), is fond of this democratic-sounding label for a strong everyone-should-have-unlimited-access-to-abortion-and-the-government-should-pay-for-it agenda. "Women's ability to make their own reproductive choices free from coercion is absolutely fundamental to genuine reproductive freedom, and every woman is entitled to genuine reproductive freedom regardless of her economic status" *Houston Chronicle* (7/18/94).

God's heart is one of compassion for a woman in a crisis pregnancy. But once she has had sexual relations and conceived, then there is a new life to consider. Would God counsel a woman who has (in most cases) consented to sexual relations to then have her baby ripped out or poisoned? A baby that He has created, known, and nurtured in the womb?

Pro-choice supporters often raise the question of rape or incest—the hard cases—to support their position. The "hard cases" are a really tough objection. When Jack first challenged my thinking on the rape objection, I became very uncomfortable. I could not bear the thought of anyone requiring me or anyone else to give birth to an eternal reminder of rape. But I could not escape the poor logic of my position: namely, if A injures B, then B is justified in killing C. A, the rapist, is the guilty party. C, the unborn child, is completely innocent. Additionally, this principle was upheld in Old Testament law. "Fathers shall not be put to death for their children, nor children put to death for their fathers; each is to die for his own sin" (Deuteronomy 24:16).

In His time my gracious heavenly Father helped me trust Him to take care of me should something so terrible ever befall me. He gave me the grace to believe that "in all things [even rape or incest] God works for the good of those who love him" (Romans 8:28). I do believe that protecting the unborn children of rape is the most just and biblical position, but I can certainly sympathize with those who think the way I used to think.

The truth is that most abortions are done for convenience. In an abortion survey of 1,900 women conducted by the Alan Guttmacher Institute, the "hard cases" accounted for only 7 percent of all abortions (mother's health—3 percent, baby's health—3 percent, and pregnancy from rape and incest—only 1 percent). The other 93 percent of abortions were matters of convenience—women who were not ready for responsibility—21 percent, couldn't afford it—21 percent, had a relationship problem—12 percent, etc.—all problems that adoption and prospective adoptive parents could help solve. Sadly, what we see at work in abortion for convenience is the Darwinian principle of the strong asserting their power over the weak.

"Even though I am strongly for abortion rights," states Camille Paglia, outspoken feminist humanities professor and author in *America* (10/94), "I feel that feminists have been outrageously unjust to the pro-life position. . . . Career women are arguing from expedience—that it is inconvenient or onerous to bear an unwanted child. The pro-life position is arguing from ethics."

A NATION IN TENSION

Ethics versus convenience, the absolute value and sanctity of human life versus the social usefulness of a mother's right to kill her child. We and our children can take a strong pro-life position based on what God's Word says about the unborn child, on ethics, and on common sense. We may feel tension when we confront a pregnant teenage gal deserted by her boyfriend and kicked out by her parents. Abortion may *seem* so easy, so compassionate, but I would much rather point that teen mom to Jesus' forgiveness and comfort and the support services of the church and a crisis pregnancy center than hold a position that justifies "the attack on something so primordial, so given, so foundational to human community as a mother's love and responsibility for her child." If you can do that, writes Catholic apologist Richard John Neuhaus, "you have to come up with a new explanation of fundamental reality, a new worldview, and finally a new religion. . . . If you can justify abortion, you can justify anything" (*World,* 7/17/93).

The progressive pro-choice person must face the tension of valuing the mother's convenience or well-being so much that she will approve the killing of an innocent child. As Francis Schaeffer wrote, she will try to bury this tension, but like Mother Teresa, we must help her find it with compassion and mercy.

Our legal and medical communities treat the unborn in ways that further reveal the tension. An abortionist can legally kill the unborn for almost any reason. But if a pregnant woman is murdered, her killer can be legally charged with causing the death of her unborn child as well and can be tried or sued. The court legally recognizes the unborn as a victim. Mothers can kill their unborn babies, but they can't injure them. The *New York Times* (8/96) reports that since the later 1980s "at least 200 women in more than thirty states have been prosecuted for behavior while pregnant that posed danger to their fetuses." Usually involving alcohol or drug abuse, most of these cases have been dismissed, although the South Carolina Supreme Court has ruled that a pregnant woman who took drugs could be prosecuted for child abuse.

In our nation's hospitals and clinics, one doctor destroys the child in the womb; another fights to save its life, treating it as a patient. Late-term abortions kill children older and more developed than many premature babies that parents and physicians fight to save.

The tension felt on both sides of the debate is also reflected in the inconsistent polling data on abortion. When asked if abortion is murder, 46 percent say yes, 41 percent say no, but only 23 percent believe it should absolutely not be permitted, according to a variety of polls by CBS, CNN, NBC, *New York Times*, *Wall Street Journal*, *USA Today*, and Gallup. The same research shows that 53 percent strongly agree that the government should not interfere with a woman's choice to abort, but only 38 percent think abortion should generally be available; 37 percent want stricter limits, and 23 percent want to see abortion made illegal.

In a more specific poll taken by Roper in November 1994, only 13 percent agreed with the feminist position that the "fetus" is like an appendix or a tooth to be extracted (Focus on the Family newsletter, 11/94). And, since you can't "murder a tooth," there should be no restrictions, *and* the government should pay if a woman can't afford it (only 6 percent of the 13 percent). The same poll found that 56 percent of Americans lean toward a pro-life view (abortion is wrong with a few exceptions), while only 26 percent lean toward a pro-choice view (abortion is permissible with a few exceptions).

The Supreme Court's *Roe v. Wade* decision was supposed to settle any dispute over abortion, but, like the Dred Scott decision that perpetuated slavery, it has only aggravated the conflict. Legislative battles continue in every national election; Supreme Court nomination becomes a pro-life/pro-choice confrontation; hundreds of thousands have marched on Washington, and tens of thousands keep showing up every year; clinics are picketed; violence has broken out on both sides. Many are beginning to weary of the seemingly interminable cultural struggle over abortion. "Just take abortion out of politics—it's too divisive," they argue. "Just take all this tension and bury it!" Which is what our country tried to do about slavery. It didn't work.

Looking at the polling data, what we see is a lot of people who think abortion is morally wrong and who would support a roll-back on abortion for convenience. I've talked to some of the "take-it-out" proponents in my precinct and pointed out how much we agree on.

Using Bill Bennett's approach printed in the *Weekly Standard* (1/8/96), I've asked them, "Do you 'oppose the use of public funds to pay for abortion'?"

"Yes."

"Do you support restricting abortions after viability?"

"Yes."

"Do you support 'ending late-term and sex-selection abortions'?"

"Yes."

"Do you favor 'establishing waiting periods, informed consent, and parental notification'?"

"Yes."

"Then we shouldn't drop abortion from politics," I point out. "There's too much we agree on that needs to be addressed politically."

We as women need to make the case to other women. "The ethic of 'choice' is not good for the world or for women," as Noemie Emery advocates in the *Weekly Standard* (12/25/95). "It has not made women more valued, respected, or safe in their commerce." Increased tension and cultural conflict are by no means the main consequence of the "right to choose."

Private Choice, Public Consequences

The consequences of abortion on demand will increasingly affect the world our children face. What Francis Schaeffer called the "educational impact" of abortion has contributed to the cheapening of human life: "If one can legally kill a child a few months before birth, one should not feel too bad about roughing him up a little bit after he is born" (*Whatever Happened to the Human Race?* p. 36). I agree with Schaeffer that there is a connection between abortion and child abuse.

Douglas Gresham, American-born son of C. S. Lewis, lives in Ireland and works with the Institute of Pregnancy Loss and Child Abuse Research and Recovery. Based on years of case study and research, he reports to Focus on the Family's *Citizen* magazine (5/15/95) that abortion is child abuse in its ultimate form. Abortion and child abuse are definitely linked psychologically. The Institute has about 4,000 case studies on record, and the link is very clear. Statistics also graphically demonstrate that women who have had an abortion are more likely to abuse subsequent children, and women who have been abused as children are more likely to abort children.

If large numbers of unwanted children are being aborted, relieving pressure on parents who are "too poor" or not ready for the responsibility, we should expect to see the numbers of abused children decreasing. But with more than 33 million abortions, the number of abused children is steadily increasing. In September of 1996 the Department of Health and Human Services released a study showing that child abuse soared 107 percent in just seven years (1986-1993). According to the report, in 1993, 1.22 million children were abused (*Houston Chronicle,* 9/19/96).

Many of the millions of women who make that "private" choice for an abortion are also seeing long-term effects on their mental health. The *Los Angeles Times* (8/95) reports that the demand for counseling after an abortion is on the rise. Thousands of women are ordering postabortion counseling materials to help them deal with their guilt, depression, and "empty arms." The momentary relief afforded by the quick end to a crisis pregnancy often gives way to lingering feelings of pain and remorse. As Frederica Mathewes-Green notes in her book *Real Choices,* abortion is not the end. That dead child is out there in a landfill somewhere. And the memory lingers on.

Our children need to understand fully the consequences that these choices bring when we destroy God's image so casually.

WILL THE TIDE OF ABORTION EVER TURN?

On the one hand, the number of abortions and the number of doctors who perform them is declining. The pro-life message seems to be getting through. On the other hand, if abortion becomes a non-surgical procedure accomplished at home with drug prescriptions, numbers of abortions and doctors participating may increase again. Numbers of pro-life lawmakers wax and wane with each election. God may yet raise up leaders and judges who will ban abortion on demand, or at least give the unborn greater protection, but our children may come of age in a nation where hundreds of thousands of children are still aborted each year.

We can hope that their convictions on the subject will be as strong as their compassion for the women touched by it. Millions of American believers have strong convictions and great intentions to do something about abortion, but the problem seems overwhelming. If everyone who shared those convictions and intentions just did something once or twice a year, we could all make a significant impact on a life or on our nation in general—good advice passed on from *World* publisher Joel Belz. (See Focus Box #12.)

FOCUS YOUR WORLDVIEW #12:
WHAT ONE THING COULD YOU DO?

Here are some suggestions on what one family can do about changing hearts and making a difference concerning abortion.

1. Share a good book. Chuck Swindoll's *Sanctity of Human Life* (Word Publishing, 1990) is a short booklet (four chapters) that would be especially great to read together with older children and pass on to someone dealing with a crisis pregnancy, the guilt of abortion, or a struggle with moral purity.

   Share a picture book of life in the womb with your children. Discuss the developmental stages and ask the children to give five or ten ways in which the baby is "fearfully and wonderfully made." The best full color pictures are in *A Child Is Born* by Lennart Nilsson, but try to find the old (seventies) edition. The "Completely New

Edition" is rife with references to evolution and contains suggestive and graphic pictures unsuitable for little eyes. Also, Focus on the Family offers a booklet, *The First Nine Months* (with full-color images), which documents the babies' growth and "strongly supports the sanctity of life." Call Focus at 1-800-A-Family.

2. Volunteer time and money to your local crisis pregnancy center. They need counselors, teachers (nutrition, money-management, etc.), office workers, prayer warriors, computer programmers, maternity clothes, baby clothes, and furnishings.

3. Put together a special basket for an unwed mother. Deliver it personally, if possible, or to your local crisis pregnancy center or American Family Association representative. (This could even be a Sunday school project.)

4. Perhaps you have room enough and love enough in your family to take in an unwed mother.

5. If sidewalk clinic picketing and counseling are too confrontational for you, try joining the Life Chain—a shoulder-to-shoulder silent line of people holding pro-life signs sponsored each October. You can just see the little ones in cars going by saying, "Mom, what do these signs mean?" It is a powerful witness to the truth. Any crisis pregnancy center or right-to-life group will have information.

6. Don't give up. *VOTE pro-life.* Should we vote for or against candidates based solely on their stand on abortion? We hear a lot of talk discouraging one-issue voting. Let me put it another way. Are there single issues that should disqualify someone from public office? What about embezzlement or racism? If you would vote against someone for those single issues, then why not abortion? Surely approval of the killing of innocent unborn babies is just as serious as devaluing fellow Americans with racial slurs and jokes. Legislation comes up every year—forcing medical schools to train students in abortion, forcing states to fund some charity abortions, addressing partial-birth abortion. When you hear about these votes coming up, weigh in with your elected officials. And we may yet see the Supreme Court turn around.

7. *Pray.* Pray for teens in trouble, crisis pregnancy centers, legislators, judges, our president. Pray for doctors to forsake the practice of abor-

tion and not to use the new prescription drugs that are coming. Pray that God will change hearts and give us courage to stand for life.

RESOURCE BOX #5: LET HEAVEN AND NATURE SING

Three videos on *The Wonders of God's Creation* offer some creative opportunities to your children, aside from providing intriguing photography and research of God's extraordinary design. You can reinforce the message of this section of the book with videos on *Planet Earth, The Animal Kingdom,* and *Human Life.*
   Suggestions:

➤ Use the video clips as catalysts for family time discussion on the Scriptures or ideas from chapters 5-8.

➤ Let children make their own multimedia show on these topics by using video clips as background while they sing a song or read psalms, verses, original stories, or poetry. They could even play music or choose recorded music to play with clips as a family night feature, or if instrumental music is chosen, as additional background to stories, etc.

   Only available as a set for $44.95, the videos may be more accessible for home school co-ops or church libraries. (Extra selling point for churches with video projection: great tools for the church's multimedia efforts or for use in Sunday school rooms with TVs and VCRs.) Available from Gateway Films Vision Video 1-800-523-0226. (Perhaps a nature special from a video rental place could serve the same purpose.)
   Another recommendation for church library or Christian school, the video series, *Whatever Happened to the Human Race?*—a powerful documentary by Francis Schaeffer and Dr. C. Everett Koop (in his pre-Surgeon General days) addressing abortion, infanticide, euthanasia, and the principles behind assisted suicide. Price: $360. Available from Moody Films.

What does God expect of us when it comes to a huge, overwhelming problem like abortion? I believe He just expects us to be faithful and obedient where we are. We can raise up future leaders of conscience (our children perhaps) who will keep this issue before the American people and win hearts to the truth. Perhaps your family has the opportunity to change just one mind, to soften one heart to choose life. Even that would be an opportunity with eternal consequences. It might be that the heart you touch would be one like the birth mother of Jessica, who wrote this letter to the pro-life Pennsylvania governor, Robert Casey:

Dear Governor Casey,

Hi! My name is Jessica Stobaugh. I am ten. I was adopted. My birth mom chose life for me. I would stand up like you for life. I think what you are doing is right. I would do the same thing if I were governor. . . . Thank you for fighting for unborn children, even when it's a hard thing to do.

From your fan and friend,
Jessica.

From *World* magazine (10/1/94)

God bless you, Jessica, and Governor Casey. And "God bless us every one," as we endeavor to change hearts on this issue.

WATCHING
"GREAT-MOTHER" DIE

8

*The Life Not Worthy
to Be Lived?*

22 January 2023

Dear Mom,

Gosh, can you believe it's 2023 already? I'm still writing 22 on nearly everything. Seems like just yesterday I was sitting in first grade celebrating the century change!

I know we haven't chatted since Christmas. Sorry. Anyway, I have a few things to tell you, and I really didn't want to call or talk face to face.

Ted's had a promotion, and I should be up for a hefty raise this year if I keep putting in those crazy hours. You know how I work at it. Yes, we're still really struggling with the bills. You were right about over-buying on the house, but it is nice.

Timmy's been "okay" at kindergarten, although he's still not happy about going. But then he wasn't happy about day care either, so what can you do?

He's become a real problem, Mom. He's a good kid, but quite honestly he's an unfair burden at this time in our lives. Ted and I have talked this through and through and finally made a choice. Plenty of other families have made it and are much better off.

I don't expect you to "understand," but you need to be sensitive to our circumstances. I can't afford years of parenting Timothy and have any sort of career, much less any time with my husband. Do you know how long it's been since we just went out together?

Our pastor is supportive and says hard decisions sometimes are neces-

*sary. The family is a "system," and the demands of one member shouldn't
be allowed to ruin the whole. He told us to be prayerful, consider all the factors, and do what is right to make the family work. He says that even though
he probably wouldn't do it himself, the decision really is ours. He referred
us to a children's clinic near here, so at least that part's easy.*

*I'm not an uncaring mother. I do feel sorry for the little guy. I think he
overheard Ted and me talking about "it" the other night. I turned around
and saw him standing on the bottom step in his pj's with the little bear you
gave him under his arm and his eyes sort of welling up. The way he looked
at me just about broke my heart. But I honestly believe this is better for
Timothy, too. It's not fair to force him to live in a family where there isn't
enough money or room.*

*Please don't give me the kind of grief Grandma gave you over your abor-
tions. It's the same thing, you know. We've told him he's going in for a vac-
cination. Anyway, they say the termination procedure is painless.*

I guess it's just as well you haven't seen that much of him.

Love to Dad,
Jane

(From the *Spiritual Counterfeits Project Journal*,
vol. 16:2, 1991. Used by permission.)

Poor Timmy. Remember the words of ex-Surgeon General
Jocelyn Elders: "Every child a planned and wanted child." Timmy may
have actually been "planned," but as it turns out, he wasn't "wanted."
If you think about it, Jane's letter is consistent with the logic in Elder's
statement. It goes like this: "Timmy was conceived in a family without 'enough' money or room. Timmy is a drag on his parents' quality
time together. Timmy's life is not worth living because he is an unfair
burden on his parents. They don't want him. If Timmy were a pleasure to his parents—i.e., a 'planned and wanted child,' his life would
be worth living."

At this point, over a million Timmys a year are being done away
with—those unplanned, unwanted babies who qualify for "termination" under *Roe v. Wade*. But if we as a nation embrace the logic of "the
life not worthy to be lived," what will the future hold?

Our children's generation may determine whether we hold the line
of "thou shalt not kill" where it is, excepting unborn babies, or whether

the exceptions grow to include any life not considered worthy to be lived. Or if we're unsuccessful on our watch, they may face a world where becoming "unwanted" is lethal, no matter how old you are.

This chapter, no doubt, contains the grimmest, most difficult considerations in this book. In fact, I wondered if I should even include this topic. But if you skip this chapter because you fear getting depressed, then you'll perhaps miss the most powerful part of the book. Powerful, because when people act in God's love, the contrast of their faith and courage shines even more brightly against the darkness of the "right to a wanted life." I've also included in this chapter my own story of God's grace as I've struggled with rheumatoid arthritis. So please stay tuned.

As we and our children stand for life, we, too, will have unprecedented opportunities to show God's grace and mercy to the truly needy. We can also be a voice of influence to prevent laws even deadlier than *Roe v. Wade* from coming on the books.

To do this we must make a logical, articulate defense of life in the face of arguments for "the life not worthy to be lived" that seem so compassionate. But, like the appeals for abortion on demand, this "compassion" desperately needs to be informed by the head, not just manipulated by the heart.

DRAWING THE LINE ON
INFANTICIDE AND EUTHANASIA

We can picture human life as a time line that begins at conception and, if uninterrupted, ends at natural death.

CONCEPTION	BIRTH	DEATH
♥	♥	♥

Back in chapter 8 we talked about how, in deciding on a socially useful criteria for protecting life in the womb, the Court could have drawn the line at the heartbeat (three weeks) or the brain waves (forty-three days), but instead chose "viability" (seven months), where the baby could possibly survive on its own outside the womb.

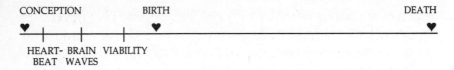

It is chilling to note that, as genetic research identifies more and more genes causing deformity and disease, some doctors are calling for the line protecting life to be drawn at three days *after* birth, so that a genetic checkup can be conducted. This used to be called *infanticide*—the killing of the infant.

At the other end of the continuum, the practice of "mercy killing," or *euthanasia*, is being recommended by many who want to see that people who are comatose or terminally ill will be "liberated" from their suffering. In the light of these proposed "interruptions," Jane's letter is just one more suggested end point on the continuum.

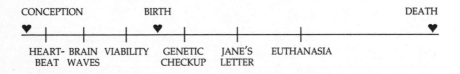

How did we come to be a society where pressure is building on families and doctors to consider infanticide and euthanasia as possible solutions when babies and people of all ages, especially the elderly, are judged as having a "life not worthy to be lived"?

MEDICAL MIRACLES AND THE HARD CASES

Modern medical technology is a two-edged sword. It cuts through centuries of ignorance to provide miracle cures and treatment, and yet pierces us to the heart as we struggle to apply these treatments with justice and mercy. The medicine that affords me significant relief from the pain of rheumatoid arthritis wasn't available even twenty years ago. Documenting the history of these medical miracles, *New York Times* reporter Lisa Belkin discusses their impact on our modern attitude toward caregiving. Her book *First Do No Harm* explores the heartbreaking dilemmas faced every week by the doctors and ethics committee of Houston's Hermann Hospital.

Before the advent of sulfa drugs (1935), penicillin (1941), ventilators (1950s), and heart transplants (1982), hospitals focused more on caregiving. Now they can cure and rehabilitate to a much greater extent. The death rate has declined "from 841 per 100,000 in 1950 to 556 per 100,000 in 1982" (p. 131). Life expectancy rose just as suddenly from 68 years in 1950 to 74.5 years by 1982. "Between 1961 and 1975 only 6 percent of babies weighing less than 1,000 grams . . . were able to survive. During the first half of the 1980s nearly 50 percent survived," writes Belkin (p. 93).

But there is a flip side to this raised expectation of medical miracles: caregiving without hope of rehabilitation, which used to be the norm, is now considered a burden—a *costly* burden. In the "old days," families just took care of their own the best they could, focusing on caregiving.

My friend Patty tells of her great-grandma, half out of her mind and often unable to sit up on her own. She was a fixture in their family kitchen every day, tied to a kitchen chair, occasionally shrieking and carrying on about something in Italian, but for the most part, quiet and watchful. Family would pass through and kiss her on the forehead and exchange knowing smiles at the eruptions. Inquiring children were reassured, "Oh, that's just Grandma."

Today Grandma's life might fall into the "not-worth-living" category, according to many. Along with changing our expectations, medical miracles have changed the nature of caregiving. Ventilators, feeding tubes, extraordinary surgical procedures—they weren't available even fifty years ago.

Families, doctors, and lawyers have struggled increasingly over the last twenty years with how to balance caregiving against the modern expectations for "quality of life." Following is a brief summary of a few hard cases that have led us to the brink of legalizing infanticide and euthanasia.

Infanticide

➤ 1972: Documentary by John Hopkins Hospital and Medical School shows Down's syndrome infant allowed to die by "inattention"—in effect, starvation.

➤ 1982: Indiana Supreme Court upheld parents' decision to deny standard surgical care to connect Baby Doe's esophagus to stomach. Without the surgery the baby died. Parents and only one of Baby Doe's many doctors contended that Baby Doe's other birth defects meant a life not worth living.

➤ 1983: Courts upheld parents' decision to refuse surgery to enclose exposed spinal cord of infant with spina bifida.

➤ 1983: Baby Doe Regulations—federal regulations put major responsibility for care of handicapped infants in hands of hospital committees.

Euthanasia

➤ 1975: New Jersey Supreme Court required parents of comatose Karen Ann Quinlan to meet with doctors and ethicists to rule on removing life support, based on chance of Quinlan's recovery. Respirator was removed; Quinlan lived another nine years.

➤ 1990: Nancy Cruzan—after seven years on feeding tube, courts agreed with parents' desire to remove tube and "let her go." Cruzan died of starvation/dehydration. Court ruled that State has no interest in "quality of life," but agreed with parents that "right to liberty" has no meaning if not protecting her from force-feeding.

➤ 1992: Christine Busalacchi—Even though video tape made by nurses showed her alert and responsive, after six years father was allowed to pull feeding tube. According to *World* magazine, she starved to the point of dehydration and died of cardiac arrest.

Time (3/19/90) asks the question: "Once it is acceptable to stand by and allow a patient to die slowly, why is it not more merciful to end life swiftly by lethal injection?"

It *is* more merciful, insisted Dr. Jack Kervorkian. So he has assisted scores of people in taking their own life. The champion of the euthanasia movement frustrates many of his supporters by being so obnoxiously consistent. Jack, "the Dripper," has advocated harvesting the organs of execution-bound prisoners, using cadavers for blood transfusions, and expanding hospitals to include something like Departments of Killing. In spite of his macabre consistency and in-your-face tactics, juries have failed to convict him, and he is winning public support. One sympathetic legal expert quoted in the *Houston Chronicle* (8/24/96) observed, "The public has begun to perceive this like abortion. Nobody likes assisted suicide, but it is a necessary consequence of living in 1996."

"You act only if it is justifiable," claims Kervorkian, who began by assisting only terminally ill patients to commit suicide. But Kervorkian's resolve to minister "relief" only to the terminally ill caved under the pressure of people in pain and depression. Only half of his subjects were dying. His thirty-fifth assist was a very depressed woman who claimed to have chronic fatigue syndrome, but autopsy results showed no evidence of the disease, only that she was obese. Subject number twenty-one was a seventy-two-year-old woman with rheumatoid arthritis who had lost both legs and an eye due to complications from diabetes. Whoa! When people with severe arthritis are classified in the life "not-worthy-to-be-lived" category, I get nervous. Kervorkian's practice shows in microcosm what the lessons of history teach—that setting aside the sanctity of life for even the most compassionate reasons is the first step down a slippery slope.

WATCHING "GREAT-MOTHER" DIE

A family gathers in a hospital room in suburban Houston. Uncles, aunts, children, grandchildren, cousins gather around the bed of the eighty-nine-year-old matriarch suffering from a liver blockage. Once a vibrant pillar of support for our extended family, she lies wan and frail, her eyes brightened by the circle of familiar faces. She is my grandmother, and the doctor tells us she is dying. Hymns are sung; tears are shed; embraces are held a little longer, a little closer than usual. All have the opportunity to say what's on their hearts—to thank her, to bless her. Prayers are said for her deliverance from pain and suffering, as God wills.

Another family gathers at a home in suburban Amsterdam.

Uncles, aunts, children, grandchildren, and cousins gather around their grandma. Although not yet bedridden with terminal cancer, they can see the pain in her eyes. And so, with cake and champagne, the family celebrates Grandma's farewell. Tears are shed, hugs and kisses linger, toasts of appreciation are offered. The precious moments are captured on video. All have every opportunity to say what's on their hearts. In the morning, her doctor comes and administers a lethal injection that sedates and then kills her.

The American studio audience watching the home video of the Dutch grandmother's farewell (shown in the making of a PBS *Frontline* special) is quiet and then comments on how painless and compassionate it looks. And I, listening to their comments and having watched my grandmother struggle on five more months after her farewell gathering in the hospital, had to agree. It did *look* more compassionate and merciful.

Like the virtuous woman in Proverbs 31, my grandmother was "clothed" with strength and dignity. A prayer warrior who knew how to approach the throne of grace, she taught me how to pray. She embodied the caregiving mentality of the "old days," taking in two sisters and her father for months, even years at a time. Her nine grandchildren and seventeen great-grandchildren were the delight of her life, and she loved to gather the family in for countless holiday dinners, decked with china, silver, and fine linens. My son could not quite get a handle on "great-grandmother," so in our family she became "Great-mother."

Until the last six months of her life, she drove her car, got her hair done, and signed checks in her office, as chairman of the family business. Every day she was outfitted in hose, high heels, and what I remember even from childhood as an impressive lace-up "Spirella" girdle (now a family heirloom).

And while she suffered physical discomfort and some pain for the months she lingered after her hospital farewell, I'm sure for her the worst part was the indignity of it all. Baby food, diapers, needing others to tend to her most basic physical needs, coupled with the loss of mobility and freedom, led to a battle with depression and despair. She was ready to die, she *wanted* to die, and yet for five long months, God did not take her home. Where was God's compassion in the face of such need? In situations like that, God's law, "thou shalt not kill," may seem to many to be cold and hard and unmerciful. Why shouldn't God's tender mercies include "mercy-killing"? Because euthanasia rejects the sanctity of life and reflects a utilitarian ethic.

BREACHING THE WALL

Our culture is prone to reject the wisdom of the ages and substitute an ethic where we try to provide the greatest good for the greatest number of people based on our *own* understanding of what it means to be compassionate.

As with abortion, the call for assisted suicide and euthanasia rejects God's moral laws that serve as walls of protection and blessing. *"Compassion!"* Always "compassion for the hard cases" is the trumpet call leading the attempt to breach the wall of God's law. And the reason is obvious: What surer way to reach a people who make laws and choices on the basis of their *feelings*? But the result of breaching God's protective wall is disastrous—waves of unforeseen consequences pour through the breach and flood us with more pain and hardship than existed before.

Before we knock down God's walls, maybe we should consider why they were put there in the first place. God's laws regarding the sanctity of life establish a protective wall around each life He has created. We bear His image as a unique spiritual being, designed for intimate relationship with our Savior. If man or beast destroys that image, his life is forfeited. The Bible only tells of one assisted suicide—King Saul. Fatally wounded in battle, the king prevails on an Amalekite to save him from capture and certain humiliation and torture. Out of compassion, the Amalekite complies. But he soon forfeits his own life for the deed when King David condemns him to death for taking the king's life (2 Samuel 1:1-16).

It may be hard, standing on this side of God's wall around the sanctity of human life, to imagine the potential for human suffering restrained on the other side. Especially when all that fills our thoughts and prayers is the suffering face of one we love so dearly. As women, we are deeply affected by this issue. Beyond the burden of another's pain, statistics tell us that the average American woman will spend eighteen years in the "daughter track," caring for an elderly parent. Maybe you are there and wondering what could be worse than the pain and indignity of a life of suffering and limitation.

Let's consider two grave consequences of breaching that wall. First, once the wall of "thou shall not kill" comes down, history shows that no one can erect a new one that protects us as well. In almost 2,000 years of Western civilization, since the moral authority of the church was established, euthanasia has been permissible only in two countries: Hitler's Germany and the Netherlands. (One Australian territory recently permitted it as well, but they have no track record to examine.)

A TALE OF TWO COUNTRIES

Hitler's euthanasia campaign started with the aged, the infirm, the senile and mentally retarded, and defective children. It then proceeded to include epileptics, amputees, and bed-wetters. And finally over 6,000,000 racially undesirables—Jews—were gassed and cremated. All the world looks back in horror and condemnation.

How did the homeland of Martin Luther and the Protestant Reformation come to tolerate such a great evil? Because the protective wall of the sanctity of life was breached in the name of compassion.

Films include *The Accused* (starring the actor who read the nativity story over German radio each Christmas), which portrayed two married musicians playing in a string trio. In one scene the wife, playing the piano, begins to make mistakes that she can't seem to control. Shaken, she stares at her hands and runs out. Soon she is diagnosed with multiple sclerosis. Together she and her husband agree that her life is no longer worth living, and he assists her suicide.

While tugging at the heartstrings through the arts, the Nazis also campaigned to capture the minds of its citizenry. In their book *Whatever Happened to the Human Race?* (p. 106), Francis Schaeffer and Dr. C. Everett Koop describe Nazi educational strategies. Documentaries juxtaposed stark images of mentally disturbed patients succeeded by bureaucrats fortified with charts and graphs explaining how it takes 100,000 deutsche marks to keep each one alive. Student textbooks drove the point home, posing math problems such as: how many new housing units could be built, and how many marriage allowance loans could be given to newly wed couples for "X"—the amount of money it cost the state to care for the crippled and insane?

The Nazi strategy for breaching the wall of God's standard was two-pronged: using the arts to reach the heart and education to reach the mind. On many issues like abortion, extramarital sex, and homosexuality, we see the same strategy at work in our culture. We have seen an attempt at death education in the schools. (I've wondered if the reason we don't see Hollywood carrying the torch for euthanasia is because of the large Jewish influence there.)

In the Netherlands, they have breached God's wall of the sanctity of life, and they have tried to erect a new man-made wall in its place. The new code would allow only terminally ill patients like the grandma mentioned earlier to be euthanized. But the *Frontline* audiences who approved of her "merciful death" were soon dismayed as PBS showed tapes of others getting the lethal needle: a twenty-five-year-old anorexic who just couldn't beat her condition, a Down's syndrome child with a small intestinal blockage—easily correctable, but his parents didn't want him.

A *Time* article (7/4/94) reports that the Netherlands has now approved lethal injection for depressed but physically healthy patients. The country's highest court refused to punish a doctor who felt that his patients' "intolerable psychological suffering [was] no different from intolerable physical suffering." They have breached the wall, and they cannot build a new one that really holds and protects. The lessons of Nazi Germany and the Netherlands are excellent examples for our children to see what happens when we breach God's wall of protection. The line of what is acceptable keeps moving further and faster, prodded on by one more call for "compassion."

FEELING THE WEIGHT OF BEING A BURDEN

There is a second consequence of accepting euthanasia and assisted suicide that hits much closer to home for me. Once the wall is breached and the line is legally crossed, pressure will mount for people who are ill, depressed, or handicapped to cross it.

If you are young and going strong, the threat of living with pressure to consider euthanasia may seem remote, but it gives me a knot in my stomach. Even at midlife I know what it is to be a burden to my family.

In our culture's measure of value (as discussed in James Dobson's *Hide and Seek*), I grew up trading profitably with the "gold coin of beauty" and the "silver coin of intelligence." A high school beauty queen and first runner-up for Miss Teenage Houston, I graduated from high school with high honors and from college with honors in three years. I have a personality profile (DI for those who speak "DISC") that values looking good and getting a lot accomplished, which I seemed to be doing pretty well until I was twenty-nine.

Then I became ill with rheumatoid arthritis. We had just arrived in Costa Rica to begin language training for a church planting and theological teaching ministry with CAM (formerly Central American Mission) when I was diagnosed. My joint pain skyrocketed, while my energy plummeted. I felt as if I were free-falling into an abyss of suffering and grief. As a long litany of physical limitations set in, I began quietly to grieve—my lost health, my mobility, my expectations . . . and the list goes on.

On a bad day, I could not stand up from a chair without Jack's help. In bed, the weight of the sheet on my toes was crushing. I would lie awake at night and want desperately to turn over but couldn't stand the pain it would cause. Though I didn't cry all the time, I tended to get overwhelmed by the little signposts of loss along my painful way—the day I could no longer wear my wedding ring, the day I could no longer play my guitar, the day I realized I could never run with my child or sit on the floor to play together.

I had to leave Costa Rica for medical care by myself. A dear friend rode buses all across town to bring me a farewell gift—Chuck Swindoll's booklet *For Those Who Hurt*. She helped me with one of my most daunting tasks—pulling on my underwear. Jack took me to the airport, and I will never forget this sight as long as I live—taxiing down the runway into a future of shattered dreams, Jack standing by our car at the end of the runway, waving and throwing kisses. When I could see through the tears, I read Swindoll's book and wept some more. Like salve on a gaping wound, his words of comfort from 2 Corinthians 4 soothed my aching soul.

God's grace has certainly been sufficient through all the hard times, but it does not take away the pain or the consequences of my illness. I have struggled with the crippling and debilitating effects of rheumatoid arthritis for seventeen years. At various times, I have had to rely on my husband to cook the meals, do the laundry, care for our son, lift me in and out of transportation, and as I mentioned, even to help me stand up. There have been times when my whole life seemed like an imposition on a wonderful man who already struggled with the demands of a full-time ministry.

Even with loving Christlike care and support, it's hard not to feel like a burden on those you love. Add to the imposition the pain and the loss of mobility, and I can understand why Dr. Kervorkian's twenty-first "patient" was a woman with rheumatoid arthritis. Currently I am in remission enough to write and teach and carry on a somewhat normal life. But I know my symptoms can flare badly again at any time. As I get older, I may get much worse.

I have a Christian family and church family with a wonderful track record of caregiving and a close relationship with my heavenly Father that helps me to lay my fears of the future at His feet. But what of people like this eighty-four-year-old woman who wrote a letter to the editor of the *Santa Rosa* (California) *Press Democrat* (3/14/93) and publicly confessed her fear of the future? She has lived with her daughter for twenty years.

> Everything went fine for many years, but when I started to lose my hearing about three years ago, it irritated my daughter. . . . She began to question me about my financial matters and apparently feels I won't leave much of an estate for her. . . . She became very rude to me. . . . Then suddenly one evening my daughter said very cautiously she thought it was okay for older people to commit suicide if they cannot take care of themselves. . . . So here I sit, day after day, knowing what I am expected to do when I need a little help.

As I read this, my heart broke for this dear lady, and I wondered, *What if she had quite a large estate to pass on to her daughter, and her daughter hated to see it "wasted" on medical bills?* This grim scenario is where the trumpet call of "compassion" is leading us.

We cannot open the door to "personal choice" for death without

welcoming the greed and aversion to self-sacrifice that will ultimately determine the personal choices to be made. We have certainly
seen this happen with abortion. A crusade for "personal choice" for
the mother has resulted in increased pressure from parents, husbands, and boyfriends who do not want to shoulder extra responsibilities. Often those who seek abortion feel that it has become the
only choice. If you think it is stretching to say that the choice for
euthanasia will become the lifestyle choice of hundreds of thousands
with physical and emotional problems and the choice of thousands
more under subtle-to-strong pressure from their families and care-
givers, remember this: *Roe v. Wade* was argued on the basis of compassion for a hard case—rape. No one believed in 1973 that a million
and a half women a year would exercise that personal choice. But
they do. Or that they would be pressured into killing their babies.
But they are.

In the legal arena the right to choose to kill the unborn has provided the foundation upon which the "right to die" movement has
tried to build. Reporting in *Christianity Today* (8/15/94), Peter Bernardi,
a Catholic priest, reveals that at least thirty-four termination of treatment cases in the courts cite *Roe v. Wade* with its "right to privacy" and
"choice" as proof of the legitimacy to euthanize.

The lessons of history from Nazi Germany, the Netherlands, and
the short history of *Roe v. Wade* demonstrate clearly what is at stake.
More importantly, God's Word speaks to the issue and lays out for us
principles of showing compassion. The postmodern ethic of the ultimate in disposability—disposable life—stands in stark contrast to the
Word. Our children will be blessed by embracing *this* ethic toward the
weak and frail. This review of biblical principles adds to those already
mentioned in chapters 6 and 7 dealing with the image of God and the
great value of every human life.

> ➤ Job 14:5; Psalm 139:16; Exodus 20:13: The length of our lives
> is ordained by God before we are born. We should not under-
> take to kill another or kill ourselves or assist in killing.

> ➤ Job 3:20-26; Job 42; James 5:11: Sometimes, like Job, we may
> think that there is a life not worthy to be lived (even our own),
> but God clearly shows Job he is wrong. He is in control even

though we may not understand His purposes. God is full of compassion and mercy and will use suffering for eternal good. Job understands and repents.

➤ 2 Corinthians 4:17; 2 Peter 3:8: Joni Eareckson Tada points out that these verses taken together tell us that since a day of suffering is achieving an eternal weight of glory, and since, to the Lord, a day is like a thousand years, then even one day of bearing up under pain and grief could be rewarded a thousand-fold. The key is in bringing glory to God, no matter what your limitation—this coming from a quadriplegic. In her excellent book *When Is It Right to Die?* Joni encourages others who suffer:

In a mysterious way each day that you live, each hopeful thought you think, however fleeting, each smile you muster brings God incredible joy. That's because your positive attitude and actions, however small and faint, are fingers pointing others to a God who is larger and finer and grander than they thought. That's what it means to glorify God as you lie in that bed, sit in that wheelchair, or persevere through that depression.

➤ 1 Peter 1:6-7; James 1:2-4: Pain has been called the gift that nobody wants, yet suffering can bring great redeeming value to our lives. Testing and proving our faith, it results in perseverance and mature character in the present—and praise, glory, and honor when we stand in Christ's presence. (See Focus Box #13.)

➤ Isaiah 50:10; Psalm 71:20; 34:17-19: When we walk in the blackest and most oppressive darkness of pain and suffering, we can cry out to God, entrust ourselves to His care, and rely on Him to carry us through.

➤ Colossians 3:12: God's compassion is frequently ministered through people who can patiently set aside the "tyranny of the urgent," spend time with those who hurt, and give practical care.

FOCUS YOUR WORLDVIEW #13: THE REDEEMING VALUE OF SUFFERING AND THE BEAUTY OF TRUE COMPASSION

Our children hear a strong cultural message: Life with dignity means we should be healthy, clean, alert, and able to take care of ourselves. "Death with dignity" means the right to opt out when you are no longer any of the above. "Death with dignity" is coming to mean death by suicide.

Not so. Following is a list of stories (books and videos) that show how human suffering can be terrible, but costly caregiving can be a thing of beauty, and both have great redeeming value. Most may be too strong for younger children, but those old enough to be getting the cultural message will see the power of the Christian alternative.

BOOKS

Joni—the autobiography of an active young girl who had a diving accident in her teens and became a quadriplegic. How did Joni's attitude change from wanting to die to wanting to live?

Jonathan's Journey by Katherine Bell (Thomas Nelson)—a big musical family prepares for a new baby, a surviving twin, the other twin having died earlier in his mother's pregnancy. Jonathan's special needs (including cerebral palsy) launch his family on a journey of tears and joy. (This one is great for younger children.)

VIDEOS

The Hiding Place—Corrie ten Boom's Dutch family hid Jews during the Holocaust and were sent to a Nazi prison camp for punishment. Use information in this chapter to discuss with your children how what happened in Germany came to be socially acceptable. Point out how our culture is coming to share some of the same presuppositions that launched the Holocaust. Can they name them? In what way was the suffering of the prison camp a refining fire in Corrie's life? Why is the smile on Betsy's dead face so beautiful?

Shadowlands—This story of C. S. Lewis's loss of his wife is painfully sad but also exquisitely beautiful. What aspects of the story make it seem so beautiful? Lisa Belkin has written, "So much about death, the dignity of death, depends on who is nearby when it takes place." How is this truth reflected in the story? How does Joy's suffering and Jack's caregiving demonstrate the redeeming value of both in their lives?

Elephant Man—Anthony Hopkins plays a doctor who takes in a battered freak from a carnival. The movie skillfully treats the idea of how different people *look* at the elephant man—like the voyeurs at the carnival? Do they see him as an animal? Or as a fellow human being? What is the carnival owner's affectionate name for John? Cite specific examples of how he and the night watchman treat John like an animal. How do the doctors and high society look at John? How does caregiving change how the following characters look at John: Dr. Treves? The head nurse? Mrs. Treves? Mrs. Kendall? The hospital staff?

How did the way you look at John change as the movie progressed? How does John change as he receives their care? How does the carnival owner's affectionate name for John really prove to be true?

THE ARMOR OF HARSHNESS
OR THE CLOTHES OF COMPASSION?

How does the world see us as we respond to this trumpet call of "compassion" that leads the charge to breach the sanctity of life wall? Does it see us suited up in the armor of harshness totally focused on defending God's wall?

Or does it see us in the "clothes of compassion"? The world needs to see what true compassion looks like. "Therefore as God's chosen people, holy and dearly loved, clothe yourselves with compassion, kindness, humility, gentleness, and patience." We can come alongside those who are suffering and hold the hand of a dying grandmother, feel the loneliness of an AIDS sufferer, show a smile, and share God's comfort with one who has none. (See Focus Box #14.)

FOCUS YOUR WORLDVIEW #14: CREATING CAREGIVING

We and our children can offer to meet the needs of the weak and frail around us in many creative ways. Following are suggestions for ministering to individuals who are hurting and then to families trying to manage costly care to their own members.

INDIVIDUALS

Ask around to find individuals in your neighborhood or church who are shut in or disabled.

➤ Read to those who are unable to read.

➤ Visit shut-ins, especially at holidays; take a fruit basket and sing carols.

➤ Drop in and offer to help around the house for an hour or run an errand.

➤ "Adopt-a-grandparent"—someone who needs help or a little encouragement. Visit, send notes, celebrate special days.

➤ A home-schooling family we know takes their children to the nursing home to visit and help trim fingernails.

➤ A group of women from our church have a hair-washing ministry once a month at the nursing home. They dry and set hair and lift a lot of spirits.

FAMILIES

There may be some families you know who have special-needs children or infirm aged parents living in. They may look like they're coping just fine, but it means so much when people drop by to help.

➤ Deliver meals once or twice a week. (Sometimes Mom is so busy the kids are eating peanut butter and crackers for dinner.)

➤ Offer to care for a special-needs child or older person there in their home so Mom has a break or time to spend with other children.

➤ Offer to spend time with the other children who often need attention or don't get out much.

➤ Make a run to the grocery store.

➤ Learn to administer prescribed therapy and offer to help with it regularly.

As we demonstrate that we truly value the suffering one, we say by our actions, "Your life *is* worthy to be lived; there is no life that is not." The push to legalize euthanasia is always portrayed as a compassionate solution to suffering. We can show that caregiving, ministering to the hurting with love is more compassionate than sending them off to what they may think a peaceful rest, but what will either be an eternity without God or an early arrival in His presence that breaks His law in the process.

This is not to say that those with a high biblical view of life should always feel compelled to pursue extraordinary measures to keep the sick and frail alive. While it is a difficult distinction to make, I agree with Schaeffer and Koop: Once the rightly motivated person "believes that the technical gadgetry he is using is merely prolonging the experience of dying, rather than extending life, he can withdraw the extraordinary means and let nature take its course, while keeping the patient as comfortable as possible" (*Whatever Happened to the Human Race?* p. 91).

In many cases, it is easier to kill than to give care. But, as I look back on my illness, it has certainly been the people of God who have shown me tenderness and comfort and who, clothed with compassion, have reached out and helped me through the valleys. I think of my parents who took me in when I got back to the States from Costa Rica and cared for me for three months until Jack was able to join me, of Greatmother who came by and treated me at Red Lobster and my weekly pregnancy-induced-shrimp-craving-fix, of Cindy who cheered me up on weekends, and then the parade of faces and gifts through the hospital when Zach was born. In later years it was Karen who did my grocery shopping for a couple of years, Teresa who cleaned my house for a while, and during surgeries and emergencies Mom who washed clothes and managed the house, Fran who coordinated months of meals, Rick who arranged to videotape my Bible study teaching from a hospital bed, Sandy who came with books, Marilyn with a teddy bear, Erin with a wreath, Cal and Mollie who threw a party in my hospital room every night and put a big, grinning poster of Simba on the wall, and many, many more kindnesses.

Through fifteen years of illness, two surgeries, and a fractured hip, we have probably received over a hundred meals, multitudes of cards, deeply needed gifts of money, help, and just time spent lifting my sagging spirits. In countless ways, Jack and Zach have learned to be real servants. At age five, Zach could run the clothes in to the dry cleaners. And what could be more romantic than having your husband empty your porta-potty?

Through the ministry of our church families and individuals, God has blessed my life so richly, *and* He has even given me a challenging ministry. I look at other people in my church, like the Kiltz family, and I think that I haven't *really* had to suffer.

DANCING WITH THE ANGELS

On May 17, 1992, we got the call from Cal and Mollie at the hospital. Something was wrong with her sister's baby. Lacking muscle tone and feeling kind of floppy, Gracie turned out to have Down's syndrome. Throughout her pregnancy, Erin Kiltz had felt that God was preparing them for something special. Waiting for this third child, they had for the first time really prayed over her name. God gave them "Grace." The birth announcements already at the printer's had the verse, "This is the Lord's doing" (Psalm 118:23).

Reeling from shattered expectations, John and Erin began to take comfort in God's sovereignty and goodness. They were not victims. This was God's plan for Gracie. At least it was the beginning of God's plan.

Gracie cleared tests for the typical heart problems of Down's babies and went into months of occupational, physical, and speech therapy. Erin spent hours massaging her tongue and limbs, hoping to maximize Gracie's development. Shortly after her first birthday in August 1993, small red dots appeared on her skin. They turned out to be symptoms of low platelets. Two weeks later, a chromosomal study indicated Gracie would eventually develop leukemia.

Like a black line of clouds on the horizon, the threat of leukemia hovered over their lives. For over a year, Gracie's blood counts continued to drop. Finally, in October 1994 the numbers indicated full-blown leukemia. Treatment—more than a year of chemotherapy. That evening, in the calm before the battle, Val, Erin's dear friend, remembers just sitting together drinking coffee as they always did but finally saying the words, "This is it. It's really here."

The sixth floor of Texas Children's Hospital is a bright and friendly war zone where precious little bald-headed children fight for their lives. Gracie's hair lasted for about one week. In the hospital for one to two weeks a month for ten months, Gracie went through cycle after cycle of zeroing out her white blood cell count and being very susceptible to infection. Even a slightly cut finger would be cause for hospitalization. The good news was that she went into remission after the first round.

Doctors, nurses, and other patients fell in love with the little almond-eyed girl, who became known as "Amazing Grace." Her bright smile seemed to radiate out from her and fill a room. Through Gracie and Erin and the Christian family and friends that constantly surrounded them, many families saw the reality of Christ's love and heard the Gospel.

Out of the hospital over Memorial Day, three-year-old Gracie charmed our whole church family at our annual picnic, coyly playing with her hat, and, as Erin had patiently taught her, using sign language to answer questions and "talk" about family and friends. Val finally had the courage to ask Erin what Gracie's prognosis was. Erin responded that her chances at the outset were fifty/fifty, but she had come so far and done so well that at this point she couldn't imagine what could go wrong.

A week later, Gracie developed a fever that went up and down and then stayed up. While John stayed home with their other children, Erin ran Gracie in to the hospital. They had entered Texas Children's Hospital through the Emergency Room probably twenty times before, but this time they hit some snags. During the four hours they waited in the emergency room, no one recognized the telltale signs of a massive bacterial infection.

On the way to her sixth floor room, Gracie started shaking. A nurse recognized she was in trouble, grabbed her, and called in an emergency crew. They put Gracie on a ventilator and began pumping blood pressure medicine into her, one syringe after another as fast as they could. When Gracie started vomiting blood, Erin left the room.

After being on the ventilator for ten minutes, Gracie went into cardiac arrest. The emergency crew worked on her for ten, fifteen, twenty minutes. In the family room, Erin and a Christian nurse prayed for God to spare her life. He did. After twenty minutes, her heartbeat came back, stabilized, and they never lost it again.

At that point the doctors gave Gracie no chance for survival. They began to prepare John and Erin for her death. But she didn't die. After a week in ICU, Gracie opened her eyes. Immediately Erin knew she was not the same. A few days later, neurologists confirmed her worst fears. Gracie had sustained a "major insult to the brain."

From well baby to Down's syndrome to leukemia to brain damage. Erin and John had managed to adjust their expectations each time the bad news came. But this loss was by far the greatest. Erin felt torn between her human perspective and God's other purposes. She felt that it would have been easier to let Gracie go than to accept her in an even weaker state. On the other hand, it was so obvious that God had purposed her weaker state and spared her life for His infinite reasons beyond her understanding.

The neurologists gave their bleak prognosis: Gracie would never smile again or talk or walk or eat on her own. Erin began to absorb the tremendous loss, and in the following weeks grieved over the Gracie who was no more, and yet at the same time was still there, needing constant care. When she held her in her arms, she almost looked at her as a new person.

In the passing months, Erin has had time to grow and reflect. She has had to hope in God alone, not what she hoped He would do to improve Gracie's condition. As it has turned out, God has had some surprises for the neurologists. Gracie is off the ventilator and eating by mouth instead of through the button into her stomach. One week before Thanksgiving she started to smile again. Although still a bit wobbly, she can hold her head up, reach out for things, and she looked for all the world like she was giving her daddy open-mouth "kisses" on his cheek as he held her at church last week.

Through all the suffering, Erin praises God for accomplishing great things, especially among the families they met at the hospital: for Blake with cancer who prayed with her to trust Christ two days before he died; for the Korean mother of a leukemia patient who lost her faith in Buddha and began praying in Jesus' name; for her son who professed his faith in Christ; for scores of others who have heard the Gospel and seen the Kiltzes' witness for Christ. She and her family have learned to persevere and trust, really *trust* in God.

"Nine out of ten people would say that Gracie's life is not worth living," Erin reflects. "But God chose an 'unworthy vessel' to do eternal good. You realize in a season of suffering how short life is. It is *good*, even in the light of my suffering and Gracie's being a sacrifice. Before Gracie, I used to think life was blue skies and rainbows, but now I understand and talk about the privilege of suffering. Through this I want my children to have a relationship with God and a passion to serve Him."

Erin muses, "I see God's work in my life and my family's, but I wonder how God is working in Gracie's body. Our value of a person tends to be based on their mind." Erin takes comfort in the fact that God does not seem to need a developed mind through which to work or reveal Himself. She thinks of John the Baptist who leaped for joy in his mother's womb and who was filled with the Holy Spirit from birth.

"Who knows?" Erin smiles a beautiful smile. "Maybe every day Gracie dances with the angels."

THE COMMON THREAD

John and Erin look at Gracie's needs and decide to unload their nice house to free up time and funds for her care. Timmy's parents keep the nice house and decide to unload their child to free up time and funds for their lifestyle. Gracie . . . Great-mother . . . Me . . . the common thread between our stories is the great value of our lives to God and the way the body of Christ has responded with costly care-giving. In contrast, the common thread between evolution, abortion, infanticide, and euthanasia is the devaluing of human life and the way our culture has responded with options for disposal.

"The fear of the Lord is the beginning of wisdom." "For whoever finds [wisdom] finds life and receives favor from the Lord. But whoever fails to find [it] harms himself; all who hate [wisdom] love death" (Psalm 111:10; Proverbs 8:35-36).

WORK, LEISURE, AND THE RICHER LIFE

I'm tired of paddling!
Are we there yet? I'm bored!

CONFESSIONS OF A
FELLOW FROG

9

---

*Balancing Motives for Work and Contentment
with the Pursuit of the American Dream*

MOST OF THE ISSUES WE'VE BEEN ADDRESSING WERE SPAWNED IN the cultural revolution of the sixties or before, but have sparked rapid social change and development in the last few years. The cultural shift in an ethic of work and leisure, contentment, and the pursuit of the American Dream is not as much of a headline grabber. This particular "kettle" has been heating up slowly over a long period of time. And like the proverbial frog who got boiled in the kettle because the heat was turned up so slowly he didn't notice, the shift has been so gradual that it's hard to get a perspective on the issue or realize how treacherously close to boiling the water is.

In the proverb, the other frog that jumped into an already boiling kettle immediately registered the high temperature, noted the roiling, bubbly water and the steam wafting upwards, gave a little froggie yelp, and jumped right back out. I was recently struck by the parallel yelps of frustration coming from children of immigrants and foreign students as they have first plunged into the kettle of American youth culture.

"When I first came here, it was like going into a crazy world," exclaimed Paulina, a Polish student studying in America. She explained to a *Washington Post* reporter that "in Warsaw we would talk to friends after school, go home and eat dinner with our parents, and then do four or five hours worth of homework." Now she is "going to Pizza Hut and watching TV and doing less work in school." Paulina was shocked by our affluent, leisure-bent society but admits she is "getting used to it."

When immigrant children tease each other about slacking off or being lazy, they say, "You're becoming American." The frogs who know better keep a safe distance from the kettle.

But those of us who've been born in the kettle, grown up in it, and are raising our children in it are in danger of getting cooked! The American Dream has always been founded on the idea of limitless opportunity. But opportunity for what?

"WE BUILT THIS CITY ON" . . . THE PURITAN WORK ETHIC

Contrary to the popular song, rock and roll did not build our civilization. Can you believe that as recently as 1947, market analysts felt that corporate America's greatest challenge was to convince citizens to become major consumers? To believe that the "hedonistic approach to life was a moral, not an immoral one" (Guinness, *The American Hour,* p. 78)? To their dubious credit, corporations seem to have met that challenge. Recent polling by Roper reveals that when Americans are asked, "What constitutes the good life?" most rank "material aspirations" well ahead of a happy marriage and children (Anderson, *Signs of Warning,* p. 144).

How do we develop a Christian worldview of work and the "good life"? It helps me with my "kettle" perspective if I back up and think about the Puritan work ethic. The Puritans worshiped God through their work whether it was manufacturing or raising children. As Harvard professor and Puritan expert Perry Ellis has documented, the Puritans who founded the Massachusetts Bay Colony saw themselves as having embarked on a great *Errand into the Wilderness.* They had a vision of establishing a "city on the hill," a truly Christian community that would be a beacon of light to the rest of the watching world. According to organizer John Winthrop, "the end is to improve our lives to do more service to the Lord, to increase the body of Christ, and to preserve our posterity from the corruptions of this evil world" (pp. 5-6). They also believed they would enjoy better economic opportunity in the new land, but that motivation was secondary.

If God blessed you financially, then the creation of capital was supposed to be largely poured back into business to provide jobs and enterprise for the whole community. The more the business grew, the more jobs were provided for everyone, and the more prosperity grew for everyone. What a wonderful business ethic. Individual effort was recognized and rewarded with profit. But a good measure of profit was reinvested as capital. This was the norm. Today it is the exception.

VISION FOR COMMUNITY VERSUS THE LOOTER'S MENTALITY

"I really haven't done anything! Corporate America has made it so that when you behave the way I did, it's abnormal" (*Time*, 1/8/96). The story of Malden Mills and its devout Jewish owner, Aaron Feuerstein, splashed across TV screens and newspapers in late 1995. Just a couple of weeks before Christmas the mill caught on fire, sustaining severe damage.

Mr. Feuerstein had a commitment to his workers and his community that had withstood not only the pressure to pursue cheaper labor overseas but even a period of bankruptcy in the early eighties. The mill's development of Polartec, an extremely light and warm fiber, quick-to-dry and easy-to-dye (and made from recycled plastic bottles), had attracted buyers such as L. L. Bean and Eddie Bauer. Corporate revenues skyrocketed.

While the mill was shut down, the owner fully funded his entire work force, even with a payroll of $1.5 million a week. News of Feuerstein's action prompted clients, the mill's bank, and the local Chamber of Commerce to send in more than $300,000. In about three weeks the mill was 80 percent operational. Its client support and some of the highest textile wages in the world seemed secure. Union chief Paul Coorey spoke for everyone: "Thank God we got Aaron." Mr. Feuerstein's commitment to a biblical work ethic inspired the loyalty of his employees, his clients, his banker, and the community at large.

In seeking a biblical perspective on our motive for work, it helps to look at the bigger picture. If the American Dream is narrowly taken to mean the license to pursue unlimited wealth, then we shouldn't be surprised at the income gap between executives and the average worker. In 1995 chief executives' total compensation rose almost 21 percent while that of the average worker rose 2.9 percent (*Parade*, 6/23/96). In 1960 the average CEO made 41 times the pay of the average worker. Today he makes 187 times more (*Houston Chronicle*, 6/9/96). Nor should we be surprised that workers' loyalty and productivity are declining. We've got to see the Kettle of American Affluence for what it really is—how the breakdown of the Puritan and biblical work ethic hurts us all.

Why is the work ethic declining? Surely greed and a "looters' mentality" have played a central role. The "looters mentality," coined by Chuck Colson and Jack Eckerd in *Why America Doesn't Work,* is the idea that greed is healthy. It should be honored as the engine that drives our capitalist, free-market economy. "Greed is all right, by the way. . . . I think greed is healthy. You can be greedy and still feel good about yourself," opined financier Ivan Boesky at U. C. Berkeley's School of Business Administration commencement address in 1986.

Inspired by Boesky, Oliver Stone preserved these words for posterity in an art-imitates-life speech in his movie *Wall Street.* Gordon Gecko, a ruthless merger-maniac, told his audience, "The point is, ladies and gentlemen, that greed is good. Greed works. . . . Greed has marked the upward surge of mankind, and greed will . . . save . . . that other malfunctioning corporation, the United States of America."

"The point is that you can't be too greedy," amened Donald Trump in *The Art of the Deal.* The Puritan dream of building a "city on the hill" and prospering by God's blessing translated culturally into an ethic of hard work, sacrifice, and sharing with the community. But our children face a world where the American Dream has come to mean making lots of money—to enjoy the superabundance that characterizes our "kettle."

Reflecting on the American Dream's devouring excesses, Os Guinness (*The American Hour*) writes, "As abundance became superabundance, high consumption was transformed from an excess into an ethos and an ethic. . . . In America, to be mall-adjusted is the opposite of being maladjusted—its central philosophy summed up in the bumper sticker, 'Veni, vidi, VISA'" (p. 78). (I came, I saw, I . . . you know!) (See Focus Box #15.)

≈

FOCUS YOUR WORLDVIEW #15: RICHER THAN SOLOMON?

In Ecclesiastes 5:19 Solomon wrote, "When God gives any man wealth and possessions . . . this is a gift of God." Everyone's conception of wealth is relative—usually to the Joneses next door or people in *Forbes* magazine. But have your children shift gears. Compare your wealth to someone historical, like Solomon. Read the following passages to get a good idea of this king's net worth: Ecclesiastes 2:4-11; 1 Kings 3:10-15; 7:1-12; 10:14-29.

Now ask your children to name things your family possesses that Solomon would have loved to have had (car, air conditioning, etc.). What do you think Solomon might have traded for a ticket to *Star Wars?* A CD player? How does your family life compare to Solomon's in terms of comfort and ease? If we could time-travel with our "wealth and possessions" back to Solomon's time, would he think we were rich? Why can't we see ourselves as rich?

≈

THE VIEW FROM THE KETTLE

I look out there, and I say, "Yes, our culture has gotten so greedy." And I shake my head sadly. But what about in here? In my house? In your house?

Writing this chapter has been an exercise in self-examination and conviction. I've been swimming around in the kettle of superabundance for a long time, and in my heart I know it's gotten way above room temperature. Whereas in the other chapters of this book I think I bring objectivity and expertise based on years of study and teaching on these subjects, in this area I feel like an "expert consumer" (not to be confused with "consumer expert").

Kerby Anderson's book *Signs of Warning, Signs of Hope* helped me to understand that my struggle with contentment is somewhat generational—not that it's okay, but that it's widespread. We forty-something moms grew up in the fifties and sixties. What we thought was a normal life was really the greatest period of "unprecedented affluence in our nation's history."

Anderson points out that we have absorbed a "psychology of entitlement" from the days when housing and cars were easily affordable. Our parents paid 14 percent of their income for the median-priced home. We now pay 44 percent. They paid about eighteen weeks of wages for a car. We pay an average of twenty-three weeks or more. Through the fifties and early sixties our parents "saw their family income double in real purchasing power" (p. 34). In one six-year period their disposable income increased by 12 percent.

We struggle just to maintain the lifestyle we had when growing up. All the while the technology advances, seducing us with additional payments for cable TV, compact disc stereos, no-rinse dishwashers, voice mail answering machines, pentium computers, and the list goes on. "Consumers are buckling beneath nearly $1 trillion in installment loans—almost twice the level of a decade ago," reports *Time* (11/27/95). "The average household carries $3,900 in credit card debt alone." Eager to gratify our "psychology of entitlement," credit card companies mailed out 2.1 billion applications in 1994. I'm sure I've received about ten. Zach has received one. According to the paper the other day, even a French poodle received an invitation to "go for the Visa gold."

Scripture tells me in 1 Timothy 6:8 that I should be content with food and clothing. Not even *shelter* is on the short list, much less the nicely decorated and landscaped shelter that passes for the median-priced home in America.

I've pursued a share of the American Dream like the rest of my fellow frogs (minus the credit card debt), and I now claim a wonderful family, a good education, a challenging and flexible job, a dog, two cars, and a house in a country suburb. Sadly, I suppose, I've resolved some of my struggle with contentment by getting where I wanted to go. But I can remember so well being in one place in my life, but wanting to be in another—single and wanting to be married, without child and wanting to be with child, leaving America and wanting to stay, renting and wanting to purchase a home, sick and wanting to be well.

God has dealt with my contentment struggles in various ways according to His mercy, not according to my performance on the test. When we returned from the mission field in Costa Rica because of my arthritis, we parked in one situation until Zach was born. Then, since

I felt too sick to return to the field, we looked for a permanent position. When we found it in the Houston area in 1981, we were counseled to rent a home. But I was so convinced the inflation train would go on forever that I desperately wanted to buy. Two years after we purchased, the value of our starter home fell almost $20,000. Each yearly postcard from the tax assessor's office was a gut-wrenching reminder of our equity loss.

Every time I thought of it, I had a knot in my stomach and a flash of anger. Then one day my friend Nancy Wallace, also in ministry and also having lost what savings they had in the Texas real-estate bust, said, "I figure it's the Lord's money, and if that's how He wants to spend it, it's okay, and I can be content."

Wow! Her words were convicting but also encouraging. I began prayerfully to let go of that lost money and ask for the Lord's help in focusing on what I had. And in God's gracious provision, we had enough money to put down on a just-right-for-us house on an azalea-and-dogwood-filled half-acre when we moved to our current pastorate. We still lost a lot, but at the table at the title company, I was content (well, at least 99 percent).

I've also struggled to be content with my rheumatoid arthritis. I miss running, sitting on the floor, skiing, and playing the guitar. But for the most part, I struggle less with RA, including all the pain and surgeries and fractured hip, than I do with contentment over material things. God has given me such grace for my illness. I still struggle on the occasional recreational outing with my guys, but in the little pig trails of my everyday life, God's grace is amazingly sufficient. My clothes or entertainment budget is often a different matter.

One thing that has helped me in the long run with my "psychology of entitlement" and pursuing my share of the American Dream, is to literally have gotten out of the kettle for a while.

¿ANDAN VENDIENDO ROPA?

The old woman approached our Suburban with sad, dark eyes. She moved slowly, a little bent over. Her Guatemalan woven shift bore a faded, frayed resemblance to the decorator pillows on my neighbor's couch. We were refueling at a gas station in "God knows where," out-back-Guatemala. She eyed the vehicle full of boxes and the bar behind the front seat packed with clothes. The contents of that car, plus about fifteen boxes that had been air-freighted on to Costa Rica, comprised the sum total of our worldly goods (except for a few pieces of furniture loaned out to friends before we left).

We were about two-thirds of the way through our journey from Houston to San Jose. I was road-weary and at that point unaware of what was happening—the arthritis was moving up from my knees to my hips. Waiting for Jack to finish paying, I sat in silence, my mind in the "O-zone" (as we say in our family).

Suddenly her face appeared at my open window, and her voice asked quietly and deferentially, "*¿Señora, andan vendiendo ropa?*" (Are you going along selling clothes?) She eyed the crammed clothes rack.

Caught totally off guard, I could only think to respond honestly, "*No, toda esta ropa es nuestra.*" (No, all this clothing is ours.) She nodded and quickly retreated as Jack returned to the car. As we pulled back out on the highway, the full impact of what had just transpired began to sink in. The encounter lasted about fifteen seconds, but those three words have been etched in my memory forever. "*¿Andan vendiendo ropa?*" If only I'd been thinking faster, I could have pulled something out for her. The reality of her perspective settled in slowly. To many of our stateside friends, it seemed that we were garage-saling almost everything, leaving the "good life," picking up our cross and following Jesus into a missionary life of deprivation. Of course, sitting on top of all my nice dishes and clothes, color TV and microwave crammed into that Suburban, I thought they overstated our case.

It gradually occurred to me that to the poor wondering woman, the only possible explanation for two people to have so many clothes was that we must be selling them. In the silence that followed our encounter, my built-in lust-ometer dropped quite a few points.

Cross-cultural encounters can have a tremendous impact on our affluent kettle mentality. We truly see how the other half lives. No, not half. Make that the great majority. If the last forty years have been an affluent blip in time as we have discussed, then America today is an affluent blip on the map. We may not be able to take our kids back to the war years or the depression or the frontier, but we can expose them to cross-cultural situations. (See Focus Box #16.)

I spent only three months in Costa Rica before I returned to Texas for the best medical care in the world. But the impact of my cross-cultural experience was deep. I can remember my mom asking me what I wanted for Christmas that year. I could honestly think of nothing. That was the first and last time I remember thinking that way. By the next Christmas the "kettle" creep was apparent. Having a new baby and buying a new home, my lust-ometer resembled a seismograph during the Mt. St. Helens episode.

Living the comfortable, busy life of the American suburban scene is synonymous with turning up the heat on the kettle. All the frogs are reveling in the nice warm water, but I'm reminded of Eugene Peterson, whom I quoted in chapter 2—our "soggy suburbia" makes it harder to think, harder to pursue God, harder to maintain the fire in our own souls.

FOCUS YOUR VIEW #16: THE VIEW OUTSIDE OUR KETTLE

Having extolled the virtues of cross-cultural experience, here are some practical ways to provide these experiences for yourselves and your children:

1. Drive around some distressed neighborhoods (preferably during the day, with Dad). I remember one time we drove into Houston and cruised the elite River Oaks section during azalea season. So taken was our son with the beauty and affluence that he was ready to knock on a few doors to see if any of these folks would take in a promising fifth grader. To balance the day's activities, we decided to drive over to Houston's Fifth Ward where the occasional neat little house and yard was an island of civility in a sea of unpainted, unkept houses with broken-down people sitting on broken-down chairs on broken-down porches. After that, home looked really good.

2. Volunteer in a soup kitchen for a week, or even a day. Take sandwiches to the homeless. Join or organize a church ministry that reaches out to an inner city or rural poor church or neighborhood.

3. Use your gifting or talents for the benefit of the urban or rural poor. A gifted cook I know offered cooking lessons at a day care center in

urban Atlanta. Women learned to cook, and the preschoolers got a wonderful lunch.

4. Join or organize a church ministry that reaches into Mexico or another developing country or an inner city area. Zach went this summer on a two-week youth mission trip to Mexico. During the day they worked on improvement projects at an evangelical church and orphanage. Evenings, their mime and puppet troupes performed in the square, and they sang and shared the Gospel through interpreters.

5. Encourage your private Christian school to link up with students at a disadvantaged school and help with tutoring or mentoring.

6. Take a family vacation to visit a missionary, or spend a week church-planting in a foreign culture with Dallas-based Global Missions Fellowship. The Davis family from our church participated in their evangelistic outreach to Cuernavaca, Mexico, last summer. This year the Davises have invited a number of other families to return with them to visit neighborhoods and share the Gospel through an interpreter and invite people to evening evangelistic meetings. (For more information contact Global Missions Fellowship at P. O. Box 742828, Dallas, TX 75374, or call 972-783-7476.)

WORK AND THE RICHER LIFE

Few parents I know these days are impressed with the industrious tendencies of their offspring. Recently Zach's basketball coach complimented him. "Zach has tremendous endurance," he enthused. "Yes," Jack laughed, "but you should see him when it's time to do yard work!"

Parents in our Bible studies commiserate that our children are absorbing a modern utilitarian work ethic: work is a means to an end, namely, leisure time and money to spend. This produces the "Friday Eve" mentality, a label I picked up from a local deejay. He starts celebrating on Thursday the fact that it is actually "Friday-Eve," and the weekend is in sight! Work is a necessary evil endured from coffee break to lunchtime to afternoon break to quitting time, so that we can afford to enjoy ourselves in the leisure time that makes life worth living. This can be a battle of perspective for both our children and ourselves.

In a survey of young people's career goals, the American Association of University Women noted that at every stage of adolescence large numbers of boys want to be rock stars and sports stars. When asked, "Do you *really* think you will ever end up being a sports star?" fully 67 percent of African-American boys said, "Yes." How do we get our boys to shake the stardust off their shoulders and prepare for a more realistic view of the future? How do we help our boys and girls aspire to that "richer life" beyond the American Dream? Beyond affluence, beyond sports, video games, drama, and dating games—a life that includes a great deal of work?

Reexamining our forefathers' work ethic can help us. Cross-cultural experiences can make us adjust our lust-ometer. But how do we renew our minds to resist the relentless calls to acquire more toys and endure the weekday work-grind so we can play with them on the weekend?

Again we have to train our children to think critically, to know how Scripture speaks to these issues in a holistic way. God's Word doesn't just warn us about greed; it calls us to a view of service, and by extension our work, that sees whatever we do as ministry and an opportunity to use our God-given gifts and talents.

GREEDY AMBITION—"MUD PIES IN THE SLUM"

What Scripture has to say about money, greed, and contentment would fill a book of its own, but I'd like to address just a few high points.

Remember how the Old Testament kind of harps on Israel's idolatry? Sometimes I can read it and pat myself on the back. "I'm glad we New Testament Christians don't struggle like they did." Then I read Colossians 3:5 and find out greed = idolatry. "Uh-oh. I'm in big trouble."

After all, Old Testament idolatry was simply worshiping and calling on foreign gods of sun, fertility, etc., to send the rain, bless the crops and the herds, and grant financial prosperity and the safety to enjoy it. Ezekiel, Jeremiah, Isaiah—they all described how God's wrath would be poured out on idolaters. Isaiah also wrote that God "was enraged by his (man's) sinful greed" (Isaiah 57:17), and Paul warned that among us "there must not be even a hint of . . . greed" (Ephesians 5:3). God hates greed as much as he hates idolatry, for to Him they are one and the same—looking somewhere besides Him and His provision for our contentment.

Scripture tells us how greed opens us up to deceit, bribes, emptiness, and broken relationships. Greed tempts us to cheat on everything from tips to taxes. "Greed can create anxiety," observes Wheaton College Professor of Psychological Studies, Robert C. Roberts, in *Christianity Today* (4/8/96). "It can foster depression and loss of meaning that often comes in middle age after a 'successful' life of acquiring the 'goods' of this world." Greed's focus is on self-fulfillment rather than generous serving. In setting standards for servant-leadership for elders, Peter reminds us all that " . . . God wants you to be; not greedy for money, but eager to serve" (1 Peter 5:2). Struggling with greed? Work on your "serve." Introduce your children to service for family, church, and the needy. We can cultivate generosity. Give away things that you value.

Every time we have the opportunity, we must teach our children that greed is like the grave and death—it is *never* satisfied (Habakkuk 2:5). The more we indulge it, the more we want. Solomon, who evidently spoke from more experience than we will ever have, assures us, "Whoever loves money never has money enough . . . is never satisfied with his income." As goods increase, so does consumption. "And what benefit are they to the owner except to feast his eyes on them?" (Ecclesiastes 5:10-11). Our eyes love to feast, but they get tired of the same meal, even if it's a lovely banquet. We can discuss the point as we clean out closets, prepare for garage sales, and ponder new wish lists at the mall.

The mall is great for eye-feasting, for appreciating innovation, creativity, for stimulating all our aesthetic sensibilities, for observing new cultural trends, and for just getting out with the "fam." Professor Roberts warns that a trip to the mall for the greedy is akin to a leisurely stroll through *Playboy* for the lusty. In his estimation, both titillate the appetite with a kind of "frustrated gratification." Roberts's assessment seems an over-psychologization of my experience, but I may be speaking as a frog that is too far gone to have any perspective.

At any rate, it's good to be reminded that while mall-cruising, one should frequently check the lust-ometer. (See Focus Box #17.)

≈

FOCUS YOUR WORLDVIEW #17:
CALIBRATING OUR LUST-OMETERS

How do I know when I've crossed the line from appreciative eye-feasting to greed? Here are some appetite check-up questions. (Thanks to Professor Roberts for his inspiration for some of the questions.)

➤ Does my longing for a nicer (fill in the blank) undercut my happiness and thankfulness for what I have now?

➤ Am I using a credit card to finance what I can't afford from my monthly budget or what I haven't saved for?

➤ When I visit the "Better Homes and Gardens" of my peers, or when my children play with their children's bigger playhouse or bigger computer system, or watch their exhaustive library of videos on a 2,000-inch TV, are we glad for our neighbors' material success and appreciative of their generosity, or do we somehow feel deprived, that we "deserve" the same perks and privileges?

➤ Lots of us might find ourselves imagining, *What if . . . we won the lottery (even if we don't play), or Publisher's Clearinghouse cameras arrived at our door?* But do we really dwell on these fantasies and revel in the imaginary acquisition of lots of things?

➤ Do I always see gift-giving as score-keeping? Do I feel cheated if the total amount I spend on Christmas or weddings or another friend or family doesn't equal what they spent on my family? Even if I have fewer kids?

➤ When I look at my total yearly amount of giving to church or charities, do I do it out of duty and then secretly compute how I could have enhanced my lifestyle the past twelve months with that money?

➤ If I have the opportunity to distribute anything to a group (food on the table, seating at an event, free samples or favors), do I take the best first for myself?

➤ Am I willing to sacrifice a friendship because I am envious of a friend's things or because of a disagreement over how some resource should be divided?

Actually, the mall can be a great place to convert hard-earned profits to meeting valid wants and needs. Exposing the bankruptcy of greedy ambition is not to dismiss or denounce the profit motive for work. "Who serves as a soldier at his own expense? Who plants a vineyard and does not eat of its grapes? Who tends a flock and does not drink of the milk?. . . . When the plowman plows and the thresher threshes, they ought to do so in the hope of sharing in the harvest" (1 Corinthians 9:7, 10). "The worker deserves his wages" (1 Timothy 5:18). The just compensation of individual effort is biblical, and without it a good work ethic gives way to laziness. (Witness the Communist system.) Our children should always link the idea of profit and hard work. (See Focus Box #18.)

The larger point to drive home to our children is not, "Don't be greedy," but rather, "Life does not consist in the abundance of possessions" (Luke 12:15). "The richer life" is found in relationships—first with God, then with others. Bankrupt materialistic values of excessive spending, possessing, and "feasting our eyes" have replaced the values of sacrifice and saving in the Protestant work ethic. When we are swept up in the pursuit of things, the "private enjoyment of life," (Mumford) or "personal peace and affluence" (Schaeffer), we miss the richer life. Instead we embrace the mediocrity of an endless shopping spree for good things and good times—a devotion that numbs our hearts and our imaginations. I'm reminded of all the well-conditioned, well-entertained, well-off, well-"soma"ed characters who populate Aldous Huxley's *Brave New World*.

God's offer of abundant life, indifferent to the pursuit of abundant possessions, is so much richer. C. S. Lewis provides a stunning analogy. In his sermon "The Weight of Glory," he chides us. "Our Lord finds our desires not too strong, but too weak. We are half-hearted creatures fooling about with drink and sex and [greedy] ambition when infinite joy is offered us, like an ignorant child who wants to go on making mud pies in a slum because he cannot imagine what is meant by the offer of a holiday at the beach."

The fun, the ambition that drives our children into a lifetime of work and service should not be the sparkle of new "toys," but the development of their unique gifting before God.

FOCUS YOUR WORLDVIEW #18: A WORD ABOUT WORKING FOR PROFIT—THE ALLOWANCE

In our home hard work (especially certain grade points) are rewarded with privileges—computer game time, stereo listening, TV/video viewing. Lack of effort translates into sharply curtailed privileges. (Profit can mean more than money.)

Some families give allowances based on work done; others supply allowances for being a part of the family team. Either way, money should be offered for extra above-and-beyond maintenance-type jobs.

Christian economist Ron Blue suggests an envelope arrangement of banking the children's allowance or money earned. Each child has envelopes for certain percentages of his income. (If children work in summer, the savings percentage goes up, possibly to half.) Suggested envelopes are for giving, saving, gifts, clothes, school lunches, and general spending. It usually means a trip to the bank to get the proper denominations, but it's a great way to teach fiscal responsibility. When the envelope is empty, "Sorry, Charlie!"—unless for some compelling reason, the child needs a loan. In which case the borrower signs to certain terms of repayment and interest.

TRAIN UP A CHILD ACCORDING TO HIS "BENT"

Some biblical scholars, Chuck Swindoll among them, take Proverbs 22:6 to mean, if we train a child in a way that is understanding of his natural bent (the way he should go), he'll not depart from it when he's older. It also follows that if we are dedicated students of our children's ways, of their "bent," we can discover how to motivate and develop their current work ethic, as well as help them prepare better for their life work.

God has given each of us a unique "bent"—an orientation to people and tasks, a unique personality and work style. Several assessment schemes of these traits are popular in Christian literature and in the workplace. Tim LaHaye introduced an updated version of the Greek concept of temperaments in the book *Transformed Temperaments*. His approach has been updated by others. John Trent and Gary Smalley have used animal labels, and Dr. John Geier's D-I-S-C scheme has popularized the concept in secular business settings.

A brief explanation of the four personality styles combining the above labels follows:

Choleric/Lion/High-D (Dominance)

Extroverted, task-oriented, high-ego strength; takes initiative, decisive, authoritative, good at developing the big picture, but weak on follow-through of details; often lacks concern for the feelings and views of others.

Sanguine/Otter/High-I (Influencing)

Extroverted, people-oriented, optimistic, verbally enthusiastic, trusting and affirming of others; confident but often is too sensitive and yields to social pressure.

Phlegmatic/Golden Retriever/High S (Steadiness)

Introverted, people-oriented, accommodating, patient, amiable, calm, easy-going, team player; very pragmatic, but resists change; undone by disharmony or instability.

Melancholic/Beaver/High C (Compliance)

Introverted, task-oriented, systematic thinker, quality-control person, well-prepared; concerned with accuracy and precision, but sometimes to a fault—can be too perfectionistic and demanding.

Obviously dealing with our children according to their main pattern or patterns (people usually are a combination of two) can give us insight into many aspects of their lives: their relationships, their scholastic orientation, their work styles and work goals; it can even be related to their spiritual gifts. The material in this chapter has been extremely helpful in my own development of my talents and gifts, both in employment and ministry. (Initial exposure to the D-I-S-C also had a profound impact on our marriage—thanks to good friends, the Larsens!)

≈

RESOURCE BOX #6: HOW DOES A LION (D) ENCOURAGE AN OTTER (I)?

The best resource I can recommend on this is a book, and especially a workbook published by Moody. I prefer *Understanding How Others Misunderstand You,* not just because I know Ken Voges, one of the authors, but because we have used these materials in our church for a whole series at our Women's Bible Study.

The materials focus on interpersonal relationships, but also discuss teamwork, leadership, or management style, dealing with stress, and commitment to Christ. They incorporate extensive Bible study and point out biblical role models for each personality pattern. The workbook contains an instrument to help assess your pattern and those of your spouse and children.

≈

If I had known when growing up what I know now (that I'm a high D, high I), I would have pursued a teaching credential in college instead of as a postgraduate. I would never have gone to work in the State Treasury crunching numbers. Knowing our pattern can help us pursue more compatible vocations sooner rather than later. And with today's cost of tuition, our children may not have as much liberty to cast about for the right program as we did.

Knowing and understanding Zach's pattern (high I, high D, some S), helps me in assisting his course selection in high school—honors English and humanities, but not honors chemistry. It guides us to think in terms of career goals that involve high verbal and expressive/creative skills, rather than those that are extremely process/detail-oriented. (We can all do many kinds of work, but we pay dearly in terms of physical and emotional resources when we're working outside our God-given strengths.) Beyond helping select *what kind* of work to pursue, knowing your children's patterns will enable you to facilitate the way they work. It helps for Zach (and for me as a fellow D/I) to do housework/yard work with a people-oriented treat promised upon completion. Have company over. "Work on your room for two hours, and then we'll go to the park with Spencer and Chris." Zach and I enjoy working on a project with someone else rather than solo. Verbal praise for work well done is very important. However, our "lick-and-a-promise" approach often needs a "quality control review" by Jack, who, conveniently, is a D/C. (How do opposites always wind up together?)

If our children are believers, they need to be encouraged to develop and use their spiritual gifts. Often we see certain clusters of gifts related to certain personality patterns, so discovering one can help lead to discovery of the other. I think we find our greatest joy in using our gifts and talents for service in the body of Christ. Our gifting is our calling. The earlier our children taste the joy of that kind of service, the richer their lives will be, and the more they can delight in serving God and knowing Him through their service.

Surely our best shot at countering our children's tendency to absorb the "Friday Eve" attitude toward work is to direct them toward work that complements their personality patterns, their spiritual gifting, and their other God-given talents: music, art, athleticism, intelligence, creativity, mechanical savvy, etc.

Life in the kettle of superabundance is so *easy*. By contrast, it requires so much thinking and many hard choices to be "in the world but not of the world" and to teach our children a truly Christian worldview that is at times countercultural. The single-minded pursuit of the American Dream may afford us a richer lifestyle, but not the richer abundant life God had in mind. In April, 1995, Bill Bennett addressed Hillsdale College's Shavano Institute for National Leadership. He concluded, "If we have full employment and greater economic growth—if we have cities of gold and alabaster—but our children have not learned how to walk in goodness, justice, and mercy, then the American experiment, no matter how gilded, will have failed."

When we stand before God's throne to give an account of how we used the time and talents God has given us, we may face a simple question: "What did I require of you? Did you act justly? Did you love mercy? Did you walk humbly with me?" (Micah 6:8) To the extent that our superabundance contributed to those pursuits, it will count for eternity. Otherwise—what do you think the eternal "market futures" will be for wood, hay, and stubble?

SHE WORKS HARD FOR NO MONEY?

10

*Developing a Biblical Work Ethic
for Home and Workplace*

*For ten long years she's cooked and cleaned
and she's washed a lot of jeans.
She's in four different car pools:
piano, soccer, ballet, and gym.
What to cook for dinner?
She's down to the dregs.
There's no hamburger, no chicken,
maybe . . . scrambled eggs!
She eats right and works out twice a week
to try to stay thin!*

She works hard for NO *money.
So hard for* NO *money.
She works hard for* NO *money
So you'd better treat her right!*

This song parody has become something of a women's retreat anthem
at our church. Hair in curlers, house robes, slippers, and yellow rubber
gloves waving, five of us hit the stage for a choreographed, hard-driving
version of this seventies tribute to working women.

Now you're on retreat while he *cleans and feeds kids . . .*

(Roars of response, women jump to their feet.)

And he gets a glimpse of just why you need *this!*

(More shouts, laughter, hands waving, fists clenched)

On Mondays she's back in the Mommy track—
no more time in the sack—no!—no!
She works hard!

The boisterous response to this song has rivaled, I'm sure, the intensity with which many feminists go about literally beating their drums. But I don't think the yelling and arm-waving is because Christian moms don't like to work hard. Granted, the "no-money" part gets old, but I think what really galvanizes the crowd here is a rare moment of profound recognition and tribute to women's work in the home. Not only is a "woman's work never done," but neither is it commended or rewarded very often.

Mary Kay, the makeup magnate, has obviously tapped into this great need for recognition. When my husband and I attended a convention at the Dallas Convention Center earlier this year, we could hardly find a parking space amidst all the pink Cadillacs and burgundy Trans-Ams. Inside, women in mauve suits and red blazers decked with enough ribbons and medals to make Saddam Hussein jealous were excitedly sharing makeup sales figures and anticipating a ritzy, glitzy gala in their honor.

Of course, it is fun to work hard for some money, but more than that, after all the recognition, the honors, the "attagirls," and countless trips across the stage, these women spilled out of the elevators, jumped into their pink-and-burgundy-mobiles, and headed for home motivated to work harder than ever.

I sometimes think that life would be easier for women everywhere if more good, old-fashioned appreciation were expressed for all our hard work on the home front. What about some applause and "attagirls" for the housework, where it seems the only notice given is something like: "Where are my clean socks?"

Perhaps we could recruit corporate sponsorship and offer a "Bathroom Duck Clean Toilet" award, or how about a "Johnson Baby Wipes Shiny Hiney" award to the one who has changed the most diapers? Moms with one child after another in diapers could go for their five- or ten-year pins.

Not likely.

Whether we work outside the home or not, almost all of us get stressed out or bogged down by housework. So it is fitting, in a discussion of a biblical work ethic, to consider briefly a couple of issues that relate directly to moms and indirectly to our children. First issue: the "H" word. Housework is thankless, and the never-ending routine of the same jobs that have to be done again and again can seem so meaningless.

HOUSEWORK DRIVES ME CRAZY!

Chuck Colson tells a story in *Why America Doesn't Work* of a bunch of POWs in a German prison camp who were made to do back-breaking, bone-wearying, meaningless work. After a bombing raid, the prisoners spent days and weeks just picking up piles of rubble and moving it from point A to point B. Then they were ordered to pick it up from point B and move it back to point A. As the process was repeated, men began to fall apart. They began to run so the guards would shoot them, or they tried to impale themselves on the electrified fence.

The German commandant was actually conducting an "experiment" in mental health. He discovered that, deprived of meaningful work, men and women lose their reason for existence; they go stark raving mad.

Now I know what some of you may be thinking. *Aha, so I'm totally justified when I feel that day after day of washing dishes, making beds, and doing laundry drives me crazy!*

Maybe that's why so many housewives throw themselves, not on an electrified fence, but into an electronic pit of escapist, mind-numbing soaps and endless strings of Geraldo-Sally-Maurey-Montel-Jerry-and-Ricki.

But escape is not the answer, whether to the media or to the workplace. If we're going to model and teach a biblical work ethic to our children, we need to see our work and our role as God sees them.

When we look at ourselves in the mirror of God's Word, we see a woman made for work. Our children should also understand that they were made for work as well. Let's now focus our thoughts on the development of a biblical work ethic of responsibility and the pursuit of excellence, and then we'll consider whether we (and our daughters) should engage in work outside the home.

WORKING IN OUR FATHER'S IMAGE

Work is our God-given responsibility. Remember Genesis 2:15? Adam was put in the garden "to work it"—and this was *before* the Fall. Then in verse 18 God purposed to make Eve to be Adam's "suitable helper" so he would not be alone. This meant that Eve was to help Adam work and tend the garden. Man and woman were created primarily for relationship and work, not leisure. And the work included both manual labor (caring for the garden) and intellectual labor (some aspects of caring for the garden, naming the animals).

When we look at the example of work that God set for man, we find a ratio of six days of work to one day of leisure (Exodus 20:9-11). This is an interesting balance. We might have preferred three and a half on, three and a half off, but God knew that we have more to gain from work than from leisure.

In Genesis 1, God's response to His work of creation was *not* waiting for the Sabbath whistle to blow. Every day he looked over His work and concluded that it was "good" or "very good." And we are created in His image.

Check out Ecclesiastes 5:18-19 with your children. Ask them if their version reads, "It is good and proper to find satisfaction in our leisure and entertainment after a hard day's work." Solomon, the wisest man on earth, recognized that it's "good and proper . . . to find satisfaction in our toilsome labor" and that being "happy in our work . . . is a gift of God." We are created to work and to find happiness and fulfillment in work, even in toilsome toilet-cleaning, diaper-changing work.

It is a challenge to keep from embracing the "Friday Eve" mentality or the real frustration that "She Works Hard for *No* Money?" pokes fun at. But it is a challenge God equips us to meet as we choose to accept the truth of His Word. Work challenges us—makes us grow in character, skill, and creativity. Learning to take responsibility for hard work, day-in and day-out over the long haul, develops perseverance, one of the major traits God wants to build into our lives.

WORKING WITH HEART AND EXCELLENCE

When the biblical picture of work does not square with my reality or my child's, then I go to the Lord and pray that he will give me *His* heart and *His* attitude toward work. We know that happiness and satisfaction in our work is a reasonable expectation. And when we are distressed over dirty dishes or moaning over mounds of mending, we can come to God in prayer asking for His "good and proper" gift of satisfaction in our work, even when it seems like meaningless repetition.

If we must spend a lot of time doing tasks that don't fully challenge our minds (like weeding, washing dishes, and watching over toddlers), we can ask God to engage our minds in something more satisfying (like problem-solving, thinking about relationships, praying, planning, creating a letter or a song). Watching livestock graze all day—now there's a challenge to personal satisfaction in your work! And yet David managed to write wonderful psalms while still whacking the occasional lion or bear and taking care of those smelly sheep—all to the glory of God.

A few other suggestions: Doing our work heartily may mean putting more creativity into meals, decorating, sewing, and hospitality. It may mean being more productive by setting goals and schedules and accomplishing them. Feeling overwhelmed? Divide large jobs into smaller segments interspersed with some treats: a drink or snack, a magazine, or a little phone chat. This can help with our children as well. (For other tips on helping our children learn to work, see Focus Box #19.)

FOCUS YOUR WORLDVIEW #19: SIX HELPFUL TIPS FOR RAISING GOOD WORKERS

I must say, we've used almost all of these, but we are still learning in this area. (If you've discovered the secret for really motivating a D-I only child to work alone, please send your tips to me!)

1. *Start young*. Preschoolers can help pick up and put away toys, use a hand-held vacuum, sort laundry, water outdoor plants, set the table, dust, get the mail, and sort recyclables.

2. *Increase time spent and level of difficulty of work with age.* Grade school children can load the dishwasher, make their own bed, take out the garbage, care for small pets, sweep, do basic yard work, fold laundry, prepare their own cereal and sandwiches, and water indoor plants. Middle schoolers should be able to do more yard work (pulling weeds, using electric equipment and lawn mowers with safety features), wash cars well (vacuum interior), vacuum the house, clean bathrooms, wash pots and pans, and even begin to take care of other children. Teens can manage complete lawn service and most housework, basic cooking, and start to do all of the above *well*.

2. *Train your child to do the job.* Demonstrate, then oversee. Rather than criticize a lot, encourage as much as possible. Each new time the work is undertaken, keep demonstrating and overseeing. Call back for more effort and a better job as they get older. We can't hold younger children to our standards. (Although I've tried too often—sorry, Zach!)

3. *Have a schedule.* Grade school children who are working thirty minutes a day and two hours on Saturday may need to be reminded, since they don't have much to do and will tend to forget. It helps for older kids, too. Make a seven-day work calendar and post it in the kitchen. Make adjustments *in writing* on the calendar.

4. *Make a card file for each chore.* List basic requirements of each task and materials needed, even reminders of where materials are kept. Each child has a card file.

5. *Make work as enjoyable as possible.* Team spirit can make large projects seem less overwhelming. Challenge the kids with suggested completion times and rewards (deduct from reward for poor quality). Set the example. Do you "whistle while you work," plod silently, or grouch and complain? "A cheerful heart is good medicine" (Proverbs 17:22).

Still singing the "Work Is a Drag" blues? (Or hearing a kids' chorus version?) It helps to remind ourselves whom we are really working for and how He calls us to (and rewards us for) excellence in small tasks before giving us the larger ones. In our family we regularly remind one another of the following verses:

> *Whatever your hand finds to do, do it with all your might*
> —*Ecclesiastes 9:10*

> *Whatever you do, work at it with all your heart, as working for the Lord, not for men, since you know that you will receive an inheritance from the Lord as a reward. It is the Lord Christ you are serving.*
> —*Colossians 3:23-24*

We talk about work as stewardship in our house. God has given us another day of life, an able body and mind, and specific gifts and talents meant to be developed, sharpened, and strengthened through work. There are days when we each choose to waste time and talents in pursuit of leisure and amusement well beyond the bounds of what's needed for rest and renewal. But as we talk about it, we admit that the overdose of amusement and leisure leaves us feeling kind of numb and dissatisfied. Whether it's during the fifth six-week grading period, the laundry marathon, or endless sermon preparation, we encourage one another with these verses. We work for the Lord. He sees the loving labor *and* the shortcuts. He promises a reward for work well done for Him. In reality, our work is never thankless if we're children of the King.

I love the advice of Norman Brinker. He is profiled in Newt Gingrich's video series *Renewing American Civilization.* Brinker started with a small coffee shop in Dallas around the corner from Dallas Seminary. Having done that well, he expanded to a small restaurant, Steak and Ale. Eventually, he developed an entire chain of Steak and Ale's, where he introduced the concept of a salad bar and trained his waiters to interact personally with customers. His "Good afternoon. My name is Mike, and I'll be your waiter today" has been copied by thousands of restaurants across the land. In 1976 he sold Steak and Ale for $102 million. Then, as chairman of the Pillsbury Restaurant Group, he took on a succession of restaurant chains—Burger King,

Bennigan's, and Chili's—greatly improving service, product, and the bottom line.

Brinker's advice to young workers is great for our children:

> Know who you are. Know what you are. Know what you enjoy doing. [As in, understand your pattern and your gifts.] If you do something you're really good at, then the money may come. Set clear-cut goals to accomplish what you want. Become the very best in that line of business, and then go do something on your own. The people I know who've accomplished a great deal do it step by step by step. Don't wander around looking for the big deal—that never happens. It's step by step by step.

While we don't have time to mine all the gems out of Matthew 25:14-30, the parable of the talents, several similarities to Brinker's advice are evident: The master gave different amounts of money to invest to three different servants, "each according to his ability."

God gives us different innate talents and gifts as He pleases. We expand or diminish our overall "ability" for success by how we apply what He's given us to the smaller tasks first. Then the general pattern is, He rewards our demonstrated ability at smaller tasks two ways: By inviting us to share in His happiness at a job well done (verses 21, 23), and by giving us a greater opportunity for success. The master promoted both the five-talent servant and the two-talent servant to be "in charge of _many_ things."

Sheep-watching, housework, yard work—they may be two-talent jobs, but, pursued with excellence, they pave the way for bigger-talent jobs. We can choose to depend on the enabling power of the Holy Spirit to renew our commitment to responsibility and excellence in our work (even when we don't feel like it, even when a halfway job would get by). When we make this choice, we deepen our relationship with the God who desires to share His happiness with us and give us His gift of satisfaction in our work—and perhaps more responsibility.

TCF: Taking Care of Family

Conference speaker and author Steve Farrar has stated, "God's blueprint for the family centers around the two nonnegotiable needs of every family: 1) every family needs provision (money), [and] 2) every family needs care."

Focus Box #20 brings out the fact that God has given women a major role in the caretaking of our families. While this is a culturally sensitive statement, if we take this as God's design, then acknowledging this role can be another source of motivation for excellence in the dailiness of our housework. We can see it as a vital part of carrying out our God-given assignment. Our work is truly never meaningless because we work as unto the Lord, and we see our caregiving as the glue that holds our family together. We have only to look around at families where the mom is dysfunctional or has abandoned her role or her family to see such a family struggling or falling apart.

Obviously, there is much more to caregiving than housework, but that seems to be our least favorite part of it. It requires a greater degree of sacrifice—just laying down our desire for self-fulfillment and tackling a dirty job for the thousandth time. It helps me to think that this may be the one area in my life where I can most consistently expect sacrifice—where I have the opportunity to take up my cross daily and follow Jesus Christ. It also helps to remember Steve Farrar's admonition, "In order to provide care and provision, someone has to *sacrifice* or *be sacrificed*."

Part of teaching our children a Christian worldview is challenging them to embrace a biblical view of feminine and masculine roles. (See Focus Box #20.) If our boys are to be servant-leaders and provide for their families, they need to discover their role in Scripture and see it modeled at home. If our girls are to learn biblical submission and caregiving, they need to see what it looks like. Remember, as Bill Bennett talked about, the "moral power" of our "quiet example." They need our countercultural example to correct for the change that has occurred in our cultural ideal. Caregiving may have characterized a wife's role in the fifties, but by the eighties she was fully replaced by a sexy woman who brought home the bacon, fried it up in a pan, and "roared" in a voice that was too loud to be ignored.

FOCUS YOUR WORLDVIEW BOX #20:
WOMAN WAS DESIGNED TO BE . . .

1. *Equal with man.* The *egalitarian* position is held by many Christian women today, many of whom I admire deeply and many of whom take a high view of Scripture. They believe that submission is to be taken as mutual submission, that rulership resulted from the Fall, that women should minister in the church according to their spiritual gifting as freely as men (including the office of elder), and that both women and men should share in the nurture and training of their children.

   With all respect, as I read Scripture, I deeply disagree. I think that this view is more a reflection of the progressive influence on our culture than Scripture's intent. I believe in what is termed the *complementarian* position—that men and women are equal in value and in sharing the blessings of salvation, but different in roles.

2. *A complement to man.* As I read the creation account, I do not read that God formed Adam and Eve both out of the dust and breathed life into them, establishing them as fifty/fifty partners. I see a definite primacy in Adam's role. Paul's instruction to "not permit a woman to teach or have authority over a man" in corporate worship (1 Timothy 2:12-13) is based on that primacy of creation. ("For Adam was formed first, then Eve.") It is not a cultural consideration at all. Our role, like Eve's, is to be a helper suitable to our husbands, whom God has established as servant-leaders in our marriage and family (Ephesians 5:22-33).

   I understand the curse to mean that man's servant-leadership was corrupted into a harsh, tyrannical "rule"—the Hebrew word used in Genesis 3:16. And I see both Adam and Eve cursed in the area of their primary roles—Adam in provision (Genesis 3:17-19) and Eve in care (Genesis 3:16). I see God's design in our bodies— man's strength designed for provision (needed until just the last century), and woman's reproductive system and breasts designed for care. Provision is also emphasized as the man's role in 1 Timothy 5:8 and care as the woman's in Proverbs 31:10-31 and Titus 2:3-5. Scripture admonishes both parents to exercise leadership in the training of children. Obviously fathers involved in the care of their children will find more opportunities for training as well.

   I believe that we have opportunities for flexibility within these primary roles, depending on the presence of children in the home, health, and economic difficulties. But, on balance, this is the role I try to live before my child while I encourage him in his development as a servant-leader.

≈

THE GOOD WIFE GOES TO WORK

Over the last four decades, a woman's role has shifted increasingly from caregiving to provision. By 1972 the number of working women surpassed the number of housewives for the first time in history. Women who had focused on caregiving for centuries, yea, even millennia, considered the question, "Shall I work outside the home?" and most concluded, "Yes, I shall."

It's a good question, one most modern moms face. For many trying to honor biblical wisdom on the subject, the question is rather, "*Should* I work outside the home?" Fortunately, God has given us the freedom in this area to answer the question individually, based on biblical criteria. Even Paul, who takes a licking from the feminists, nowhere requires women to refrain from employment.

The way we answer this question not only affects the care and provision of our own family, but also that of our children's future family. They will either take their cue from our example or reverse course in order to spare their children the wrongs they feel they suffered.

Why have women gone to work? According to Kerby Anderson in his book *Signs of Warning, Signs of Hope,* there are three reasons.

1. *Ideology.* If you peruse your children's textbooks today, I doubt that you will find anything remotely resembling this excerpt from a 1950 high school home economics textbook. It gives an example of "How to Be a Good Wife."

Have dinner ready. Plan ahead, even the night before to have a delicious meal on time.

Prepare yourself (with a fifteen-minute nap and a ribbon in your hair). He has just been with a lot of work-weary people. Be a little gay. [Ah-the original usage!] His boring day may need a lift.

Clear away the clutter. Then run a dust cloth over the tables

[Now I always dust daily, don't you?]. Your husband will feel he has reached a haven of rest and order.

Prepare the children (wash faces, comb hair, change clothes). They are little treasures, and he would like to see them playing the part.

Don't greet him with problems. Don't complain he is late for dinner. Count this as minor compared with what he might have gone through that day. Have him lean back in a comfortable chair or suggest he lie down in the bedroom. Have a cool or warm drink ready for him. Arrange his pillows and offer to take off his shoes. [At this point I always throw in a fifteen-minute foot massage.] Make the evening his.

Now this was *serious* caregiving!

The newspaper article quoting this old textbook was titled "The 'good wife' is gone, but should we miss her?" If the "good wife" is gone from her pedestal in society, what happened to her? I'll give you my best guess: Betty Friedan pushed her off and stomped on her.

Sixties feminist and author Betty Friedan (*The Feminine Mystique*) took a long, hard look at the "good wife" and concluded that her devotion to the caregiving role came at the expense of developing her own talents and abilities and her right to self-fulfillment. Friedan, Gloria Steinem, and a chorus of other feminists have asserted that sexual roles are interchangeable. Women have just as much right to the perks and power of the provision role as men, and day care can assume the caregiving role.

2. *Opportunity.* The ideology gained great momentum in the sixties and seventies due to a second factor: opportunity. One has only to read about Abigail in 1 Samuel 25 to be glad we are no longer subject to arranged marriages to fools like Nabal. Similarly, I could not help but inwardly grimace at the limitations of life in Jane Austen's England as I watched Emma Thompson's screen version of *Sense and Sensibility.* The beautiful, sensitive women were completely dependent upon the affections of some gallant young man to deliver them from the life sentence of spinsterhood. And too often the young man's affection or his family's blessing was withheld, not because of the girl's character, but due to her social or financial status.

The twentieth-century Western woman has been much freer to

choose and be chosen in marriage. More women are college gradu-
ates, and the trend continues. Women now comprise over half of the
students currently enrolled in higher education. We have options to
limit the size of our families. Add to that the labor-saving devices
introduced in the last thirty years (washer, dryer, dishwasher,
microwave, etc.), and a woman's opportunity to devote much less
time to caregiving and much more time to something else has
increased significantly.

I remember visiting the General Electric Pavilion at Disneyland as
a child. We sat in a large "carousel" theater where the stage slowly
revolved to show us the history of labor-saving appliances. You may
remember that the advantage touted by their manufacturers was a
great *increase* in leisure time. Why, the four-day work week was just
over the horizon! The Disney theater showed Mom petting the cat
and playing with her children while the dishwasher purred in the
background.

Funny how things turn out. Perhaps what really ignited the feminists was the appliance manufacturers' success. Deprived of the challenge of caregiving work, too many moms played too much bridge,
watched too many soaps, and ate too many bonbons, and the feminists
recognized that too much of too many women's lives was a colossal
waste of time. Perhaps they were on to something (remember we
were created to work), but they made the sad mistake of dismissing
caregiving as meaningless, unfulfilling work.

3. *The "Need" of the Times. Ideology* has intersected *opportunity*—more
personal freedom and education and less time needed for caregiving.
Add to these, the real needs of an increasing number of single moms
and the perceived need for two incomes as Boomer women try to
equal or better their parents' standard of living. The corollary question for many moms asking, "Should I work outside the home?" is,
"How much is enough?"

We considered this question at length in the last chapter. And we
talked about how Boomer moms, having grown up in the most affluent time in our nation's history, have developed what Kerby Anderson
calls a "psychology of entitlement." We are, as Anderson notes in *Signs
of Warning, Signs of Hope,* mixing a recipe that reads, "Take one part

heightened expectations, mix with psychology of entitlement, place in climate of lowered expectations = envy" (p. 117).

I remember as a young mother feeling that Zach and I were bobbing in the wake of my career-minded friends as they zoomed by en route to corporate offices and exotic vacations. I struggled with envy and greed. I just wanted a little nicer house, to replace my late-basement-early-Holiday-Inn-period furniture with something a little nicer, just a few more outfits—just a little more, more, more. I had to come to grips with the fact that my expectations were very culture-bound. God's priorities are not. I needed almost all of my limited physical energy for caregiving. Like Paul in Philippians 4:11, I had to _learn_ "to be content whatever the circumstances"—a tough assignment for a ministry wife with medical bills and a _long_ wish list.

SUPERMOM'S REGRETS

Given the confluence of ideology, opportunity, and the need of the times, millions of moms chose to pursue the Supermom image, trying to juggle career, marriage, children, and caregiving. But there has been a trade-off for "[bringing] home the bacon and [frying] it up in the pan."

Mary Ann Lindley, the Knight-Ridder newspaper reporter who dug up the old textbook describing the "good wife," had an interesting reaction to her find. She commented that she "wanted to cry" when she read it. It reminded her of when her mother visited her. Every day when she came home from work, her mother had a "wonderful dinner underway."

She woke up the next day "wondering how life had changed so. How it had ever been so lopsided? Or if it is better now, when all of us would adore such extraordinary nurturing, but none of us is available to give it" (_Tallahassee Democrat_, 11/95). As our cultural pendulum swings toward overemphasis on _provision_, we heave a collective sigh over the loss of _caregiving_. A "good wife"? Many moms today would love to have one.

In 1990 Barbara Bush delivered a speech to a graduating class of Wellesley women. "At the end of your life, you will not regret . . . not winning one more verdict or not closing one more deal," the First Lady courageously prophesied. "You will regret time not spent with a husband, a child, a friend, a parent" (*Time*, 6/11/90). Students smugly complained that Mrs. Bush did not reflect "the self-affirming qualities of a Wellesley graduate" and that her success was the result of her husband's career, not her own. But surveys and headlines of the nineties reflect a growing change of heart in these "self-affirming" women and their predecessors. In a 1994 survey of 800 women with children, *Child* magazine (5/94) reported their regrets: "They wish they had had more children, gone back to work later, quit rather than continued to work, and made career less of a priority and family more of one."

A caption from a 1996 *Orlando Sentinel* reads, "Study shows working moms aren't happy with their lives." They work hard to help provide "necessities" (the number one reason given to *Child* for being in the job market), and at the same time fret over the loss of care for their families. "It was my duty to cook for the children at dinner, but I'm doing it less and less," confides one columnist. "Having snacked when they came home from school [spaghetti sauce slathered on shoestring potatoes], they're usually not hungry again till right before bedtime when they eat cereal as I cast a blind eye." "The Good Wife" would shake her head in disbelief at a whole new genre of books and articles reintroducing moms to the value of family dinnertime. (See Focus Box #21.)

Add up all the guilt, regrets, stress, sleep deprivation, and longing for time alone, and we have a new nineties trend: "Large numbers of women are leaving the workplace and making the sacrifices required to stay home while their children are young," observes Dr. James Dobson in his August 1994 Focus on the Family newsletter. He quoted a recent issue of *Barron's,* a business journal, reporting "the exodus of women from the workplace as a demographic sea change." More and more women are finding ways to work at home. (See Resource Box #7.)

We hope that our children will grow up in a culture where women temper the "careerism" of the previous decades with consideration for caregiving to families. Given the choice to be at home full time, to work full time, or to work part time, guess which option most women polled by *Child* chose:

11 percent to work full time
41 percent to be at home full time
45 percent to work part time

Ideally, over half of the moms (56 percent) would still like to work, although most would rather work part time. This reflects their number two reason for wanting to work: "Because I enjoy my work."

Christianity Today writers Don and Carol Browning join Harvard social scientist Jacqueline Olds in a 1992 research paper entitled "Part-Time Employment and Marital Well-Being" (10/18/95). "Their research shows that the families with the most marital, parental, and child satisfaction are those that work one and a half jobs or approximately sixty hours a week between them."

———————————————————≈———————————————————

FOCUS YOUR WORLDVIEW BOX #21:
THE LOST ART OF DINNERTIME

Even for the at-home mom, convening the entire family at the dinner table all at the same time can be a challenge of Olympic proportions. Coordinating three to six or more separate schedules of work, school, music, dance, drama, and church activities becomes an assignment for a good data base. And then there's the battle against TV and the telephone.

Many families concede a night or two to the activity blitz but carve out breakfasts or several nights a week where family time is guarded. It's a wonderful time to teach the social graces of dining etiquette and also to develop conversation skills. It can be a rich time of storytelling and building relationships. Here are a few helpful tips, some from *Table Talk* by Mimi Wilson and Mary Beth Lagerborg published by Focus on the Family:

➤ No television and let the phone machine do the talking.

➤ Ask questions that require more than a yes/no, one-word answer. Any parent who can't be more creative than "How was your day?" deserves the uncreative "Fine" for an answer.

➤ Encourage each one to listen with respect so that each member, no matter how young, has a hearing; no one leaves the table until he or she is excused.

➤ Sometimes you may want to plan a discussion. You can bring your subject to the table with a post-it note by your place, recording your inspiration from earlier in the day.

➤ Use an interesting "centerpiece," such as a globe, to focus a discussion on current events, or use an interesting picture, comic, quote, or verse.

➤ Some families use a decorative box or jar full of interesting questions written on folded slips of paper to stimulate discussion. Each night a different person pulls one out and asks, "What would be your dream vacation?" or "If you wrote a book, what would it be about?"

News anchor Katie Couric relates that when she was growing up, her dad asked each child to bring a new word to the table each night. Ted Kennedy's dad requested that each one come prepared to tell about a current event—and look how the children in this family turned out.

RESOURCE BOX #7: WORKING AT HOME

Perhaps one solution to the need to balance care and provision for children would be to consider a home-based business. An excellent resource to help you probe this possibility is the book *A Christian's Guide to Working from Home* by Lindsey O'Connor. Lindsey's book is an enjoyable and practical read based on a biblical perspective. She helps her readers determine if working at home is right for them, suggests numerous ideas for home-based businesses, and then follows up with step-by-step recommendations for how to get started. As a journalist, author, and the mother of four children ages four to twelve, she gives solid advice on making it work with a full house. And any resource you could possibly need is fully referenced in the final section.

RUBY PLUS OR SAPPHIRA THE SECOND?

Now this is progress! We've gone beyond the "Good Wife," beyond Supermom, only to wind up . . . in Proverbs 31—the part-time working mom who puts her priority on caring for her family. This is an encouraging trend! If our children want to see a woman who has worked out the balance of her primary caretaking role and using her gifts and talents outside the home, introduce them to Ruby Plus, the wife of noble character who is more valuable than . . . (you know).

Ruby Plus is a woman for all seasons and ages. She teaches our girls who to be and our boys whom to marry. Ruby Plus's role is not culture-bound but perfectly reflects God's priorities.

Priority Number One

➤ First and foremost, the care and nurturing of her family. This is where she spends most of her time. (Granted, she had household help, but she didn't have a vacuum cleaner or Campbell's soup.)

➤ Within the family, her top priority is her husband—being that "suitable helper" (vv. 11-12).

➤ She works hard for no money on clothing (vv. 13, 19, 21-22), food (vv. 14-15), and interior decorating (v. 22).

➤ She is responsible for the moral training of her children (v. 26). If she had a TV, she would no doubt turn it off to be heard.

Other Priorities

➤ Ministry: to poor and needy (v. 20). Verse 26 may mean a teaching ministry beyond the home.

➤ Work for pay: real estate, agribusiness (v. 16), clothing business (v. 24).

God Rewards Her Priorities

➤ Her trading is profitable (v. 18).

➤ The real bottom line of her whole story: the praise of her children, her husband, and even the whole city (vv. 28-29, 31).

It is no coincidence that an Old Testament portrait reflects today's poll results of the most popular choices. Subtract Ruby Plus's entrepreneurial pursuits in two verses, and she is full time at home, where many Christian women are wonderfully content. Include her business ventures, and she is a part-timer. After the children arise, bless her, and leave, she may even have spent more time pursuing business interests or perhaps ministry.

God is certainly most concerned with our heart and our priorities. I believe that is why His Word teaches that there is great flexibility in how we address those priorities. As we consider whether to work for pay and as we teach our children about their future on the subject, it can be helpful to review our motivation and our priorities with the following questions:

1. Can I work for pay and still give account to the Lord that I have given my husband and children the care they need?

2. Am I just bored? Do I need to be more creative in the use of my gifts with my family or in my ministry?

3. Do we really *need* extra provision for our family? Does my sense of "need" reflect a heart of greed or envy?

4. If I have extra time and talent, would the Lord have me use that in ministry at my church, crisis pregnancy center, etc.?

5. Do we want more money or more time? How much money will I really net? (See Resource Box #8.)

RESOURCE BOX #8: COULD YOU AFFORD TO QUIT YOUR JOB AND STAY HOME WITH YOUR CHILDREN?

Maybe you identify with the longing many career women have for just a part-time job or no additional job responsibilities at all outside the home. But can you afford to quit? While you prayerfully consider your "needs" on one end, you might get out your calculator on the other and compute exactly how much of that second paycheck you actually take home. The following table from Debra White Stephens, a certified financial planner with Financial Network Investment Corp., can help you clarify your possibilities (used by permission).

HOW MUCH IT COSTS YOU TO WORK

ANNUAL GROSS INCOME *before taxes*   _____

Child care   _____
Transportation   _____
Bus fare   _____
Gasoline and oil   _____
Vehicle maintenance   _____
Increased auto insurance   _____
   (classification changes from "leisure only"
   to "to and from work")
Parking   _____
TOTAL   _____

Clothing:
   Purchase price   _____
   Dry cleaning   _____
   Pantyhose   _____
TOTAL   _____

Personal grooming:
   Nails   _____
   Hair   _____
   Makeup   _____
   Massage or other stress relievers   _____
TOTAL   _____

Food:
   Lunches out   _____
   Dinners out or take-out food   _____
TOTAL   _____

Communications:
   Cellular phone   _____
   Pager   _____
TOTAL   _____

Taxes:
   FICA *(Social Security and Medicare)*   _____
   Federal income tax *(individual tax bracket)*   _____

Add'l income tax on
spouse's earnings if your earnings increase   _____
your joint bracket

TOTAL   _____

NET INCOME (*actual take-home pay*)   _____

After doing your math, you may discover that you're working forty hours a week for $3.50 an hour (minimum wage was $5.15 as of September 1, 1997).

Still in doubt? Try living on one paycheck for a while or request a leave of absence from your employer.

———————————————— ≈ ————————————————

God has made us to find satisfaction in our work. At home, where we work hard for no money, He wants us to look out over a clean room or a savory dinner and say, "It is good." He has given us unique talents, spiritual gifts, interests, and passions. He may lead us to use those gifts in provision as well as in caregiving. I would love for this book to be a critical success at the "city gates." But much more than that, I long for Zach to look back after he has "arisen" and bless me. And for Jack to think I "do him good and not harm" all the days of our life together.

May we and our daughters follow in the footsteps of Ruby Plus, and may our sons "find" someone like her. Much better Ruby Plus than her worldly modern cousin, Sapphira the Second. With profound apologies to the author of Proverbs 31, I offer this tongue-in-cheek portrait of an example to avoid:

SAPPHIRA THE SECOND

A wife of worldly character who can find?
   She is worth far more than her unborn child.
Her husband has full confidence in her and knows that
   he is one of her top priorities.
She brings him good, not harm
   (so long as it is personally fulfilling) all the days of her life.
She selects influential friends and progressive schools
   for her children and works to help them with eager hands.
She is like a merchant ship,

always bringing home fast-food dinners from afar.
She gets up while it is still dark to do her workout video
_____while her household provides breakfast for themselves._
She gets an insider tip on a vineyard future and buys it.
_____Out of her huge earnings she plants a trust fund._
She sets about her work vigorously
_____but has precious little energy left for family._
She sees that she is moving up her career ladder;
_____her overtime lamp does not go out at night._
In her hand she holds the Dictaphone
_____and grasps the "mouse" with her fingers._
She opens her checkbook to the charity with the biggest gala
_____and always gives a dollar to the homeless man_
_____who squeegees her windshield._
When it snows, she has no fear of animal rights activists.
_____All her furs are fake._
She redecorates regularly
_____and is clothed in new Donna Karan fine linen_
_____and Ralph Lauren purple every season._
Her husband is respected as a leader at City Hall,
_____but at home he knows he is strictly a fifty/fifty partner._
She knows the ready-to-wear business inside and out.
_____She undercuts all the competition for her line._
She is clothed with "openness" and "tolerance."
_____She can laugh at the "religious right."_
She speaks at Wellesley College and gives faithful instruction
_____based on her own career (not her husband's)._
She neglects the affairs of her household,
_____and her children eat the bread of idleness._
Her children arise and say,
_____"Back off, Mom. Don't even go there."_
Her husband praises her saying,
_____"Many women try to have it all, but you surpass them all."_
Charm is delightful, and brains are even better,
_____but a woman who fears nothing and no one—_
_____she is to be praised._
Let her enjoy her rewards and perks now,
_____because her works may bring her problems at the pearly gates._

A TIME TO KILL, FLOP, AND CLICK

11

Leisure and the Entertainment Culture

Dear Diary: Woke up late. Great to sleep in. Ate cereal while I watched some old cartoons. Had my Star Wars *fix for the day—22nd time for* Return of the Jedi. *(Followed along on the script I found on the Internet last night.)*

Took the boom box out on the driveway. Shot baskets and listened to my new Jock Rock CD till Chris came over. Then we went inside and played video games. A little later Spencer and Andy came over. We pulled on our "camo" and videotaped another segment of our movie Space Cadets. *After lunch we headed to FuncoLand to scavenge for cheap old Nintendo games.*

So goes the ideal leisure day for most teens—floating from one technology to the next, either as focus or background, but never completely unplugged from their own media world. They may even end the day with their Walkmans in bed or their stereo on sleep setting.

What do you do when you can do anything you want or nothing at all? That is basically the definition of leisure time. From the beginning of civilization up through our grandparents' time, the stewardship of leisure wasn't nearly the cultural issue it is now. Mainly because (A) they didn't have much and (B) the options of how to spend it were pretty tame.

If your grandparents were around in 1934, they probably only had half a day off on Saturday and reserved Sunday for church and proper Sabbath activities. The top seven leisure pursuits of the day were: "eating, visiting friends, reading, listening to the radio, sports, motoring for pleasure, and various types of public entertainment" (Witold Rybczynski, _Waiting for the Weekend_).

In 1940 the five-day work week was written into law, but it upset many in the Christian community. The departure from the Ten Commandments' prescription of six days of work and one day of rest worried them. What would people do with all that leisure time? As it turns out, they mainly watch TV. While the increase of leisure time has been called "the most important megatrend of the century" (_Time_, 12/24/90), the American Use of Time Project reports that women's gains over the last twenty years have been transferred to the tube. We spend 40 percent of our free time parked in front of it (Schultz, _Winning Your Kids Back from the Media,_ p. 42). (If it's any consolation, men spend 50 percent.)

In Nielsen rating terms, that translates into four hours of TV-viewing a day. Our children follow our example and average three hours a day, although viewing time for ages two to twelve is declining as they shift over to video and computer games and computer on-line services. You may have noticed your own preteens and teens pulling out of watching TV with the family. _Time_ reports that the average postadolescent spends thirty dollars and forty hours a week on his preferred media entertainment.

So much has been said on this subject. But if the tendency is for media consumption to be a part-time job for us and a full-time job for our children, or if we are continually fighting that tendency (like playing Whack the Mole at the pizza parlor), then this chapter can offer some insight and encouragement. "Keep up the good whack!"

Blue Recliner + Remote = Sanctuary

I can certainly empathize with the ranks of part-time-job TV viewers. And I can attest to the fact that the most subtle, yet most profound impact viewing has on us and our families is that we wind up having the time of our life . . . go by.

For many years I probably spent twenty to twenty-five hours a week with my Sony. After a day of trying to keep up with a toddler, I rounded the corner into the just-make-it-through-dinner-and-into-my-big-blue-recliner homestretch. I would turn on the TV at 5:30 to catch the news while I cooked dinner. Sometimes (often?) it stayed on through dinner and cleanup.

Kitchen duty completed, I usually collapsed into my wingback recliner, allowing the throbbing pain of my arthritis to gradually subside. Except for a brief time-out for Zach's bedtime routine, if Jack wasn't home to do it, I would watch till the 10:00 P.M. news and beyond if Johnny's guests looked interesting.

Looking back, I realize that to a certain degree, I was emotionally bonded to the TV. I really enjoyed the shows, looked forward to my favorites, and talked about the characters and recent episodes with friends, especially with Mary.

I didn't think I was watching "too much" TV or that it had too large a place in my life. I knew *other* people who always had the tube on— day and night. You call over there, and they watch TV while you're trying to talk to them on the phone. They interrupt the conversation to laugh at a commercial or exclaim about a story. Now *that* was too much TV.

Or take the Trekkies. We met some of them at Universal Studios in L.A., lined up hours ahead of time at their Mecca, the Star Trek attraction. Hundreds of video-taped episodes at home on their shelves. Veterans of umpteen Trekkie conventions.

They reminded me of a skit William Shatner (Captain Kirk) did on "Saturday Night Live" as a gentle rebuke to their watchful affection. He was fielding questions like these from a Trekkie convention audience sprinkled with Star Fleet uniforms and Spock ears.

"Captain Kirk, Captain Kirk, in episode number twenty-four, "The Hidden Planet," didn't the Klingons wear their sashes on the wrong side?"

Shatner shrugged. "Well . . . I really don't . . ."

"Captain Kirk! How many crew cabins did the *Enterprise* actually have?"

Blank look. Exasperated, Shatner responded, "Before I answer any more questions—having received all of your letters over the years and—I've spoken to many of you. . . . Some of you have traveled hundreds of miles to be here. I'd just like to say, 'Get a life, will you people?' For crying out loud, it's just a TV show! You've turned an enjoyable little job I did as a lark into a colossal waste of time!"

Alas, poor Trekkies. Now *that's* excessive. I laughed with the audience.

GETTING A LIFE

Zach is sixteen at the time of this writing. I am . . . also older. So far I've watched three hours of TV this week, two with the family and one while Zach and Jack were scanning the Internet locating articles for Zach's biology report. Twenty-plus hours down to under five—that's pretty typical. What has happened? How did I come to give up my part-time job?

To oversimplify, I "got a life." I started by making choices to move back into my area of gifting (teaching), first at the community college and then in women's ministry. At about the same time Mary, my media-mate down the block, accepted the role of leader of a large women's Bible study.

It's not that we took the twenty-plus hours a week and suddenly invested them all in ministry. Rather, once our lives began to fill with more meaning, purpose, and joy in using our gifts in ministry to others, the old habit patterns broke down. The change whetted an appetite for more creativity, more communication, more experiencing, more *real life.* Our emotional bond with TV lapsed as our interests refocused on ministry and family. It also helped that my health has improved over the last five years. It's hard to engage more people and activities and use more creative energies when in pain.

When I was first writing up this material for my class notes, I called Mary and asked her for her thoughts on her waning involvement with TV. "It's as if we've grown apart," she reflected. "I have new priorities of ministry and people. And in the meanwhile, the content of TV has gotten worse and worse."

As I've prepared for my teaching on this topic, I feel like the teacher who has learned more than her students. And I've been struck by this quote from Quentin Schultz (*World*, 3/13/93): "Christians should be more concerned about the loss of time spent watching TV than the content of shows. . . . [They] negate their God-given role to communicate with others when they are stuck in front of the tube. The Christian community loves to blast all the secular humanists in

Hollywood, but a lot of that anger is there because we don't have our own houses in order."

God made us to find great meaning and fulfillment in communication and the imagination, the beauty of art and culture. But we're getting soft. It's easier to flop and click than to talk, phone, or write. It's easier to surf and scan and just stare at "whatever's on" than to sift, evaluate, seek out the good and the beautiful, and say no to our children.

Most of us struggle with TV-induced inertia. But if after careful, prayerful consideration, we realize that our family leisure time is dominated by the tube or other electronic a-musement (lack of thinking), then it's time to consider the ant: "O sluggard." Get up. Be social. Enjoy the outdoors. Go for a walk. Dial up a friend. Discover a gourmet coffee bar. Break the hypnotic spell of the teasers that hook you into the next program and the next. (See Focus Box #22.)

The book of Proverbs often associates laziness with poverty. This holds true for poverty of income as well as our "poverty of values," Dan Quayle's coined phrase. "The sluggard buries her behind in the couch; she is too lazy to open her mouth (and communicate)" Proverbs 26:16 (Arrington Substandard Version). Communication, the *essence* of relationships, can be largely ceded to the tube, or it can be encouraged by wise parents who make the effort to turn TV off and talk with their children.

Is it any coincidence that TV consumption differs greatly from affluent to low-income homes? "Various data, including [a] recent *New York Times* (5/96) survey, indicate that the children in the most affluent homes may be the ones spending the least time on television of any sort," reports Geraldine Fabrikant. And Quentin Schultz summarized what his wife had observed as a home-health nurse: "Especially in lower-income neighborhoods, the media blast away all day long, diverting attention away from parent-child relationships . . ." (*Winning Your Kids Back from the Media,* p. 129). Our Angel Tree Christmas gift distributors to children of prisoners noted the same trend at our follow-up meeting this year. In many of these struggling families' homes, the TVs blared loudly during our entire visits, and no one offered to turn them down. Communication was difficult.

As I consider my weaning from TV, I gratefully acknowledge that God was at work wooing me gently to a richer life. The pursuit of leisure is most decidedly a free-market enterprise. With the available free time we tend to choose to do what we most enjoy (that we can afford). Getting ourselves to enjoy electronic media less and other kinds of leisure more is a major challenge. Sometimes we have to decide that this is the right thing to do and trust God to enable our heart to follow our head.

Beyond the stewardship of our time, media consumption greatly affects the stewardship of our imagination. It has been said that our imagination is profoundly connected to our hearts and our will. Our children's imagination can fire their hearts with a vision of the richer life to pursue God and the beauty of His kingdom, or it can inspire them to turn their hearts away from Him to pursue "the kingdoms of the world and all their splendor." Satan tempted Jesus with that kind of vision (Matthew 4:8). You can bet he's milking the media to tempt our children and us in the same way.

FOCUS YOUR WORLDVIEW #22: NUMBERING YOUR MEDIA DAYS

When David struggled with perspective on his circumstances and his battles, he would ask God to teach him to number his days and show him how fleeting were his life and times (Psalm 39). We can also get a perspective on our struggle to control media use if we start by numbering our days and hours.

Prepare a one-week time sheet to put by each major media component in your home (TVs, stereos, computer, even car radio). You could call it the "(Your name) Family Ratings Sheet." List each person's name who would use that component across the top and the days of the week down the side. Ask each person to track carefully his or her media use. (Time in, out, and what was watched, listened to, played, etc.) Check the charts daily and follow up to make sure they're being used.

At the end of a week, analyze your media use. (Let the computer users put it on a spread sheet and really figure lots of statistics.) You could even put in some fun categories—most (and least) popular component, biggest (and least) user, most popular time frames or days, etc. Or just compile a few simple statistics.

Meanwhile, you keep a chart of how much time the family spends in good communication together. This is much more elusive, but you can estimate time each night as you reflect on the day.

Share all the results with the family. Compare media time with "face time" with family. (Quentin Schultz recommends a three-to-one ratio face to media.)

Prayerfully consider any adjustments that you may want to make. (Lord, is there a balance here? Is communication down and media up? Are my kids on media auto-pilot? What do You desire for my family?) (Also see chapter 12.)

LAUGHING AT MR. LOOPY

"Just because I watch *Bridges of Madison County/Birdcage* doesn't mean I'm going to have an affair/become a homosexual." Many Christian moms and older children acknowledge the immoral or progressive bent of much of today's media, but we fall into the trap of thinking that it has no effect on us. We may not see media-influenced behavior in our children. But we can't see the monumental effect on the inner person—how the media affects our imagination.

Like most responsible people, we are well aware of the gratuitous sex and violence, crude language, and coarse behavior common in the media. Orthodox and progressives alike regularly engage in media-bashing. In her inimitable style, Reagan/Bush speechwriter Peggy Noonan gently chides: ". . . the Ghetto Boys on channel 25, rapping about killing women, having sex with their dead bodies and cutting off their breasts. Really, you have to be a moral retard not to know that this is harmful, that it damages the young, the unsteady, the unfinished. You have to not care about anyone to sing these words and put this song on TV for money. You have to be a pig" (*Life, Liberty, and the Pursuit of Happiness*, p. 65).

Kids know this stuff is toxic to their imaginations and their hearts. A large majority of them (ages ten to sixteen) told the advocacy group Children Now that TV encourages them to lie, be disrespectful to parents, become more aggressive and violent, and engage in sexual activity too soon. The same survey said that 54 percent had TVs in their bedrooms where they tend to watch what they like in private (*World*, 6/17/95).

If you're clueless or doubtful as to how bad it is, check *Learn to Discern* in Resource Box #9. Most concerned Christian moms are steering their children away from MTV, soap operas, and talk shows. We realize how they epitomize the truth of *Time* magazine's assessment that "in American TV, a spirit only modestly gifted and sometimes flat stupid—sits at the wheel of a trillion-dollar vehicle. That vehicle has a tendency to veer toward the ditch, seeking the lowest common denominator."

But there are other kinds of programming we need to thoughtfully consider. What about the rise of infotainment? Watergate-buster Carl Bernstein wrote in the liberal *New Republic,* "For more than fifteen years we have been moving away from real journalism toward the creation of a sleazoid infotainment culture in which the lines between Oprah and Phil and Geraldo and Tom and even Ted . . . are too often indistinguishable."

He describes a media genre and a culture where the "trivial is significant," the "lurid and the loopy are more important than real news," and he rebukes fellow journalists who "pander" to viewers who, "sadly, seem to justify our condescension, and to kindle at the trash." He believes that journalists are creating "the idiot culture. Not an idiot subculture, which every society has bubbling beneath the surface," but one where the "stupid and the coarse are becoming our cultural norm, even our cultural ideal" (p. 25).

Whether we absorb it through infotainment, sit-coms, drama, or movies, we are all witnesses to the process of desensitization to sex and violence, the "lurid and the loopy," that often begins when one pervert or "expert" hits the news. A "scholarly" debate about Mr. Loopy begins on *Nightline* and is followed up by Loopy's guest appearance on the talk-show circuit. Here audience shock gives way to scolding, although a few nonconformist souls stand to Loopy's defense. In less than a year, Loopy's story is made into a TV movie of the week, and the next TV season features several "must-see" sit-coms with Loopy look-alikes, and everyone laughs at them. Through humor they endear themselves to us. What was loopy is just another average lifestyle. What's average is normal. What's normal is acceptable. Long live Loopy!

How did we get to the point where TV's "family hour" is filled with "smirk and smut" comedies with so many "big boob" and "hooter" jokes that our local newspaper TV critic lost count? As media expert Al Menconi puts it, "One television show at a time." How did the Ghetto Boys music video wind up in the heavy rotation in channel 25? One music video at a time. How have my own standards for what I'll watch or what I find shocking declined? One movie at a time. That's why drawing the line at *Birdcage* and *Bridges* to me is important. I know I'm on the Loopy downward spiral, and at some point, before God, I have to get off.

I may not watch *Bridges* and then go out and have an affair, or *Birdcage* and embark on a homosexual escapade. But exposure to vivid, tender images that I never thought of before can have a strong, quiet impact on my imagination.

TECHNICOLOR VISIONS OF GREENER GRASS

Media images are so strong because, through the power of our imagination, we begin to *identify* with the images. I remember Zach "flying" around when he was little in his Superman pajamas. No doubt about it, he did not fly and leap around like that when he wore his other pj's.

As we get older, we observe certain boundaries on our behavior, and our imagination goes inward. Flying and leaping are no longer cool, but Zach's imagination is still greatly stirred by the books he reads and movies he watches. I see the influence occasionally in the way he acts, the cartoons he draws, stories he writes, or videos he films, but mostly I think it ranges around in the private spaces of his thoughts and feelings. It is the same for us; and if our private spaces are at all empty, unfilled by intimacy with God or with our husbands, the media's vivid images of romantic fantasy are gladly offered as a substitute.

There may be physical boundaries that we would never dare cross, but movies like *The Bridges of Madison County* can inspire us to gaze longingly over the fence. I read one reviewer complimenting Meryl Streep for making "completely clear" what's driving the Iowa farm wife. Portraying a character that feels "invisible and uncherished" and longs for true intimacy, Streep "details each step in the progression by which her character's attraction to the photographer [Clint Eastwood] turns from the *idea* of him, to the physical reality of him, and ultimately to the necessity of him" (*Houston Chronicle*, 6/2/95).

Sounds a bit like Eve in the garden, doesn't it? The idea, the appeal of the reality, the desire, the necessity, and then sin and death—only the movies never show that part (James 1:15). Spurred by a movie or a book, our imagination can paint the idea in a technicolor vision of reality. That vision can lead to emotional involvement. For the record, huge numbers of American women get emotionally involved with romantic fantasy novels to the tune of $885 million a year. The genre is also growing in Christian bookstores.

What does it mean? A little relaxation in the bathtub at the end of a weary day? (Harlequin, take me away!) Or at some point does it become what Professor Roberts in chapter 10 called the "frustrated gratification" of our titillated appetite—in this case, for intimacy rather than greed? I suppose our response hinges on how well the story engages our imagination. How much do we *identify* with it and get emotionally involved in it? Do the *ideas* lead to thoughts about and attraction to the physical reality of other men?

Whether it's a romantic fantasy or a real live other man besides our spouse, do we tolerate a developing emotional attraction? Do we savor it? If it's a fantasy, do we indulge in daydreams? If it's a real person, do we begin to make slight changes in our dress or schedule to encourage it?

We may take comfort in the secure belief that we would never cross the line and do anything about it. Question: What's worse? *Emotional* involvement with someone besides our husband, or *physical* involvement with someone else?

Let me ask you. Reverse roles. What would hurt you more? If your husband had a one-night stand with another woman, or if he had a deep affair of the heart with her—spending lots of time alone, verbally expressing his affection, becoming her main pillar of support?

As I have posed this question to many women in my classes, all agree that the affair of the heart would be much more painful. The emotional involvement threatens as a great betrayal. And yet we cross that line so much more easily than the physical line. It's so . . . private.

Not really. "Before a word is on my tongue you know it completely, O Lord" (Psalm 139:4). And while we focus on outward appearance and action, God looks on our hearts. Jesus strongly cautioned us against the "adultery in the heart" (Matthew 5:28).

The movie *Camelot* is a powerful portrayal of unlooked-for desire nurtured as a secret longing and then exploding into a passionate affair. Early on King Arthur sees the sparks fly between Lancelot and Guinevere and cries out in pain, "Be it sin, or be it not sin, I can see it in their eyes, and that's far sin enough!"

If Lancelot had done the right thing, he would have left the court before intermission (but then there would have been no movie). Our family generally avoids films where the plot is driven by adultery. But Zach and I talked about the power of desire portrayed in *Camelot* and its consequences. Three lives were destroyed, as was the Round Table and everything they had worked to build.

It is very difficult to hold marriages together and be faithful in these times. The media is a big reason why. A friend and fellow pastor burst out of his office a few weeks ago and vented to a staffer, "If I hear of one more marriage on the rocks, I'm going to explode!" No Christian I know has ever purposed to become involved in an extramarital affair. People take small, incremental steps—dreaming the dream, savoring the smile. They ignore the red flags, then the stop signs, and, as pastor and friend Joe Wall put it, "When they finally see the red light, they discover they have no brakes."

For us as Christians, it's not likely that we or our children will be persuaded logically that the Bible is a lie and our faith worthless. It's much more likely that Satan will derail us spiritually and invalidate our message and potential to minister to others by seducing us morally. This was his very effective strategy with the nation of Israel (see Bible Study #11), and today he uses the media to full advantage in his schemes. "Above all else, *guard your heart,* for it is the wellspring of life" [italics mine] (Proverbs 4:23).

The evidence is pretty clear that the media touches a woman's imagination most deeply through the vision of romantic fantasy.

When it comes to our children, it offers a vision of identity and attitude that also requires some serious heart-guarding.

PLASTIC FEMALE, HE-MAN, AND MAJOR ATTITUDE

The media packs a strong cultural message for our daughters: "You are what you look like," and "The Babelicious gets the guys." This message is amplified into a monolithic assault on their fragile, developing identity. The cultural ideal of the "plastic female," as Quentin Schultz calls it, finding meaning and intimacy by tumbling into bed is a complete fiction found only in the media. But the high anxiety it produces in young girls who feel they never quite measure up, and the not-too-subtle pressure to "find a guy" that it generates in the preteen and teen culture are felt in every home.

If the media's cultural ideal for girls is the "plastic female," then for boys, "male identity is patterned after power, what I call the 'butt-kicking he-man' . . . who takes authority by lording it over others," writes Schultz (*Winning Your Kids Back from the Media*, p.148). What could be further from the biblical manly ideal of servant-leadership, of the male crown of authority in his family—a crown of thorns—than the football-spiking, body-slamming, beer-guzzling, stage-strutting "manly men" who populate the media? If so many of our boys want to be sports stars and rock stars, it just means they *do* get it. They get the media message of young male identity loud and clear.

Plastic female, he-man, sports and rock stars—most of these media icons inspire our nation's children to copy their exploits *and* their attitudes. Our own children may not be acting out the more aggressive sexual or violent behaviors so prevalent in the media, but what about the "attitude"? The sassy, mocking, know-it-all, authority-defying Roseanne/Bart Simpson/"Dear God, we bought all this food ourselves, so thanks for nothing" attitude? Don't you love it when you see it glorified on TV and then turn around and see it in your children?

"Casual cruelty, knowing sex. Nothing could be better designed to rob youth of its most ephemeral gift: innocence," muses columnist Charles Krauthammer. "The ultimate effect of our mass culture is to make children older than their years, to turn them into the knowing, cynical, pseudoadult that is by now the model kid of the TV sit-com" (*Houston Chronicle*, 7/92).

It is only a few short steps from the cynical, sassy "attitude" of the sit-coms to the rage and despair of so much popular music. And it's little wonder that so many teens identify with it, considering the built-in frustration of trying to find meaning and real personal value in the plastic female and he-man media ideals. Nowhere is our postmodern crisis of meaning more apparent than in the sad tunes and lyrics booming from boxes, splashed across clothing, and hanging on bed-room walls across America.

> *Your God is dead, and no one cares.*
> *If there's a hell, I'll see you there.*
> —*Nine Inch Nails*

> *Emptiness is loneliness,*
> *and loneliness is cleanliness,*
> *And cleanliness is godliness,*
> *and God is empty just like me.*
> —*Smashing Pumpkins*

The postmodern movies that dazzle with style and image (forget the substance and content) give us violence with a wink and a smile (*Natural Born Killers, Pulp Fiction*) and plots that float in midair, full of gaps, holes, and reasons (*Mission Impossible*).

We need to *assume* that the media is massaging our imagination and that of our children in the hidden nooks and crannies of our minds and hearts. *Take the media very seriously.* One cautionary word before we continue: Don't suddenly get overwhelmed and start ripping posters off the wall and trashing Nine Inch Nails CDs. Remember, as Al Menconi says, that teens often view an attack on their media choices as a personal attack, since they may identify closely with their choices. If you decide to try to effect change, come alongside your teen, focusing on loving communication, especially listening. And get some good advice. If you'd like some recommendations of thoughtful, helpful resources to help you sort through the teen media culture, check Resource Box #9.

RESOURCE BOX #9: TUNING IN TO THE MEDIA

For me, the key to finding good media advice has been finding someone I could trust—someone who shares my definition of "coarse" and "crude," yet who eschews sensationalism and parent-teen polarization, and who really seeks to understand the heart and needs behind the media choices.

GENERAL (TV, MOVIES, MUSIC, INTERNET)

Winning Your Kids Back from the Media, Quentin Schultz, InterVarsity Press, 1994. Great emphasis on developing communication, offsetting the negative with the positive.

Learn to Discern, Robert DeMoss, Jr., Zondervan, 1992. A shocking wake-up call to parents with their heads in the sand, but less information about working with teenagers over choices.

MAINLY MUSIC

Staying in Tune, Al Menconi, Standard Publishing, 1996. A reworked edition of *Today's Music: A Window to Your Child's Soul.* The best, especially if your child is already into the music scene, and you have concerns.

It's All Rock 'n Roll to Me, Dave Hart. Profiles of today's top rock stars from a Christian perspective. Available from Al Menconi Ministries, 800-78-MUSIC.

Menconi's 900 Line. Recorded profiles of many of today's most controversial secular artists. Updated monthly. 1-900-872-1717.

MONTHLY REVIEWS

Most of these will send a sample upon request.

Plugged In, Focus on the Family. News and reviews. 1-800-A-FAMILY.

Media Update, Al Menconi Ministries. (Bimonthly) News, reviews. Focus on secular and Christian music (8 pp.). 1-800-78-MUSIC.

Preview, The Family Movie & TV Review, 1309 Seminole, Richardson, TX 75080. Rates both artistic content and acceptability.

Ted Baehr's Movie Guide, bimonthly reviews of major new releases, subscription 1-800-899-6684. Latest reviews available on recorded phone message 1-900-234-2344.

In addition to influencing the stewardship of our time and our imagination, there's one more way the media subtly affects our inner person. The electronic media exerts a profound conditioning effect upon us—and upon our children even more so.

"EVERYBODY'S HAPPY NOW"

In Aldous Huxley's *Brave New World,* a utopian vision of the world at peace is finally achieved by massive totalitarian conditioning programs. Engineers genetically breed different castes of workers in bottles, tailoring them to perform at various skill levels needed for a prosperous economy. These workers are then propagandized by subliminal slogans whispered in their sleep. In their off-hours they pursue pleasure. No sexual desire is denied ("everybody belongs to everybody else"); evenings and weekends are a blur of "obstacle Golf," "synthetic music" clubs, and the "feelies"; and, to quench any lingering dissatisfaction or aggravation, everyone is supplied with a steady ration of a feel-good drug with no aftereffects—"soma."

Reading the book aloud on our vacation last year (yes, we read as a family with teenager and friend!), we were impressed with the parallels to the increasing pleasure-seeking bent of our own times. When we read the part about the "feelies," the theater where every viewer actually *feels* the kiss on the lips, the bearskin rug, the conk on the head, and the wild helicopter ride, we were reminded of our last vacation to Disneyland and Universal Studios—the Virtual Reality sensation of the *Star Wars* and *Back to the Future* rides. "The 'feelies,' the 'feelies,'" we laughed.

I've read that the top of the pyramid-shaped Luxor hotel in Las Vegas is a similar 3-D cinerama, and the entire floor pitches and rocks. Guests emerge from these experiences thrilled and awed. The advancement of computer technology is Genesis 11:6 come true. We seem to have overcome the confusion of languages at Babel, and now, reunited with a binary computer language, everything we can imagine we *will* be able to do. But what happens to us in the process—to our minds, our hearts, our affections?

Have you ever looked at a copy of *WIRED?* This premier magazine of the Information Age is published by people who have been conditioned to absorb information in a way that makes me feel absolutely antique. "Golly, Margaret! Look at that fancy cover and them pictures of all those celebrities!" Processed in contrasting hues of gold and fuchsia, indigo and fluorescent green, or orange and red, they look, well . . . different. The table of contents is physically arranged in a spiral. The departments include "Rants & Raves" (letters to the editor), "Geek Page" (technology update, I think), "Fetish" (new gadgets), and "Deductible Junkets" (travel). Slick advertisements and features arrest, shock, and titillate: a computer seamlessly inserted in an impressionist painting, a bald head with Medusan snakes writhing out of the mouth, and barracudas cruising through a deserted subway station. An ad for a conference on computer graphics reads, "imagine it. do it. celebrate it."

Perusing many of the articles, I feel like Einstein's wife: "I understand all the words. I just don't know what they mean." What I do understand seems ominous and troubling, like Dickens's Ghost of Christmas Future.

". . . people involved with high tech are frequently more inquisitive, more open to new experiences, and right now the cutting edge of new experience is transgender."

Oh wow. And while that glimpse of cyberscape seems so out there and remote, here's one closer to home.

"My three-year-old son, Gavin, learned about computer interactivity by passive participation in action-packed games like Marathon and Doom. Potential psychological effects aside, his taste in CD-ROM entertainment stretches far beyond his years. When he hits a key or clicks the mouse, he expects *something exciting to happen*. Flimsy electronic storybooks won't satisfy this boy" [italics mine].

What about picture books? What about the Bible? Can the miracles of Jesus compare with the magic of CD-ROM or even Aladdin's blue genie?

As Sven Birkerts points out in the *Gutenberg Elegies,* it's not just that you take your kids to see *Beauty and the Beast* these days. You see it several times in the theater, buy the book, read it endlessly as you play the sound track tape "until the emulsion [wears] thin." Then there's the lunch box, underpants, teapot set, Burger King toys, and finally at Christmas . . . (drumroll, please) . . . the video! Potential for hundreds more viewings. Our children live in an "entertainment environment," writes Birkerts, that reinforces the "tyranny of the movie."

Good phrase, that. It aptly describes my son's enthusiasm for the summer blockbuster season now upon us. This child, who is continually surprised by the due dates for homework and tests, has memorized the release dates of the summer's hottest hits. A TV commercial for *Dragonheart* prompts a spontaneous "we're not worthy" kneeling homage—tyranny indeed.

I clutch with Birkerts and join him in wondering, "what tale or rhyme or private fantasy will be able to compete with the high-powered rendition from Hollywood's top talents?" (p. 29). It shapes not only our children's imagination, but the very way they process information. The threshold for what gets their attention and holds it is getting higher and higher. The quaint special effects employed for God to inscribe the Ten Commandments or part the Red Sea pale in comparison to the flight of our *Back to the Future* virtual DeLorean ride or the seventy-five-foot-tall Stadium Theater experience of *Twister*. What if the little Gavins of the world enter a classroom, open a book, or listen to a Sunday school lesson where nothing "exciting" happens? What are the "potential psychological effects" that his proud father brushed aside?

Birkerts lists a few from a purely secular perspective:

- "impression and image take precedence over logic and concept"—electronic telecommunications are the perfect postmodern medium.

- "reduced attention span and general impatience with sustained inquiry"—we see it every day.

- "language erosion"—computer-speak is short on wit, irony, and nuance.

- "flattening of historical perspective"—history will appear as a body of data floating in cyberspace or a "mythology" constructed by movie producers and other dream merchants.

Birkerts's core fear: that "the more complex and sophisticated our systems of lateral access (from channel-surfing to net-cruising) *the more we sacrifice in the way of depth* . . . that we are, as a culture, as a species, becoming shallower . . . that we are giving up on wisdom [italics mine]" (p. 228). Echoing his concern, Os Guinness (*The American Hour,* p. 301) writes, "Inundated by a flood of vivid but uninterpreted images from the instant-everywhere, [many Americans] are overloaded with facts but starved of understanding." (See Focus Box #23.)

The irony of our newly conditioned species: In Huxley's *Brave New World*, the totalitarian government did it to the people. In our Brave New World, the massive conditioning program is self-administered—we do it to ourselves.

What are the spiritual implications of Birkerts's list? We Christians are people of the Book. "In the beginning was the Word." Our faith is built on words, logic, and concepts—"precept upon precept." Our knowledge of God depends on our understanding of His revelation through a rich vocabulary of poetry, figurative language, paradox, irony, and subtlety. A historical perspective on our faith is essential. Most of the Bible is written as historical narrative. The connections fostered through the Internet are no substitute for the community of believers. Think of it. God designed us for deep intimacy with Him, our spouses, our family, our church. He has called us to patiently mine the depth of His Word and seek out its riches.

"Wisdom cries out in the street," but we and our children can get caught up cruising through life in the shallows of the great leisure pursuit of pleasure, and give up on listening to her. "Besides," whispers the conditioning voice of our Brave New Electronic World, "everybody's happy now."

FOCUS YOUR WORLDVIEW #23: TRADING DEPTH FOR BREADTH

One way to visualize how the Information Age has changed our lives is to look back at a slice of life when experience was deeper—when one read and reread the same books, lived in a smaller setting and knew the place and the people deeply and well, when time was plentiful but moved more slowly, and the arrival of a letter or a person was a great event.

Two suggestions of movies to rent: *Babette's Feast* (with subtitles). You'll really have to slow down to watch it, but it's a wonderful movie, where the last scene is worth the wait. Makes a beautiful statement about the heart of the artist. Also, *Sense and Sensibility*— not quite as slow, but makes a similar point.

Talking points:

➤ Give examples of how people's lives focused on relationships.

➤ Notice the context of work in which many scenes took place.

➤ Review the ways their lives were characterized by depth. How were their lives different from ours?

➤ Do you think they were more bored or less bored than we are today?

➤ What does the movie also say about the stewardship of the gifts the Lord has given us and our children?

➤ How can we consciously seek to have more depth in our lives?

CHEERING OUR CHILDREN ON TO A RICHER LIFE

My purpose in writing this chapter and the next is to help and encourage moms struggling to navigate the white water of our "entertainment environment." I've discussed the need to go against the cultural flow because it's easier to drift. Our children are quite naturally enthralled with it, and some of its deepest effects are subtle and incremental. Sometimes we don't realize how subtle until the late teen years when their wardrobe turns black, they want lots of candles in their room, and they visit us in our world only occasionally.

Against the technicolor-digital-sound-dream machine and music-trax of America's youth culture, you and I stand with our relationship, our example, and our Bibles, trying to balance the entertainment media's influence on our children's hearts and minds. We tire of "whacking," of the endless confrontations with our children over the pull of the media.

Feeling overwhelmed? Take heart. Beside the power of God to change hearts and lives, the entertainment culture pales in comparison. And God has given us great power to influence our children with "just" our relationship, our example, and our Bibles. "For God did not give us a spirit of timidity, but a spirit of power, of love and of self-discipline" (2 Timothy 1:7). All of which we can creatively apply to the way our family spends our leisure time. How? In the next chapter we'll get specific.

"A Time to Laugh . . . Dance . . . and Be Silent"

12

Leisure and the
Richer Life

SOLOMON FIGURED THAT THERE REALLY WAS A TIME FOR everything—including leisure (Ecclesiastes 3). Laughing and dancing were high on his list. The challenge to us is to offer our children creative, enjoyable choices for leisure time that help them shake off the hypno-passivity of surfing, scanning, and viewing.

By default or on purpose, we help them set the patterns for use of leisure time. We may encourage reading, sports, music, an interest in animals, or gardening. We also buy TV sets, Nintendos, and computers and install them in our homes with our seeming blessing.

As they live with our leisure choices and begin to make their own, they need to see us not as security agents who guard the McGuffin (Alfred Hitchcock's famous nickname for the thing everybody wants), but as cheerleaders for the richer life. Our approach should be positive and proactive, leading our children to better choices.

One of the greatest gifts we can give our children is a love for a good story. The great art of good stories makes a strong impact on our imaginations. Truth blazes to life in the context of well-crafted fantasy or realistic narrative. We've already discussed the importance of story in our worldview—how as Christians we can see our lives as part of God's Grand Story. In my Focus Boxes I have used a lot of stories because art has such power. It is one thing to *talk* about the redeeming value of suffering and caregiving. It is so much more compelling to see the *story* of the Elephant Man, to be moved to tears by the beauty of his soul despite such tremendous abuse, to feel his anger echo in our hearts as he cries out, "I am not an animal!"

Perhaps the greatest reason for our cultural decline is that the Devil really does have "all the good music." Not really, but he has far too great a market share of the well-crafted TV shows, movies, and books. Commenting on this, Terry Glaspey has written, "In general, the Christian vision which most believers project today fails to effectively engage the imagination of our culture" (_Children of a Greater God_, p. 23). Glaspey notes that C. S. Lewis, George MacDonald, and J. R. R. Tolkien are renowned as such powerful authors because they knew how to imaginatively portray the power and fascination of goodness. Good stories are out there, and they can do wonderful things for our children. We can spark their imagination in the right direction and counterbalance the conditioning effect of electronic media by introducing them to the richer life reflected in great literature.

CHILDREN DO NOT LIKE TWADDLE

I owe a great debt to Susan Schaeffer Macaulay, whose book _For the Children's Sake_ I read when Zach was quite young. From the pages of that book, I caught a vision for challenging Zach's mind and spirit. That vision has already born fruit in his life, as well as in mine. Macaulay makes a case for feeding young minds the best food for thought we can find. "Children don't like twaddle," she observed; we tend to underestimate their interest and ability to learn.

So we have taken some of our family times to nurture Zach's imagination and teach him to _think_ with materials composed by great minds. Let me share some of the works we pursued. To supplement Zach's grade school curriculum, I ordered _Open Court Readers_. For kindergarten to sixth grade, they have age-appropriate stories from great writers—Aesop, Tolstoy, Dickens, etc. (This was just to enjoy; we did not home-school.) We traveled to Narnia regularly for years with C. S. Lewis's wonderful, magical books.

From first grade on, we have read classic children's novels together. We started with _Treasure Island_. Zach loved it so much that it turned out to be a pirate year. On our Disneyworld vacation, we stocked up on paraphernalia at Pirates of the Caribbean. We had a pirate

Halloween and even a pirate birthday party complete with treasure hunt, skull-and-crossbones cake, and invitations composed on photocopies of the book's inside cover. Scribner & Sons has a wonderful series of adventure novels, illustrated by N. C. Wyeth, that we have collected and will pass on to Zach's children, Lord willing.

We picked up *Shakespeare Stories* by Leon Garfield, a wonderful simplified version of our greatest playwright's histories, tragedies, and comedies. The original characters and plot are retained along with the most famous quotes and scenes. Zach loved it and read most of it on his own. Inspired by such a good beginning, he has picked out some great videos to bring home: Mel Gibson in *Hamlet*, Kenneth Branagh in *Much Ado About Nothing*. Last year for a class project, he wrote his own version of *Romeo and Juliet* and recruited a large cast of friends to film it.

As Zach has gotten older, we've read aloud Orwell's *Animal Farm,* a wonderful parable that shines the light of truth on the lies of communism. We also read aloud (after I edited out some scenes with Winston and his lover) Orwell's *1984*, a timely book on the manipulation and deceit of an all-powerful central government—the ultimate exercise in political correctness.

I realize that these suggestions may not interest a lot of moms or their children. Other families may be more into sports or camping or gardening or raising animals. But if you could only make one effort in this direction, Bill Bennett's *Book of Virtues* is a capsuled version of all the resources mentioned already. If you'd like to start somewhere in the fight against "twaddle," start here. (See Resource Box #10.)

RESOURCE BOX #10: SOME GREAT
READING LISTS AND COLLECTIONS

Perhaps, like me, you were raised in a home where parents read aloud to you a few good books early on, but you'd really like to do more. Or perhaps you're such a novice at this that you think Aslan is the name of a dam on the Nile River. The following resources provide great suggestions for children of all ages.

The Book of Virtues, William J. Bennett, Simon & Schuster, 1993. Excerpts from the best of Western literature combined with some "fun" reading on the ten virtues: self-discipline, compassion, courage, honesty, and others. Material arranged from easy to more difficult in each virtue section. Also, a sequel, *The Moral Compass,* 1996, and the *Book of Virtues for Young People.*

Children of a Greater God, Terry Glaspey, Harvest House, 1995.

Cultural Literacy: What Every American Needs to Know, E. D. Hirsch, Vintage Books, 1988. "Includes 5,000 essential names, phrases, dates, and concepts." Also *What Your Kindergartner Needs to Know . . . First Grader . . .* and on through sixth grade. An easily accessible curriculum for K-6 in cultural literacy. (Great for trips!)

For the Children's Sake, Susan Schaeffer Macaulay, Crossway Books, 1984. A wonderful case for challenging our children's minds and spirits together. On pp. 33-34, she gives a short list of recommended books.

Great Books of the Christian Tradition, Terry Glaspey, Harvest House, 1996. A book that is one, long, wonderful annotated list—over 500 entries.

Honey for a Child's Heart, Gladys Hunt, Zondervan, 1969.

Open Court Readers. For beginning and low elementary children, these readers put Dick, Jane, and Spot to shame, focusing instead on stories from the Bible, Aesop, Brothers Grimm, biographies, folk tales, Laura Ingalls Wilder, and much more. 888-772-4543.

The Read-Aloud Handbook, Jim Trelease, Penguin Books, 1982. A detailed guide to over 300 great read-aloud books.

Reissued Classics Series, illustrated by N. C. Wyeth, Charles Scribner's Sons. Beautiful hard-bound family heirloom series of books, including titles such as *Treasure Island, Robinson Crusoe, Robin Hood, Twenty Thousand Leagues Under the Sea.* Especially good for boys.

Shakespeare Stories, Leon Garfield, and awesomely illustrated by Michael Foreman, Houghton Mifflin Company, 1985. Much original dialogue and helpful narrative summaries and transitions. Makes these great plots and characters come *alive.*

STEERING OUT OF THE SHALLOWS

We live in the information age, and our children will grow up absolutely bombarded with words and information. They will be pulled toward the muddy shallows and cajoled to paddle there contentedly, dazzled by images that stroke their *feelings*. They need to be steered back into the clear, swift current where the whirlpools and rapids of ideas must be navigated by a well-disciplined sense of truth and direction.

As we discussed earlier, we are people of the Book. Our walk with God is founded upon knowing and understanding God's Word—the verses, the principles, the applications. It is essential to our children's spiritual health to be able to think critically and deeply, to figure out what is true and what is a lie. Through family devotions and being nudged into Bible study on their own, hopefully we can lead them to wrestle with what Scripture means and what it means to us—an introduction to "sustained inquiry." Additionally, reading great literature can help our children begin to acquire those skills. Here's how:

1. *Vocabulary*. Words are the vehicles that express our ideas. Great literature, including Scripture, uses a vocabulary that stretches and deepens our understanding of the world around us. Our thoughts go higher and deeper because we have the tools to express and understand greater thoughts.

2. *Attentiveness and Imagination*. We have to work to get into the context of a book, especially older books. And often we have to sustain our attention for hundreds of pages of typed words with nothing to hook us but the power of our imagination constantly interacting with the text. At every word, phrase, and sentence, our imagination must "flesh out" the concepts keyed by the text. Great exercise!

3. *Truth in Action*. Great literature shows what goodness and evil look like—the consequences of pursuing one course of action over the other. Scenes in *Kidnapped* and *Les Miserables* illustrate the blessing of forgiveness on a profound level. These scenes awaken what Glaspey calls your child's "moral imagination." They communicate a vision for doing the right thing beyond rules, beyond duty, because they reveal the power, beauty, and delight of doing right in an imaginative story.

4. *Cultural Literacy*. E. D. Hirsch's best-selling book by this name

emphasizes how deeply our communication is enriched by shared knowledge of our rich cultural heritage. He tells about the ill-fated invasion of Dunkirk where Allied troops pinned down on French beaches sent a desperate SOS for every boat available in England to help evacuate them. The appeal for help ended with, "And if not . . ." This reference to Daniel 3:18 communicated their imminent danger and their commitment to serve 'til death if deliverance was not found, just as Shadrach, Meshach, and Abednego vowed to serve God despite the fiery furnace. Their eloquent appeal, easily understood by their culturally literate countrymen, touched so many hearts that every boat available on England's south shore sailed to the rescue. Hirsch has constructed a core curriculum of cultural literacy for grades K-6. (See Resource Box #10.)

5. *Broadened Horizons.* Great literature paints the reality of people and places far beyond our own experience in living color. It enlarges our understanding of different cultures, times, and worldviews. It puts us inside another's shoes so that we see life from another's perspective and develop more empathy for someone quite different from ourselves. Our communications and relationships are enhanced. Movies and TV can do this, too, but not in the depth or detail of classic books; and too often newer versions do so from a politically correct point of view.

6. *Christian Cultural Identity.* Reading Christian classics, in particular, has its own rewards. As Glaspey points out, discovering the depth of our tradition gives us roots, fights against the flattening of our historical perspective, reveals the victories, struggles, and desire for God that we have in common with those who have gone before us. At the same time, it brings the sweep and drama of God's Grand Story to life and helps us to appreciate the multicultural and diverse body of Christ.

7. *Cultural Curiosity.* Having to accommodate into our brain-space the new people, places, and things we encounter in books naturally sparks our curiosity. Children's questions are a precious commodity, and, as we've noted before, should be encouraged. Answer their questions with questions when appropriate. Be honest when you don't know the answers. Don't let it stop there. Let the questions about one book lead to another, or to an encyclopedia, or to a Scripture verse. Be humble in reflecting on questions about ultimate issues. Even Solomon

acknowledged that we "cannot fathom what God has done from beginning to end" (Ecclesiastes 3:11). "The problem with Christians," reflected a thoughtful unbeliever to my writer-friend Helen, "is that they have all the answers, but they don't have any questions."

THIS IS YOUR BRAIN. . . . THIS IS YOUR BRAIN ON MTV

As a child reads people's ideas, he learns about logic—how to be reasonable. A child builds arguments for the truth based on facts, premises, deductions, and conclusions. If this is true, and if that is true, then this must be true.

As children get a foundation of truth, they need to read widely and determine if they agree or disagree with what they read. They need to compare what they read to what Scripture says. As a result of that exercise, they understand Scripture better because they realize it stands in sharp opposition to this new idea.

There will be huge contrasts among those in our children's generation. There will be those who know truth, who think with vertical and logical skills, building precept upon precept, and who can understand and critique others' ideas and take a stand against deception.

Then there will be those who are cut off from the truth but won't even have the thinking skills to figure it out. These will be the children of the MTV generation who do not think in a vertical, logical fashion, but in fragmented images.

Their ability to assimilate images quickly as they watch music videos and channel-surf is being hailed by some (mostly marketers) as a strategic new development far superior to cultural literacy. But fragmented image-oriented processing of information engages the emotions and bypasses the mind. The next generation will be subject to manipulation on a massive scale.

Already we're seeing the tendency toward postmodern political campaigns—votes solicited by floods of high-tech, high-impact images, especially of the visibly disabled and handicapped strumming the voters' heartstrings. Emotional appeals for *compassion* connect with the voters' *feelings*.

By way of comparison, the Lincoln-Douglas debates (1858) lasted three hours. First Douglas had an hour; then Lincoln had a thirty-minute rebuttal. Then they reversed roles. Can you even imagine? *Three hours* without a word by Dan-Peter-Tom-or-Ted "explaining" what the debaters had said!

I recently had an opportunity to watch a thirty-minute political ad produced for Barry Goldwater's 1964 campaign for president. It was a thirty-minute *speech* by Ronald Reagan, the speech that launched Reagan's career—thirty minutes of dense reasoning, facts, figures, specifics—no charts or visuals. It gave new depth and meaning to the word *progress.*

As with all child-training, the younger our children are when we set a certain course and pursue it, the more likely they will choose to join us for the long ride. I must confess that I was handed a stacked deck in this regard. Zach is very verbal and probably would have loved books even if he'd had to bum them off his kindergarten buddies. Some children are "bent" in the opposite direction.

But so much is at stake in their need to be able to read deeply for meaning and application that we need to find the best materials we can and figure out some rewards. In the summers, we've granted extra media time for time spent reading. If your child has no appetite for great literature, start with good movies of great literature and try to generate discussion. Beware of some of the recent classics-to-movie versions that became politically correct in translation (*Little Women*). Actually even these can give you an interesting additional angle to discuss. (See Focus Box #24.)

Focus Your Worldview #24: Everything I Know I Learned from TV

I, Zach Arrington, have been referred to many times throughout this book, and I felt that it would be beneficial to add my two cents about what my educational enrichment aside from school has added to my life. First off, there is an appreciation for the finer things that comes when your mother has bombarded you with "high art" since you were four. I like classical music, books, challenging movies, and the theater. I am musically inclined, and I can sort of play two instruments. Note: I am not a nerd. I sleep in, eat pizza, play basketball for the school, wear my hat backwards, participate in drama, am generally liked at school, and have friends who play sports and are normal and popular.

However, through all of these activities and relationships, I have met people who do not like classical music and books and who resent people who do. Some of these people I had the opportunity to meet during my short stint in the Tomball High School football program. It was an interesting contrast to be in both choir and football. I would come into the meeting room where all of the players would gather before practice after singing for an hour and a half with the music still in my head and hear:

"*Exultate justi in domino, rectos de . . .*"

"Man, John's a #@!!★$!"

" *. . . chet co laudatcio. Confite mini dom . . .*"

"Yeah, he's a #@!!★$!. Let's beat his ★!!@$!"

" *. . . ino inchitara, benesalite ei, in terra pax . . .*"

"Hey, John, you're a #@!!★$!"

" *. . . hominbus, bonae voluntatis gloria.*"

"$★!!@★&$$# ^ @★&#%!"

The trouble is, however, despite how much I had been taught to appreciate the finer things, it took all that I had not to call John a #@!!★$! as well. If you do not pound the richer life and the Bible into your children, they will inevitably end up as John-beaters, because that is what everyone will become if left to themselves. Despite the fact that we know more than you, you parents are ultimately responsible for how we kids turn out. Kind of scary, but true. Oh, by the way, as long as I'm telling you this, I'd just like to mention that if you'd like to really enhance your child's "moral imagination," purchase him a car and insurance on his sixteenth birthday.

Author's Note: This piece was written two months before the aforementioned birthday. His "moral imagination" may have to languish a bit.

"A Time to Build," "A Time to Keep"

Zach was gone for the evening. The yard was done. Dinner dishes were cleared away. Jack looked at the TV listing—pretty interesting movie coming on. We had made a few phone calls to see if anyone wanted to join us at Clouseau's, Tomball's finest (and only) gourmet coffee bar—no takers. We looked at each other. To veg or not to veg? Whether 'tis nobler to head on in to the coffee shop, just we two, or answer the call of the Blue Recliner? The "spirit of power and self-discipline" nudged us. To Clouseau's! Where we had a whopping good, no, a *great* conversation with two of our church leaders, flagged down on their way into Eckerd's to price some Pepcid. Not to mention the fact that I really love hazelnut hot chocolate with a mound of whipped cream.

Leisure time + self-discipline = "a time to build up" and "a time to keep." Small decisions to say no to media and yes to relationship and communication pay big dividends. We have lots of opportunities to communicate and build relationships while we're riding in the car, eating, working on chores together, and going about our daily busyness. Our leisure time affords special opportunities for focused attention on relationships.

Quentin Schultz has polled many adults and children asking, "What special activities were most important while you were growing up for building healthy family relationships?" Answers included board games, vacations, hobbies, and fellowshiping around food (*Winning Your Kids Back from the Media*, p 63). Following are some other suggestions for more "building" and "keeping" ways to use our leisure time:

Stir Up Creative Juices. Buy toys and supplies that help children build and create—not just act out what they see on TV. Musical children need instruments and lessons. The musical *and* agile will enjoy opportunities to dance. Dramatic children need hats, costumes, accessories, a dress-up trunk, a skit box. Artistic children need good color and paint supplies, quality paper, clay, crafts, books on drawing, cartooning, or perhaps a class in cake decorating. Literary children need to be encouraged to write; to have their stories read, celebrated, perhaps illustrated; to have their plays acted out; to find a pen pal or to write missionaries.

Nurture a Love for Nature. Time spent enjoying God's creation can build a deep admiration for His awesome capability for design and His incredible sense of beauty. Make time for parks, hiking, rock-climbing, beach-combing, vacations that explore His magnificent world, camping trips (highly recommended by Gary Smalley for family bonding as well), Christian camping programs, fishing, and hunting. Introverted children will naturally "recharge" in outdoor settings. For extroverts, make it a group outing with some planned fun times. Raise animals, plant a garden. My neighbor encouraged her son to channel his dirt-digging interest into a small vegetable garden. He sold fresh tomatoes and squash from his red wagon at age five. By age twelve he had saved $1,000 with which he bought stocks. Now a high school sophomore, he enjoys "digging around" for new acquisitions to add to his growing portfolio.

Marty Hair reported in the *Houston Chronicle* that "the key to gardening with children seems to be figuring out what the youngsters would enjoy [eating or seeing]." Some children might be especially drawn to creative ideas found in many gardening books and stores today. Hair mentions "a secret hideaway made of sunflowers, a teepee made of beans, potatoes growing in a garbage can, or the prospect of creating a restaurant for butterflies."

Enrich Life with the Fine Arts. "Great art gives us a life-affirming pleasure simply not available in the pallid fare of TV or Top-40 music," writes Terry Glaspey (*Children of a Greater God*, p. 173). It's true! I will never forget returning to the van after taking my high school students to a Bach pipe organ concert. The key in the ignition revived the "oh-yeah, baby, baby" tunes on the radio. A chorus of groans went up, punctuated by "Turn it off." We did.

Begin or regularly add to a collection of classical music. Glaspey's book includes a "Classical Music Beginner List." Many Christian bookstores and mass-market record stores stock some wonderful series. We've enjoyed the RCA Greatest Hits series (Bach, Beethoven, Copland, etc.) by way of introduction to various artists. Then we've gone on to purchase CDs of individual works of the artists we've liked best (e.g., Handel's *Water Music*). Rotate this richly textured, less accessible, but more enduring music into the background of your home life, especially at dinnertime.

Another wonderful series to introduce your child to classical music is *Play Beethoven* (*Mozart*, etc.). The life and music of the composer in a book *with* an electronic keyboard. Series by Barrons of New York. (For grade schoolers. Can be ordered from bookstores like Bookstop.)

Many younger children enjoy classical music regularly during bath times or rest periods. If older children lobby for music while they do homework, approve only classical selections. (Besides, research shows that Mozart improves your IQ.)

Stock up on art books at bookstore sale tables. Look at the books with your children. Guide their interaction/observation as Susan Macaulay suggests (*For the Children's Sake,* pp. 127-30). Hang your favorites on the walls.

Visit the symphony, the art museum, the ballet, the theater— "ain't nothing like the *real* thing, baby." My friend Dorothy (mother of the stock portfolio gardener) invited me to see the finest of the eighteenth-century ballets, *Sleeping Beauty.* It was the most beautiful creation of human talent I've ever seen. If the professional productions are a financial stretch, try one production a year as a special family treat. Or catch the symphony or Shakespeare in the park. Zach recently came back from dollar night at the symphony and just went on and on about how much he enjoyed the program, in large part because they played so many songs he already knew and liked. Or try your local high school productions. Often the talent is first rate. And they (mostly) produce the drama versions you see on TV or Broadway minus the language, violence, or nudity.

A challenge from me to you: Read one art history book. (A Christian art history is even better.) Art has great meaning in context. The history *is* the context. My favorite is *Modern Art and the Death of Culture* by Hans Rookmaaker. It was one magnificent "light bulb" experience. Aha!

Savor the "Thrill of Victory." And build character and dependence on God in the "agony of defeat." To the extent that involvement in sports can add richness to your family life—develop teamwork, confidence, discipline, a sense of fairness, a gracious attitude win or lose, and a desire to pursue excellence—it's a great choice for leisure time.

Caution: Sports where families purpose to picnic together, communicate with one another in the stands, and celebrate together or nurture disappointments together can build a family up. Sports can also tear a family down. Watch for red flags of too much pressure to win, too many practices and games squeezing family time, and Sunday-school-teaching parents who morph into howling banshees that blast the refs, the other team, their own team, and their own child.

A Time to Be Silent. Sometimes the greatest times for building and keeping come from leisure time spent in quiet solitude. (Mothers of little ones, don't laugh. Your season for being "home alone" is coming. In the meantime, seize the small gaps in your busyness— early, late nap time, an extra few minutes of quiet time, maybe even a sitter while you squirrel away.) Leisure can afford us time to sift, to reflect, to meditate—to figure out where we've come from and where we're going, to appraise the works of our lives and determine if they were very good, good, or at least kind of okay. We can encourage our children's reflection with photo albums, scrapbooks, or a blank book waiting to become a journal.

For a family building time, make an album together. Decorate it with captions from magazines, or make your own on the computer. Buy brightly colored paper and cut it in interesting geometric shapes with the craft scissors that cut in decorative, squiggly lines. Use the cutouts grouped as mounts for pictures. Add little stars, hearts, musical notes, and other shapes that you can punch out with the craft punches now available.

But don't just make them; review them together, especially at the beginning of a new school year or for a New Year's Eve activity. You could even share your own prayer journal and spiritual journey.

Cooking, Sewing, Hobbies, Collecting, Jogging . . . An exhaustive list of creative ways to use leisure time to build relationships, appreciate beauty and excellence, and recharge your batteries without vegging out would be endless. If you need more help with ideas, check the library and bookstores. If you need more help with motivation, pray that God's "Spirit of power and self-discipline" will really help your family's direction. The example of our Lord's life can also be good for our motivation.

JESUS' DAY OFF(?)

I reread the Gospels carefully to glean any hint of how Jesus spent His leisure time. He didn't seem to have much. I would love to find a record of His "normal" pre-ministry life, but from His baptism and the beginning of His ministry forward, the picture is one of a man on the move under continual stress. Mark is the best at chronicling His schedule. The crowds pursued Him as if he were a rock star. "So many people were coming and going that they did not even have a chance to eat" (Mark 6:31). All that and "they tell me He didn't even have a Daytimer," confided pastor and friend Ivory Varner.

Jesus fought to carve out "a time to be silent," escaping to lonely places to pray. He also used leisure to build relationships with friends (and sinners). Beyond that we're left to guess how He used His leisure hours. Although He spent a lot of time on the lake, the Gospels never mention that He went fishing, even though He knew where all the fish were. (Of course, if you really know, then it takes all the fun out of it.)

Jesus spent His free times pursuing relationships—with God, with believers, and with unbelievers. The irony of our leisure fixation on media is that it tends to reduce our face time with other people. The vast majority of what we see on the screen leads away from relationship. Great breadth, little depth. More times to "throw away" or subtly "tear down."

VEG-OUT TIME: THE NEW ENTITLEMENT

I know I've carried on against the media for quite a bit in these two chapters, and I'd like to clarify that. What concerns me is our unbalanced, undiscriminating use of it. To have CDs, TVs, computers, VCRs, and on-line access is to accept the responsibility to confront our own undisciplined tendencies and those of our children. I'm grateful for all the above in my home and for the enjoyment they bring to our lives, especially the great *depth* of fine movies, TV programming, and computer research capability. There is even a place for enjoying "veg-out" leisure—even "twinkie" music and media as Menconi calls it. Not the "building and keeping" kind of media, but not the "tear-down, throw-away" stuff either. You know, the frothy, insubstantial "Oh yeah, baby, baby" stuff. However, as Menconi points out, a solid diet of "twinkie" music (or "twinkie" leisure time in general) isn't good for us.

As with any source of enjoyment, if our "treasure" is there, our heart (our focus, our priorities) will also be there (Matthew 6:21). My sense of it is that many children, and especially teens and stressed-out dads, don't just treasure their leisure time with electronic media. They see it as a sort of entitlement. They've worked hard all day at school or the job and, by golly, they have *earned* an evening of self-indulgence with their treasure. While everyone needs a chance to recharge batteries (remember the Good Wife's poor husband), the essence of Christian discipleship is laying down our life, our treasure, and considering the needs of others. Maybe we need to put a sign like this on top of the TV: "Love is . . . the selfless presence of one person in the life of another" (Quentin Schultz).

SENSIBLE GUIDELINES FOR THE MCGUFFIN

To help us guard against letting the media be a "time to tear down and throw away," here are some suggestions gleaned from a number of sources. These ideas can enable us get the best out of the electronic media without letting it consume the best part of our lives.

TV Notes

Watch TV with your children unless you know a given program's content is trustworthy. Even Disney can get politically correct and New Age, and a new Disney (Hyperion) book promotes homosexuality as an alternative lifestyle. Some similar tendencies appear at PBS, including "Sesame Street" and "Reading Rainbow." "Wishbone," on the other hand, seems consistently good and entices children to read classical literature. Note: Oliver Stone, Steven Spielberg, Barbra Streisand, Linda Bloodworth-Thomason, Norman Lear, and Richard Donner number among legions of entertainers who view the media as their pulpit. Be careful what sermons your children hear.

Challenge the subtle, manipulative images and logic in advertisements. Os Guinness plays a game with his children—Spot the Lie—a quarter won if they can detect the deception in a given ad.

Predetermine a limited amount of tube time. Shop your TV listings for the best buys. For accounting accuracy and convenience, you might check out Time Slot, a TV management tool recommended by Focus on the Family. Your children receive "credit cards" for a certain amount of TV time. Using your parent card, you can program how much time your child can charge per week before the set goes dark. Before you get clammy hands at the thought of "programming," relax. It's more like an ATM with prompting than a VCR. Also works for VCRs and Nintendos. For a free brochure call (919) 829-3525. Focus has also recommended buying a roll of tickets and issuing one ticket per hour allotted. They suggested that parents issue themselves tickets, too!

Menconi's three-strikes-you're-out suggestion: if you find the same series offensive in three different episodes, move on to another selection.

Movies (Rental and Theaters)

This is very subjective, but here's our general rule of thumb: no "R" ratings, unless one of us is along and we hear firsthand or from a reliable review that a brief edit or extraordinary merit warrant viewing. I humbly submit that one person's "merit" is another's misjudgment. (*World* magazine called *Rob Roy* one of the best motion pictures of 1995. We thought the film could have been retitled *Debbie Does Scotland,* and we almost walked out.)

If it's PG-13, we ask questions. If it's touted as a sex-comedy, focuses on a coming-of-age theme, or trades heavily in bathroom humor, we decline. Hollywood's idea of frontal nudity as acceptable in PG-13s is not ours.

Music (CDs, Cassettes, MTV, Radio, and Concerts)

Don't let your teens withdraw into their own niche and run on media auto-pilot. Listen with them. Talk about the artists and lyrics.

No MTV. Block it on your cable package. The heart behind MTV's messages is not what we want to develop in our children.

Whether it's Top 40 ("Take your time/we've got all night/You on the rise as you're touching my thighs/And let me know what you like."—Janet Jackson); adult contemporary ("That's all you wanted—someone special, someone sacred in your life, just for one moment to be warm and naked at my side"—George Michael); or country ("It [adultery] may be wrong, but I don't want out, 'cause it's a little too late to do the right thing now"—Tanya Tucker); monitor it, edit it, punch the button in the car (and always explain why).

Robert DeMoss (*Learn to Discern*) suggests that if you want to begin a new approach with children who already have music collections, offer a full or depreciated cash settlement for offensive titles in stock. Future purchases are "buyer beware." If a new purchase comes home that's unacceptable (make your standards as clear as possible), the music is disposed of and no compensation given.

So far we've avoided Top-40 battles by listening to Christian contemporary/adult contemporary/classic rock when we're together. In his room Zach can listen to any CD that passes muster. On Sunday morning, we hear contemporary Christian only. Again I do not hold this up as a standard, but merely suggest it as a creative alternative. Sometimes it helps to know what's working (mostly) for another family.

Promote and enjoy good quality contemporary Christian music whenever possible. Offer to buy as much as your budget affords. Try and catch the Contemporary Christian Music concerts.

Not all CCM is well done or has a strong message. Some secular music is and does. (Don Henley is a family favorite.) As children get older, encourage them to make choices based on your shared values. Be open to the message of what they choose even if the form (like rap) is not your favorite.

Computer Notes

Locate your computer where the entire family has access. Learn to compute together.

Computer porn is only a mouse-click away. All your child has to do to find thousands of pornographic pictures and references on the Internet is type in S-E-X and push enter. No family member should cruise the net late, tired, and alone. To ensure safety for children and teens, purchase a software program that blocks sites with sexually oriented material. Net Nanny, Safe Surf, and Cyber Patrol have information on the net that you can download and consult. They charge a reasonable price for the software, and monthly updates are available (but not necessary) for an additional charge.

Adopt guidelines for children's usage including hours children can spend, values for games, approval of chat rooms.

Occasionally check over file names your children have stored in the computer.

Three nevers:

1. Never let children give personal information to strangers they meet on the net.

2. Never let your children arrange a meeting with a net-mate without your full cooperation and approval.

3. Never respond to threatening or lewd E-mail.

If your daughter was being stalked or our son sustained a life-threatening injury, we would quickly rally all our family resources to their defense. But too often we leave our children vulnerable to the relentless pounding of the media that erodes their innocence, monopolizes their time, and sears their imaginations. Future scholars may look back and evaluate the destructiveness of American electronic media culture on a par with the gladiatorial combat of Rome or the Indian practice of suttee—burning a widow on her husband's funeral pyre. They may shake their heads and quote Allan Bloom: "A society's greatest madness seems normal to itself."

God has always delighted in men and women who stood against the cultural flow: Abraham, Moses, Daniel, Esther. They chose God. He gave them the strength and protection to stand alone. Tired of whacking that mole? Of fighting the media battles with your kids? God promises wisdom (James 1:5) and strength (Philippians 4:13) and power, love, and self-discipline (2 Timothy 1:7).

I speak as a woman of faith to other women of faith. Be the parent. Take a stand. When the trillion-dollar entertainment mobile tantalizes your children with ritzy, glitzy, fantastic, big-bang and big-burn, rock-'em, sock-'em but unsuitable, angry, hopeless fare, don't let it take your children for a ride. Remember—it's headed for the ditch.

CITIZENSHIP

Yes, it's rougher!
Don't pull back, and keep looking up!

ABOUT DONKEYS
AND ELEPHANTS

13

*Being Good Stewards
of Our Dual Citizenship*

IT WAS ONE OF THOSE MONUMENTAL CONVERSATIONS BORN out of modest beginnings. Zach, his buddy Chris, and I were driving home from a movie (nice segue from the previous chapter here), chatting about collecting things that increase in value.

That made me think of all my dad's tools. I read somewhere that if the economy falls on really hard times and the mobs run riot in the streets, tools will be a valuable commodity, especially where demand for even basic goods far outstrips their supply. Tools and toilet paper.

So I told Zach that even if I never used them, I would probably save my dad's tools and advised him to do the same. Even if you didn't stock up on toilet paper, you could rent or trade tools for it and come up with plenty.

This led to a "group-think" exercise about the future as *Mad Max*-world or *Waterworld*. What if industrialization breaks down, and we're forced back into an agrarian mode? The guys had great fun assembling their survivalist group. They'd invite Luke because he was a mountain man at heart with skills to match and had a ranch in a remote part of Texas; Clint because his family had two huge safes full of enough guns and ammo to dispense with any Dennis Hopper types crazy enough to challenge them; Andrew the profitable gardener; and the list went on. We all laughed as we imagined the magnificent seven or eight who would stand together in hard times.

Then it was quiet, and Zach eventually asked with just a shade of apprehension in his voice, "Mom, do you really think our country's going to fall—like Rome?"

My son is sixteen. His whole life lies ahead, beckoning. The future as *Waterworld* or even DryLand World casts a depressing shadow over his hopes and dreams.

"How does our part in the Story end?" he was asking. As a nation. As a young man in that nation. And what I tell Zach is that while we know how the Story ends, we don't know how our earthly part ends. As a nation our significant role in God's Story could be winding down. We truly seem to be in spiritual, moral, cultural, and national decline. Currently we seem much more vulnerable to economic collapse than to external attack, but that could change. Our whole system is driven by confidence. And that confidence in reason, meaning, progress, and the ability to solve our nation's problems is getting shaky.

But I am an optimist. Zach is too. I told him, "I hope the decline is slow. I hope and pray for reformation and revival on such a scale that the decline would cease and renewal would begin." I love my country. I treasure my freedom, my American heritage. If anything, the threat of decline motivates me to be a witness for Jesus Christ and spread the Gospel.

I hope that by my sharing this with Zach, he will not lose heart or become pessimistic. I hope that he will take real and profound comfort in the fact of his dual citizenship. We American Christians need to remember, as Os Guinness has said, that our glory days are not in the past. Rather, our golden era lies in the future. We will celebrate and rejoice in the end of the Story, no matter how our part plays out.

COASTING WITH A BIG LEAGUE CONTRACT

But how does our heavenly citizenship and our confident hope in the end of God's Story reflect on our American citizenship? Does it make us eager to be "salt" and "light" in the community where God has placed us? Or, content that our future is secure, do we coast toward the finish, somewhat apathetic and disengaged?

My friends Dave and Patty LaRoche have been involved in Major League baseball for a long time. In the 1970s Dave's salary as a young Major Leaguer was $35,000, and that was after he had risen to be an all-star pitcher. Many of today's young Major Leaguers sign multi-million-dollar, multiyear contracts after only a few years in the Majors.

After years spent coaching these guys, Dave has told us he's seen a few of his young pitchers gain a big bank account and lose their competitive edge. They start to coast and lose their drive for giving their all and playing their best, because in a large sense their future is secure. They're busy enjoying their reward. Focusing with discipline and determination on 162 games a season is difficult.

What do we do with the blessing of a secure future and a happy ending? Like one of these well-paid, young Major League players, are we content to know we "have it made"? Are we indifferent toward our "teammates"? Do we leave it to others to shape the schools, decide the limitations on partial-birth abortions, and reach out to those in need?

Or does God call us to be good stewards of our American citizenship? His call to love our neighbor here and now is answered as we share the Gospel with them. But it is also answered through wise citizenship, fulfilling our responsibility to be salt and light.

As followers of Jesus Christ, shouldn't we really engage in shaping the democracy our children will inherit? (Don't get uptight now. I'm not heading for a pep talk on political activism. Maybe later.) What I'm talking about starts at home with our children—with teaching them values. The key values in a democracy are freedom and justice. Sharing a biblical understanding of these values with our children—showing them how we can better love our neighbors when we live out true freedom and justice is, I believe, the first challenge we face as good stewards of our American citizenship.

WITH LIBERTY AND JUSTICE FOR ALL

To many of our neighbors, especially those of a more progressive bent, talk about freedom amounts to talk about rights—rights for women, racial minorities, gays and lesbians, to name a few. And the latest to get in line for more legally guaranteed freedom? Kids.

You have the right to be seen, heard, and respected as a citizen of the *world* [italics mine].

You have the right to your opinions and feelings even if others [God? Your parents?] don't agree with them.

These excerpts from "Nickelodeon's Kid's Bill of Rights" can be found in the 1995 U.N. Treaty on the Rights of the Child (in similar wording). Are you trying to remember the last time your child read a U.N. treaty? Don't relax too soon. Bobby may just find his Bill of Rights when he opens his next Post cereal box of Alpha Bits or Fruity Pebbles. Your educationally minded food manufacturer has thoughtfully stuffed it in your breakfast food. What a way for our kids to start their day! And if you can find a copy in your box, what a great opening for talking about another piece of our children's worldview puzzle.

But the kids' rights puzzle piece does not fit in with the biblical puzzle piece of freedom. To learn more about that, take your children back to the creation of freedom in Genesis 2. God gave Adam and Eve great freedom: "You are free to eat from any tree in the garden," but He also gave the freedom and responsibility to choose—"but you must not eat from the tree of the knowledge of good and evil" (vv. 16-17). This God-given freedom to choose is the basis of our inalienable "right to liberty" recognized by our country's founders in the Declaration of Independence.

But even in Paradise *freedom* to eat from any tree was balanced with the *responsibility* to observe limits on that freedom. First Peter 2:16 repeats the connection. "Live as free men" but also "live as servants of God." What makes us truly free is knowing the truth (John 8:32) and obeying it. What truth? Jesus was not referring to a good education or the "truth as I see it." He was talking about God's truth concerning sin, redemption, and forgiveness—His truth about obeying your parents and loving your neighbor. Disobeying God's truth is sin, and slavery to sin is the polar opposite of freedom.

What we and our children must ask ourselves is: Do kid's "rights" or any "rights" lead us away from God's truth and encourage sin? In this book we've talked about a lot of "rights"—animal "rights," abortion "rights," the "right to die." Today we see many progressives push for more and more rights but, as Francis Schaeffer warns in *A Christian Manifesto,* "having no Christian consensus to contain it, that 'freedom' leads to chaos or to slavery under the state or an elite. Humanism [the view that *Man Makes the Rules*] with its lack of any final base for values or law always leads to chaos. It naturally then leads to some form of authoritarianism to control the chaos" (pp. 29-30).

We see this at work in our own neighborhood. Our teens' right to "freedom of assembly" is being revoked in our county. *Problem*: Too much teen violence. *Solution*: State-imposed teen curfew. Given a choice, most people will opt for order over freedom. They will invite the government to take away their "freedom."

Teaching a biblical view of freedom and making the biblical connection with responsibility begins with our example. What about my "right" to a certain lifestyle? What about Jack's "right" to veg-out in front of a video after a hard day? We make the connection between freedom and responsibility when we talk to Zach about expanding the "fences" on his freedom (later curfews, riding in friends' cars, consuming media). We tell him that he gains our trust by showing responsibility with more freedom, so that in turn, he can expect to see his fences widen. The process also works in reverse.

Freedom—the extension of "rights" as well as freedom from authoritarian *control*—must be balanced with responsibility. And our definition of freedom must square with Scripture—that is, what the biblical puzzle piece looks like. This is the biblical worldview of freedom that best serves families *and* governments. (See Focus Box #25.) This puzzle piece considered, now we can look at our other great democratic value—"justice for all."

≈

FOCUS YOUR WORLDVIEW #25:
THE STEWARDSHIP OF FREEDOM

Here are some suggestions:

Get a copy of your preferred political party's platform. Evaluate how it reflects the biblical balance between freedom and responsibility, justice and mercy. If the platform is extremely long, just select the party's position on a few issues.

Take your children to a political rally or a Fourth of July symphony in the park. Wave the flag. Sing patriotic songs. Renewing a childlike appreciation for our forefathers and our nation's ideals is good medicine in a cynical age.

Pray for your elected officials (1 Timothy 2:1-2). Write and tell them you're praying for them.

Take your children with you to vote. Let them observe the process firsthand. Tell them how you voted and why.

Have your children write a letter to an elected representative, a letter of thanks or request. They will enjoy being a part of the process and receiving the written acknowledgment or reply most officeholders send.

On April 15 tell your children how much you're paying in taxes and what you appreciate in return and what you don't appreciate. (Careful here!)

When you get a jury summons, go. Set a good example. Tell your children stories about the jury experience, contributing a Christian perspective.

If you have a chance to visit a military museum or installation on a trip, do it. Our visits to the Air Force Academy and the World War II aircraft carrier *Lexington* have been real highlights. It increases our respect for those serving us and makes Grandpa's stories come to life.

MATTHEW 25—"THIS IS WHY I AM A DEMOCRAT."

"For I was hungry and you gave me something to eat, I was thirsty and you gave me something to drink, I was a stranger and you invited me in, I needed clothes and you clothed me, I was sick and you looked after me, I was in prison and you came to visit me" (Matthew 25:35-36). A godly man I know, a criminal defense lawyer and a deacon in his church, looks at this passage, and out in the margin of his Bible has written, "This is why I am a Democrat." For all his life (until the last election) he has identified with the more progressive party because of its concern for the poor. Ultimately, his concern for the destruction of innocent lives by abortion has compelled him to switch parties.

As I've wrestled with the biblical puzzle piece of justice and what to teach Zach, I find it easier to talk about racial equality than about "justice" for the poor and downtrodden. (See Focus Box #26.) And yet I'm challenged by criticism from the other side, by those who say that the welfare of the poor is a bigger issue in the Bible than racial prejudice or homosexuality or abortion. And I seriously reflect when some contend that taxation is a "moral imperative" rather than a political issue because, "unlike taxpayers who waste their money in self-indulgence, government spends money on worthwhile projects" (i.e., entitlements to the sick and poor). Why let some citizens "indulge themselves at the expense of social needs"?

Two things concern me about this approach. First is the attitude of moral superiority. "We, because we are wiser (or better?), know how to spend your money, and will, and are," as my friend Donna Ballard, Texas Board of Education member, sums it up. Unlike the people who compose it, the government is somehow morally superior. Second is the call for compassion again, the same banner under which the progressive forces march to extend abortion rights and the "right" to die. And, as with the other issues, I believe the answer lies in the broader, wiser sense of God's compassion that truly provides the greatest good for the greatest number of people.

Let me explain. Just as *freedom* is biblically linked to *responsibility, justice* is biblically linked to *compassion* or *mercy*. "Administer true justice, show mercy and compassion to one another," the Lord tells the prophet Zechariah (7:9). Micah 6:8 carries the same message: "What does the Lord require of you? To act justly and to love mercy." We've already discussed in chapter 3 how God's just punishment of Israel described in Jeremiah was continually tempered with mercy and how God's justice was satisfied at the Cross by the ultimate act of mercy and compassion—Christ's death for us.

So the question is, to deal biblically with the poor and needy, how do we deal with them in justice *and* compassion? Matthew 25 is a beautiful picture of mercy, but Scripture clearly teaches, "If a man will not work, he shall not eat" (2 Thessalonians 3:10). This is indeed a significant question, since the general consensus in the United States today is that "welfare as we know it" is an unmitigated disaster.

I wish I had space to summarize all the wonderful insight and answers that University of Texas journalism professor and *World* magazine editor Marvin Olasky has offered in his book, *The Tragedy of American Compassion*. He contrasts today's mind-set of mercy ("the feed and forget" approach) with the *personal involvement* that was the hallmark of compassion through the 1800s. Our forebears practiced a brand of mercy that investigated people's needs, required work and temperance, and demanded that fathers provide for their children. "Tough love was standard." The indiscriminate dole of food or money was seen as "promiscuous charity" that makes people lazy and dependent.

Olasky urges a return to personal involvement with the poor. He wants government aid for private and religious charities so that the poor may be truly helped by a ministry of hands-on compassion properly reunited with justice *and* accountability.

As I consider Olasky's advice, I return to the example of Ruby Plus who "opens her arms to the poor and stretches out her hands to the needy" (Proverbs 31:20). Her hands, mind you, not just her checkbook. I see a need for our own family to meet the biblical challenge beyond our financial support to the children of Compassion or a hospital in Haiti.

I am encouraged to see more youth groups and Christian schools finding opportunities for young people to minister to the poor. Obviously much more can be done, and much creative thinking is being done to offer churches and individuals the opportunities to come alongside those who need help. My local American Family Association newsletter has started listing specific local programs and people that need help. Recently Prison Fellowship announced its plan to encourage church families to follow up prisoners' families over the long term using the Christmastime Angel Tree project as only the beginning. We can seek to teach our children about the biblical ideas of justice and mercy in many other ways—in discussion of current events (race riots, affirmative action), dealing with neighbors (good ones as well as bad ones), and in discussions of school and family guidelines and discipline, to name a few.

When Zach was in eighth grade, his dad gave him a profound lesson in mercy. It was the day of the school-wide pep rally sending our winning basketball team off to the Lutheran schools' state finals. Even though he was a team starter, Zach, for an accumulation of errors, had to spend it in in-school suspension. Right before the pep rally, in a prearranged deal with the headmaster, Jack showed up to take Zach's place in the little ISS room so Zach could go on to the pep rally. Zach sank to his knees weeping and profusely thanked his dad for the sacrifice. Not quite. Actually the memorable moment brought an embarrassed smile and a mumbled "thanks." But it did hit the mark, he told us later.

I believe what our children want and need from us is not always all the answers, but a life lived in authentic tension between freedom and responsibility, between justice and mercy—a worldview that incorporates *all* the puzzle pieces and helps us sort out when to emphasize one or the other. Our commitment to nurture these values should result in loving our neighbor in practical ways and should give our children the example and inspiration they need to be good American citizens as well as heavenly citizens.

≈

FOCUS YOUR WORLDVIEW #26: "CITIZEN," "PERSON," OR LIFE MADE "IN THE IMAGE OF GOD"?

In 1857 our Supreme Court held that "the Negro was not included, and not intended to be included under the word 'citizen' in the constitution." This distinction based on racial prejudice was as unjust as the *Roe v. Wade* ruling, which held that "the unborn are not included within the definition of 'person' as used in the Fourteenth Amendment." God doesn't talk in terms of "citizen" or "person" but life made "in his image."

Reviewing the verses on God's image with your children can also lead to a fruitful discussion on race. Add to the verses listed in chapter 6 Galatians 3:26-29, and use the following questions:

1. Look at Galatians 3:28. Jews and Greeks are two different races. What other race names could you substitute in the verse? What does it mean for blacks and whites to be "one in Christ Jesus"?

2. If we call a person from another race names, how does that make the other person feel, especially if the person is a Christian?

3. Can you describe a stereotype of a Jew? Almost all the Bible stories are about Jews. Do most of them fit the stereotype? How do you think the stereotype got started? (Note: Because the Catholic church

banned usury [loaning money for interest], Jews became the bankers of Western Europe.)

4. What's wrong with these statements? "All whites are greedy." "All blacks are mean." Why do we form stereotypes?

5. How can we live out our "oneness in Christ" with people from different races? I know there are many suburban Christian families who have no friends beyond their own race. May I encourage you to find some. They are a treasure. (I count it a privilege to have an African-American friend and fellow writer who prayed for me and helped me write this book. Thanks, Melvin!)

6. Perhaps you could invite a family of a different race from your church, neighborhood, school, or sports team to dinner at your house or to go out for a meal or a snack after a game.

7. Invite a classmate of a different race to go with your child to the park, zoo, or museum or just come over to play. Try to get to know the child's mother. Invite her along.

NAVIGATING POLITICAL WHITE WATER

Part of preparing our children to be good stewards of their citizenship in a democracy is helping them to be informed voters. They need to learn how to communicate to their party and elected representatives their ideas based on Christian principles. Developing a Christian view of politics means that our loyalty to God and His Word is always greater than our loyalty to a political party or candidate. Our children, and sometimes we ourselves, need reminding that God is neither a Republican nor a Democrat. Evangelical Christians are both. The *Los Angeles Times* (6/25/96) reported that "40 percent of evangelical Christians identify themselves as Republican, compared to about 25 percent who call themselves Democrats and 29 percent who identify themselves as independents."

Our goal in political action is to live out our convictions about freedom and justice and what it means to really love our neighbor—to be "salt" and "light" in the process. To do that we need to help our children with their strategy, their heart attitude, and their information source.

Concerning their strategy, I believe we need to take to heart and pass on to our children the following advice taken largely from Os Guinness's discussion of a "public philosophy" in *The American Hour.*

> ➤ We must be shrewd in our attempts to build political consensus. Ask the larger questions. What can we *accomplish* that will ultimately protect the ill and unwanted or reduce the number of abortions? Politics is the art of compromise. I'm grateful that our Christian founders compromised with the Deists. I wish we could have been *officially* founded as a Christian nation, but since the idea was defeated, I'm grateful the Christians didn't walk away from the table.

> ➤ In church and in the public square, contend for Christian principles and biblical truth through principled persuasion.

All of which leads us to a discussion about the heart attitude of a good citizen. Peter encourages us to offer a defense of our faith "with gentleness and respect, keeping a clear conscience." In fact, we should "show proper respect to everyone: Love the brotherhood of believers, fear God, honor the king" (1 Peter 3:15-16; 2:17).

I have walked around a convention hall lined with booths, a few selling derogatory T-shirts and bumper stickers about the Clinton administration ("First Gennifer Flowers, Now Us"), even piñatas of Bill and Hillary awaiting a violent encounter with a baseball bat. I whispered in Jack's ear, "How does this square with 'honor the king'?" Can you imagine the disciples sporting "First His Brother's Wife, Now Us" on their tunics as they tried to spread the good news in Herod's jurisdiction?

By our example and teaching, our children must learn how to *earn* moral authority in the public square. Humor is great, but it must be in bounds. Justifying wearing the above mentioned T-shirt because "it's funny" is no different than justifying watching the excesses of "Beavis and Butthead" because they're funny. Our children are watching, and they need to see consistency.

Passion is also great. Read Peter's "warning and pleading" with the

Jews (Acts 2) or Patrick Henry's famous speech. *Passion, humor, reason, honor, respect, gentleness*—these characteristics define the heart attitude of a good citizen.

Our goal should be to convince, not annihilate or demonize. I think of the direct mail I receive from a number of different groups. Much of it conveys the message, as columnist Cal Thomas caricatures it, of angry people cursing the darkness, threatening ominously that "our father can beat up your father," and "our group can beat up your group—if we're big enough."

In this chorus of harsh rhetoric that fails to explain subtle differences, Dr. James Dobson's newsletters stand out as a fine example of well-reasoned, argument-driven appeals, complete with footnotes. (See Focus Box #27.) And he has probably one of the largest mailing lists. If we give in to the urge to use image over argument, appeal to inflamed passions over Spirit-led discernment of truth, then we confirm the *Washington Post*'s critique of the fundamental and evangelical Christian community as "poor, uneducated, and easy to command."

Ralph Reed, former executive director of Christian Coalition, tells the story of doing lunch with a *Washington Post* reporter two days after the story on Evangelicals ran.

"Tell them to stop!" the reporter implored of Reed.

"What?" responded Reed, not getting it.

"Tell your people to stop faxing!" the reporter further explained.

"What?" responded Reed, still not getting it.

As it turned out, for two days all the available fax lines at the *Post* had been maxed out by a groundswell of correctional effort. People identifying themselves as fundamental, evangelical Christians had been busily faxing in their diplomas and W-2 forms.

The episode proved what the orthodox community has long known—the progressives who dominate the news media have little personal contact with the orthodox community. And their abysmal lack of understanding of them often shows in open contempt. The media claims their reporting of news is unbiased and objective. Just once I'd like to see someone like Connie Chung introduce herself with, "Good evening. I'm Connie Chung, and I'll give you my progressive/liberal take on the Christian Coalition," before she launches into a report that goes: "It doesn't have much to do with religion. . . .

It has to do with power," and "If the Christian Coalition had their way in America, there would be no First Amendment," and then a solemn warning, "They are recruiting your neighbors" (*Eye to Eye*, 7/22/93).

≈

FOCUS YOUR WORLDVIEW #27: "DECONSTRUCTING" DIRECT MAIL

Here's a project for the family that wants to develop "principled persuasion" in their children. Collect direct mail from political groups, Christian public policy groups, parachurch ministries, or even churches. Select a few examples of direct mail and analyze and discuss them on the following points (from James Davison Hunter's *Culture Wars*). Identify what you think is "principled persuasion" and what you think is over the line.

➤ Is there feigned familiarity—the impression that this is your close personal friend writing only you this intimate little note?

➤ Is there an honest sense of urgency? (Check the envelope for signs of urgent delivery mailed third class.)

➤ Is there a gimmick? A "card-carrying" card, fake honors, "personal" birthday cards to sign and put money in, stickers, too frequent questionnaires—anything to heighten your "personal obligation to become involved."

➤ Is there an extreme, overblown message crafted to manipulate your indignation or fear? Check for hyperbole, overuse of *incredibly monstrously, notoriously*—compelling adjectives and adverbs.

➤ Is there a "Devil factor," a nasty enemy that is an immediate threat to you and your family?

➤ Is the writing under the sixth grade level? Mostly five-letter words?

➤ Is there sound moral argument? Try and pull together some syllogisms from the letter. (If this, then this and this.)

➤ For those who want to take it further, suggest a rewrite done with "principled persuasion." Boring won't do. Boring doesn't raise money. It must be creative.

≈

WELL, THERE'S GOOD NEWS AND BAD NEWS

Our children need to understand where the media is coming from and where it wants to take them. They need to grasp how the media can manipulate public opinion, which, as we pointed out in chapter 3, is the driving force behind public values and public policy in our country today.

New Republic reporter Hendrick Hertzberg questioned media objectivity in the 1992 New Hampshire primary. He found that of forty-seven reporters polled, all favored Clinton before a single vote was cast.

Listening to broadcasts, sifting through news on-line, or picking up a newspaper, our children need to be able to detect the manipulation of the media in the editing process, the subtle mixture of fact and opinion, and the overall tone of the piece.

➤ The very inclusion of some stories and exclusion of others is an editing choice that sets an issues agenda for the nation. Provide for balance by including news sources from an orthodox perspective. (See Resource Box #11.)

➤ The editing process determines *how* a story will be reported. What you see on TV is not reality; it is an edited image. Sources quoted, sound bites sifted from a speech, selection of camera angle, etc.—it is the editor's job to shape a story.

➤ Encourage your children to read some news pieces and circle any *opinion* words sprinkled in with the facts—"extreme," "weak," "intolerant," "unacceptable," "bickering," "fanatic," "unfair," "worst, "strong," "floundering campaign." In a "Nightline" town meeting at Houston's Rice University after the 1992 campaign, top newsmakers were questioned as to why reporters from the floor of the Republican convention used opinion words such as *mean* or *sleaze* over 100 times in describing proceedings. Answer: Well, it was mean. As in Question: Why are you reporting your opinion? Answer: Because our opinion is right.

➤ More subtle than opinion is tone. Words have so many shades of meaning. Choice of nuance conveys tone. Watch for examples like these two headlines on the 1996 Texas GOP convention.

The *Houston Chronicle:* "GOP Conservatives Flex Muscles." The *Austin-American Statesman:* "GOP Ends Rancorous Convention." One paper consistently uses a more conservative tone, one a more liberal tone. Can you guess which is which? (Hint: In Texas our capital city is also fondly known as the "People's Republic of Austin.")

As moms, we will have done a great service to our country if we raise up leaders for the next generation who cherish freedom and justice, who appreciate our Christian history yet have a vision for the common good, who engage in politics with respect for all, and who are motivated and prepared to vote their Christian convictions. Apart from spreading the Gospel, it's the best strategy I can think of to address America's decline.

RESOURCE BOX #11: GOOD NEWS

"The first to present his case seems right, till another comes forward and questions him" (Proverbs 18:17). The best news sources offer some form of debate from people on both sides of an issue. For example:

➤ The editorial section of the paper, if indeed it encourages debate

➤ "The News Hour" with Jim Lehrer (PBS)

➤ "Nightline" (ABC)

➤ "Cross-fire" (CNN)

➤ My favorite orthodox (evangelical Christian) news source is *World* magazine, with a format similar to *Time* and an editorial board committed to biblical truth (1-800-951-6397).

➤ Also available for children—*God's World* student newspapers and corresponding Teacher's Helpers. Age-appropriate news summarized for grades K-8. Written to promote a Christian worldview. Making students aware of what God is doing in the world today and encouraging them to ask, "What does God think about specific current events?" (1-800-951-KIDS)

➤ Other good sources are *Citizen* magazine, Focus on the Family (1-800-A-FAMILY); *Breakpoint* with Chuck Colson—transcripts of Colson's radio commentary on news and trends (1-800-995-8777); *Washington Watch,* Family Research Council (800-225-4008); *The Family Voice,* Concerned Women for America (1-800-458-8797); the *Phyllis Schlafly Report* (618-462-5415); and *AFA Journal,* American Family Association (601-844-5036).

➤ And on the radio, "Point of View" with Marlin Maddoux, "Beverly LaHaye Live," and "Family News in Focus," which often deal with cultural themes.

➤ Another news source I appreciate is *The Weekly Standard* (1-800-983-7600)—not particularly evangelical, but morally conservative and thoughtful.

≈

LONGING FOR THE LAST CHAPTER—
CELEBRATION BAY

There's a great deal of rhetoric out there calling Christians to political action, warning and threatening that we'd better turn our country around or *else*. And I do feel that the church, the body of Christ, *is* the hope of the world. But I believe that national renewal will be the result of spiritual renewal. I'm encouraged to hear a growing chorus of voices in the political/cultural arena—Bill Bennett, Dan Quayle, William Raspberry, Peggy Noonan, George Bush, Jr., to name a few—echoing Jeremiah, acknowledging that spiritual renewal is the real challenge before us.

But in the struggle for spiritual renewal we cannot force a victory. Only God can change hearts. Whether in evangelism or stewardship of our citizenship, God calls us to be *faithful* where we are with the children, the opportunities, and the information He has given us. (Ah, there's the "wry twist." Now that you've read this book, you may be accountable to do more. If it's any consolation, I feel much more accountable having written it!)

The natural consequence of realizing that our real battle is spiritual is to conclude that no political system or strategy or even victory can meet our deepest spiritual needs. In our lifetime we have seen the excesses of liberalism and conservatism as the political pendulum has swung back and forth. Winston Churchill observed the pendulum from a generational perspective. "Any twenty-year-old who isn't a liberal doesn't have a heart, and any forty-year-old who isn't a conservative doesn't have a brain," he quipped.

To the extent that either liberal or conservative attempts to fix our problems ignore their moral and spiritual dimension, they will be no real fix at all. They merely put a Band-Aid on a cancer, like the priest and "prophets" of Jeremiah's time proclaiming peace and safety in the shadow of the temple while King Nebuchadnezzar's army was on a roll in their direction.

Our children must learn that true peace and safety—the place where we really *belong*—is in intimate relationship with Jesus Christ. In a fallen world living "outside the garden," as Christian counselor and author Larry Crabb puts it, we lose our perspective. We have high expectations of the Opportunity Society for self-expression, and of the American dream of self-fulfillment. We lose sight of the fact that America is part of a fallen world where chaos and pain are the norm. We do not "welcome" problems and pain as that which pushes us closer to God (James 1:2). "We need intimacy with God to deal with what comes next," urges Crabb. "We need intimacy with God *period*."

Which is not to say that our political expectations and longings for truth, value, meaning, and belonging are wrong—often just misplaced. These intangible needs of our soul will never be fully met this side of eternity. God Himself "has also set eternity in the hearts of men" (Ecclesiastes 3:11). He's written the Story of eternal transcendent things in our hearts, if you will, and though we get sidetracked with Lewis's "mud pies in the slum," we just can't find them satisfying. This deep connection to the Author and His Story compels us to long for God's justice—for shopping bag thieves and murderous tyrants alike. To long for His freedom, His peace. Complete healing and restoration for broken relationships and broken homes. No more war, poverty, disease, or pain. We long for the world that John Lennon "imagined." But that world is found only in true intimacy with God instead of under "only [empty] sky."

If the end of *our earthly part* in the Story looks uncertain, the end of the Story looks great. And this is how we need to encourage our children for their future: to value their heavenly citizenship, for it determines their part in the end of the Story where wonderful things happen. Satan's deception will end. The truth will blaze for all to see with crystal clarity. Paul makes it clear that God "will soon crush Satan" under believers' feet (Romans 16:20).

In his wonderful book *Bold Love,* Christian counselor Dan Allender paints a possible scenario for making the Devil pay for all his lies and destruction. "I imagine a long line of believers, who have faced the torment and attacks of the Evil One, waiting single file for the opportunity to kick Satan in the face before God delivers the final blow." By withholding his own petty attempts at revenge in this world and leaving "room for God's wrath" (Romans 12:19), Allender hopes he will find himself "near (very near) the front of the line." He wants his kicks to be felt deeply and for the pain of Satan's humiliating defeat not to be dulled by the proper revenge of too many in front of him.

Like Allender, I want Satan to pay—for seventeen years and counting of physical pain from rheumatoid arthritis, for the heartache of Jack's broken family, for the grief of my grandmother's and Gracie Kiltz's hospital vigils, and for grandmother's death and Gracie's injured brain and weakened little body. The book of Revelation's promises of "no more death or mourning or crying or pain" mean a great deal to me.

If *Star Wars* and *Pocahontas* fire our children's imagination more than the thought of heaven, maybe we need to do some picture painting of our heavenly destination ourselves. What will it be like to live in a "city of pure gold, as pure as glass" and reign with Christ? To get us started, we can reread the parts of Revelation, Ezekiel, and Isaiah (chapter 6) that describe heaven and reality in God's presence, or Aslan's joyous cry of "Further up and further in!" (*The Last Battle,* C. S. Lewis).

A sweeping, technicolor vision of heaven inspires ordinary people to do extraordinary, heroic things. The heroes of the "Hall of Faith" prized their heavenly citizenship above all the creature comforts of home. By faith they were certain of what they could not see—a "city with foundations whose architect and builder is God" (Hebrews 11:10). Many of these were quite wealthy—Abraham, Jacob, Joseph, Moses in Pharaoh's court—but they held their earthly gains lightly.

"They admitted they were *longing* for a better country—a heavenly one" (vv. 13, 15).

What a wonderful worldview to share with our children—we *belong* in that fabulous city, at home with Jesus. No matter how much we who live by God's truth are rejected now, we will ultimately live and work (reign), worship and fellowship there surrounded by beauty and plenty.

I visited my good friend Jana last week, and over lunch she laughed and squeezed my arm. "I had the most wonderful dream last night, and you were in it!" she enthused. "Valerie, you, and I were sitting on my sofa planning to go shopping. As we looked out the French doors over the pool and the yard, up above the pine trees we could see a really unusual cloud formation quickly gathering, a big windstorm from the north and clouds growing larger and piling up higher, much higher than regular thunder clouds.

"I said, 'We'd better hurry and go shopping so we can beat that storm.'

"While you and I were gathering up our purses and finding the keys, Valerie looked back out the windows and shouted at the top of her lungs, 'Jana, the Lord is coming!'

"We all three ran out on the driveway and looked up. The clouds that had been gathering up so high were not dark and threatening at all, but surrounded by a brilliant light and shot through with rainbow rays of glorious color. The wind rushed through the pine needles, and it didn't smell like rain but like something else, something fresh and sweet. And we could see *Him*. We started jumping up and down, laughing and shaking our heads, looking at each other.

"'He's here! He's here!'" we shouted. And we weren't worried about the kids or how we were going to join up with Him; we were just caught up in the utter joy of the moment. And then I woke up."

I think about Jana's dream, and I get goose bumps. In my mind I can hear above the wind a roar "like rushing waters, like the voice of the Almighty, like the tumult of an army." And I can really see myself running and jumping once again, and Gracie, too. I can see Jesus coming back for us, to take us home where we belong. And there in the ranks of saints behind Him, I can see Great-mother . . . smiling.

The white water is a distant memory. From the immense brilliant clouds, light flashes in dazzling patterns and colors like fireworks, only much more awesome. A chorus of trumpets sounds a glorious fanfare of welcome as we put our paddles down and glide into Celebration Bay.

BIBLE
STUDIES

Oh, yes,
here's the map!

CHARTING YOUR COURSE

14

A Four-star, Triple AAA,
How-to-Really-Get-a-Grip-on-It Guidebook

ALTHOUGH THEY WERE DESIGNED TO BE DONE BEFORE EACH chapter is read, these Bible studies are not just the "preliminaries" to each chapter, nor are they merely the "intellectual or academic framework" for dealing with the issues before us. They are the heart and soul of this book. For when we dare to differ with certain voices in our culture, it is not because we willfully cling to our own opinions and prejudices. It is not because we cannot bring ourselves to "just all get along." If God's Word did not exist, my people-pleasing self would be the first to go along and get along. (Of course, without His Word our lives would be disasters, and I doubt cultural concerns would even register on our Richter Scale of trials.)

But God's Word *does* exist, and so we prepare to give an answer to those cultural voices. As we stand before the majesty and beauty of His revealed moral law, what else can we do?

> *Streams of tears flow from my eyes*
> *for your law is not obeyed. . . .*
> *Though rulers sit together and slander me,*
> *your servant will meditate on your decrees.*
> *Your statutes are my delight;*
> *they are my counselors.*
> —*Psalm 119:136, 23-24*

BIBLE STUDY #1:
AS THE WORLD CHURNS

A Bible study on our hearts' response
to "destructive forces" at work in our culture

How do you prepare your children to navigate today's turbulent times, especially when *you* are the one old enough and wise enough to recognize the strength of the forces working against you and your family? You may feel like David in Psalm 55:9-11:

> *Confuse the wicked, O Lord, confound their speech,*
> *for I see violence and strife in the city.*
> *Day and night they prowl about on its walls;*
> *malice and abuse are within it.*
> *Destructive forces are at work in the city;*
> *threats and lies never leave its streets.*

1. Read Psalm 55. How did David think about responding to the threats and lies around him? (vv. 4-8) How are you tempted to escape the reality of our moral and cultural decline?

2. David's problems as king were twofold: civil war and personal betrayal—his son conspired to take his throne. In what ways was Absalom's strategy similar to that of slick politicians today? (2 Samuel 15:1-6)

When it became apparent that Absalom had won the support of too many people, what did David have to do? (2 Samuel 15:13-16, 23, 30)

And yet the thing that wounded David even more than the rebellion of his son (according to many commentators) was the betrayal of whom? (2 Samuel 15:12, 31)

3. This betrayal was grievous to David for what two reasons? (2 Samuel 16:23; Psalm 55:12-14, 20-21)

4. Dr. James Dobson has called our cultural conflicts over calls for "diversity" and "tolerance" in violation of God's moral law a "civil war of values." How has this war wounded you or your family?

Has the conflict spilled over into personal relationships with friends or family?

(Note: Perhaps our process of grieving and forgiveness begins in these next verses.)

5. Instead of running away to his stronghold in the desert, David moves his family out of harm's way, and then what does he do? (Psalm 55:16-19, 22; 2 Samuel 18:1-7)

6. How did God respond to David's prayers and petition for deliverance in Psalm 55? (2 Samuel 18:28)

7. God's response to David is no guarantee of what He may do for us in our cultural conflicts, but David's attitude certainly should be our example. How can we follow his example as we guide our children through turbulent times? (Review question #5 plus 2 Samuel 15:25-26.)

8. Regardless of the final outcome of the culture war, God will continue to work in His own way to respond to our cries for deliverance as it pleases Him. In what way did God direct the outcome of David's struggle? (2 Samuel 17:1-14)

In what ways has God already answered your cries and met your needs as you have struggled with guiding your children through challenging times?

By the way, whatever happened to Ahithophel, the traitor? (2 Samuel 17:23)

BIBLE STUDY #2:
THE HEART OF THE MATTER

A Bible study on the authority of Scripture

1. Complete this line of reasoning: If God is _____ (Romans 3:4), and if _____ breathed out the Scripture (2 Timothy 3:16), then it follows that the Scriptures are _____ (John 17:17). Can you think of some examples of situations where people have lost their belief in moral truth or their confidence in speaking out about it (i.e., the truth about what is right and wrong)?

2. What would you say to a friend if she told you she believed most of the Bible but thought that certain parts of it were not true? (2 Timothy 3:16)

3. Was human will the source and guiding force in producing Scripture? If not, who was? (2 Peter 1:20-21)

How is this source of inspiration referred to in John 16:13?

4. Read Matthew 4:1-11. Did Jesus believe that *all* of Scripture is God's Word? (v. 4) What key words indicate His position?

5. How did Jesus defend Himself during Satan's greatest attempt to destroy His ministry?

6. Jesus acknowledged the factual, historical reality of the following persons and events. Locate them in the references provided. (Matthew 19:3-5; Matthew 24:38-39; Matthew 10:15, 28; Matthew 12:40; John 5:46; John 8:39)

7. Are any of these people or events "controversial" in modern times? What does Jesus' teaching about these events and people communicate?

8. Read Psalm 119:9-16, 45-48, 89-100. It's interesting to note that the psalmist is mainly talking about God's law—Leviticus, Numbers, and Deuteronomy. And he was writing this surrounded by pagan cultures whose religious laws required sex and sodomy with temple prostitutes, and infant sacrifice. How did his spiritual environment sharpen the psalmist's appreciation for God's law? (Think of what is in Leviticus—Deuteronomy.)

 As our culture becomes increasingly pagan, how can you identify with the psalmist's heart?

BIBLE STUDY #3:
JEREMIAH AND THE EGG HUNT

*A Bible study about the spiritual, moral,
and national decline of Israel*

The book of Jeremiah chronicles the fall of Jerusalem to King Nebuchadnezzar of Babylon. The Jews have rebelled against God and His law so much that God delivers them into their enemy's hand. Jerusalem is sacked and burned. The leaders are killed, and thousands of Jews are taken captive and exiled to Babylon. Jeremiah is God's messenger to a culture in rebellion against Him.

1. For what specific sins was God judging Israel? (Jeremiah 2:13; 7:8-10, 30; 8:1-2, 10; 16:10-12; 19:4-5)

2. In what way do we dig our own "broken cisterns" (i.e., turn to other people, things, or activities to fill our lives with meaning and security)? (Jeremiah 2:13)

3. How did Israel respond to God's invitation to repentance? (Jeremiah 2:25; 8:6; 13:23; 18:11-12)

4. In our culture, what is the *perceived* cause of bad behavior? What is the real cause?

5. How did the leaders and prophets rate the seriousness of Israel's problems? (Jeremiah 8:11)

What did they prophesy and hope would happen? (Jeremiah 5:31; 21:1-2; 27:12-17)

6. How was this different from God's view? (Jeremiah 30:12-15; 21:5-7)

7. On a scale of 1 to 10, do you think our culture is in slight (1) or serious (10) trouble? Why? (Compare our cultural situation with Israel's in terms of specific sins [#1] and how we view the seriousness of our problems [#5]).

8. What was God's just punishment for Israel? (Jeremiah 4:16-18; 5:19; 11:1-8)

9. In the midst of great discipline and hardship, how did God show mercy to Israel? (Jeremiah 21:5-9; 26:1-9; 29:10-14)

10. How does God show you His mercy when you fall into sin?

BIBLE STUDY #4:
THE FLAME PASSES ON

*A Bible study about the spiritual
and moral nurturing of our children*

1. What do you think are your greatest obstacles to teaching your children to love and fear the Lord and obey His commandments?

2. Compare Exodus 12:24-28 with Joshua 4:4-9, 20-24. What is the setting in each passage for a discussion of spiritual and moral truth in the family? Is this a formal or informal setting?

What was the ultimate goal of each time of family discussion?

How can you overcome some of the obstacles mentioned above to use special occasions or holidays to teach your children about God?

3. In the Exodus 12 passage, what is the special significance of the phrase in verse 26, "What does this ceremony mean to you?"

Why does the child initiate the discussion? What triggers the child's curiosity?

4. In Deuteronomy 6:7, what is the setting suggested for the discussion of family values?

How can you overcome some of the obstacles mentioned earlier by following this example?

5. Taking the Exodus 12 and Deuteronomy 6 passages, whom does God hold accountable for the *spiritual and moral training* of your children?

Understanding God's priority then, what role should the school and church play in teaching morals to your children?

6. When we live in times of relative peace and prosperity, what danger are we warned against? (Deuteronomy 6:10-12; 8:10-18)

Why is this a danger for people living in comfort?

7. What finally happened to God's people? Did they teach God's law to their children? (Jeremiah 6:10; 8:7; 11:9-14)

8. Even God had disobedient children. Our children may know the truth, see us setting a good example, and yet like Adam and Eve, they will choose to give in to sinful desires. Especially as they get older, our greatest option to help them choose obedience and blessing may come from the following verses. Note how each verse can direct us toward a godly response to the challenges and heartaches of parenting (James 1:5; 5:13; Philippians 4:6-7).

Our prayers must be accompanied by what? What is the significance of this condition to peace?

BIBLE STUDY #5:
MOM, WHERE DID I COME FROM?

*A Bible study about the origins of the
universe and human life*

1. Scripture is very clear about the origin of the universe. How did it come to be? Or, in the famous words of the philosopher, "Why is there something, rather than nothing?" (Psalm 33:6-9; 148:3-5; Hebrews 11:3)

And for what purpose did He design it? (Isaiah 45:18-19; Genesis 1:14-15)

2. Genesis 1:1 or 1:3 quite possibly could have made a big bang. (Compare with vv. 14-18.) But the Big Bang theory says that a small ball of matter either existed in eternity past or suddenly came into being. Billions of years ago the small ball of incredibly dense matter exploded—washing out uniformly all over the universe. It slowly coalesced into stars, galaxies, planets, and gradually the earth was formed. Genesis 1:14-18 does not quite square with this sequence. How does it differ?

Does it fit with evolution to have v. 14 after v. 11? Why or why not?

3. A Hebrew verb that means "to create out of nothing" is used in Genesis 1:1, 21, and 27. What did God create out of nothing?

4. How does the phrase "after its kind" or "according to its kind" (vv. 11, 12, 21, 24, 25) help you evaluate the theory that one kind of plant or animal mutated and evolved into another kind of plant or animal?

Is "kind" necessarily the same thing as "species"? (Remember: There are many species of squirrels, dogs, etc.)

5. Read Romans 5:12. When did physical death enter the world? How might this affect the possibility of evolution?

6. Read Genesis 7:11 and 2 Peter 3:5-6. More than just lots of steady rain and flooding happened here. What phrases indicate the possibility of a giant catastrophe of "biblical proportions"?

7. Read Isaiah 45. In verse 12 God asserts His authorship of creation. In the other verses what related points is He making about His relationship with human beings?

In what ways does your belief in creation affect your relationship with God?

8. Read Hebrews 11. List seven things that these people believed by faith but could not see. List the one thing this passage assumes that you as a believer must believe by faith but cannot see.

BIBLE STUDY #6:
ANIMAL "RIGHTS" VERSUS EVE'S LEATHER DRESS

A Bible study on the comparative worth of humans and animals and our stewardship of animals

1. If one believes in evolution, how are human beings different from animals?

2. If one believes in creation, how are human beings different from animals? (Genesis 1; Psalm 8:6-8; 139:1-4; Luke 12:24; Romans 2:14-15; 5:6-8)

3. How did God set forth the relationship of humans to animals before the Fall? (Genesis 1:28-29)
How did He amend this after the flood? (Genesis 9:1-3)

4. Who was the first to kill an animal, and why was the animal killed? (Genesis 3:21)

5. According to God's Word, "without the shedding of blood there is no forgiveness of sin" (Hebrews 9:22). How was this accomplished in the Old Testament? (Hebrews 9:24-28)

6. Summarize from the previous verses the relationship God has established between humans and animals, including three situations when it is permissible to kill animals.

7. Our freedom to rule over animals should be tempered by what responsibilities? (Genesis 2:20; 7:2-4; Proverbs 12:10)

8. In Habakkuk the rulers and people of Judah are being judged for their sins. God is bringing the Babylonian army (1:5-11) to punish them. List three of their sins mentioned in 2:17.
Why do you think God takes the treatment of animals so seriously?

BIBLE STUDY #7:
ABORTION KILLS CHILDREN, BUT JESUS HEALS AND FORGIVES

A Bible study about the sanctity of life created in the image of God

1. Read Genesis 1:27. What does it mean to be created "in the image of God"? What characteristics and abilities of our heavenly Father do we uniquely reflect?

2. List five different ways God is involved in creating new life. (Genesis 21:1-2; 29:31; 30:22-23; 1 Samuel 1:5-6, 19-20; Job 10:8-12; Psalm 139:13-16)

3. How did God relate to the following in a personal way while they were still in their mothers' wombs?
Jacob and Esau (Genesis 25:23; Romans 9:11-13)
Jeremiah (Jeremiah 1:5)

4. What value does God put on human life? (Psalm 8; Romans 5:6-8)

5. Why did God institute capital punishment? (Genesis 9:5-6)

6. What should be our response to the shedding of innocent blood? (Proverbs 24:11-12)

7. The Greek word for baby is *brephos*. The same word for baby is used in Luke 1:41 and Luke 18:15. What primary distinction would progressives make between these different babies? Do they use the same words to describe the babies in both verses? What does Dr. Luke's use of the same word to describe these babies mean?

8. To anyone dealing with the guilt of abortion, King David's experience can provide great encouragement. He committed adultery with Bathsheba. Then, when he found out she was pregnant, he arranged for her husband to be killed so that he could marry her. He rationalized his sin for at least nine months, but finally confessed it when Nathan confronted him (2 Samuel 12:7-14). God forgave David's sin of killing for convenience to "take care" of the consequences of his adultery. But what were the consequences?

Psalm 51 records David's confession. After months of denial, what does David request of God, and what does he acknowledge? Not only was David's guilt forgiven, but how did he go down in history? (Acts 13:22)

How can we respond with truth and grace to those struggling with a crisis pregnancy or the guilt of abortion?

BIBLE STUDY #8:
WATCHING "GREAT-MOTHER" DIE

*A Bible study about the worth of
great suffering and the clothes of compassion*

1. We tend to view suffering as something to be avoided at all cost. Some have even called pain "the gift that nobody wants." According to James 1:2-4 and 1 Peter 1:6-7, what good can come from suffering and grief?

2. What is a day of suffering worth? (2 Corinthians 4:17) And with the Lord, a day is like what? (2 Peter 3:8)

What do these verses say about God's rewards for days of suffering and pain?

3. Something that is "precious" is not taken lightly or distributed randomly. What does Psalm 116:15 say about saints suffering to the point of death?

4. Sometimes, like Job in chapter 3:20-26, we may think there _is_ such a thing as a life not worthy to be lived. Do you agree? How does Job's perspective change in chapter 42?

5. I have stood and listened to many people tell me the story of their health crisis and how God delivered them. There's a natural feeling that any episode of crisis should have a development, a climax, and a resolution—an end. It seems unnatural that mine or anyone's chronic condition should go on and on. What encouragement can be found in these verses when there is no deliverance (yet)? (Isaiah 50:10; Psalm 71:14-22; 2 Corinthians 12:7-10)

6. Read Psalm 27. Pain, dependence on others, fear of the future—physical illness can be a great enemy threatening us. How did the attack of his enemy affect David's focus and desire? Of what was he confident?

(Note: Even David wound up bedridden and needing round-the-clock nursing care. 1 Kings 1:1-4, 47-48)

7. In Colossians 3:12 Paul talks about the "clothes of compassion." Just as clothes have different styles, compassionate caregiving can be done in different styles or ways. What caregiving "style" do you prefer? Or do you enjoy a variety of "styles"? If so, what? How often do you "wear" them?

BIBLE STUDY #9:
CONFESSIONS OF A FELLOW FROG

A Bible study on contentment and greed

1. List the hindrances to contentment mentioned or implied in these verses. How does American culture (especially TV and advertising) encourage the very hindrances you listed? (Proverbs 19:23; Ecclesiastes 5:10-15; Hebrews 13:5)

2. How did Paul _learn_ contentment? (Philippians 4:11-13) How can we?

3. Why do we tend to envy our neighbors or family members more

than we envy Bill Gates or Donald Trump? What does lack of contentment lead to? (Ecclesiastes 4:4-8)

4. List the consequences of greed. (Proverbs 15:27; 28:25; Ephesians 5:5; Isaiah 57:17)

5. The following verse is often used as one of the strongest New Testament condemnations of homosexuality. Do you tend to think of an unrepentant lifestyle of homosexuality as a more serious sin than an unrepentant lifestyle of greed? Why? What do these verses say about greed compared to homosexuality? (1 Corinthians 6:9-10)

6. What is the opposite of greed? Since Scripture says, "be content" or "don't be greedy," what are some ways people could change the desires of their heart if they're drawn toward greed? (Proverbs 11:24-25; 1 Peter 5:2)

7. Jesus says if we're greedy, we're focused too much on what? Of what, then, does meaningful life consist? (Luke 12:15-21)

BIBLE STUDY #10:
SHE WORKS HARD FOR NO MONEY?

A Bible study on a Christian work ethic

1. Were human beings created primarily for leisure or for work? (Genesis 2:15, 18-20)
   Did God call Adam to work with his hands or with his mind? Did Eve have housework before the Fall?

2. Was the responsibility of work a part of the curse, part of the Fall? Compare Genesis 2 with 3:17-19. Specifically, how was work affected by the Fall? What do you think that means?

3. What example of a work schedule did God set for man? (Exodus 20:9-11)
   Why do you think He didn't set aside more days for rest and leisure?

4. As Solomon worked at all his great projects, his "heart took delight" in the pursuit and accomplishment of all his plans. But when he thoughtfully surveyed all he had done from a purely human perspective, what did he conclude? (Ecclesiastes 2:4-11, 21-23)
   What was God's response to His work? (Genesis 1)

How does being created "in God's image" and designed for a relationship with God relate to work and satisfaction? (Ecclesiastes 2:24-26; 5:18-20; 12:13-14)

5. In the New Testament the motive for work is expanded. Explain how. (Colossians 3:17, 23-24)

6. What gifts and talents has God given you to work with? Are you finding satisfaction in your work? Why or why not? If not, what can you do about it?

7. Are you teaching your children to work? How are you teaching them to take responsibility for work? How are you teaching a commitment to excellence in work? How are you rewarding your children's work?

BIBLE STUDY #11:
A TIME TO KILL, FLOP, AND CLICK

A Bible study about the enemy's strategy
to defeat God's people

Read Numbers 22–25:13.

1. How did Moab think they would fare in open conflict with Israel?

2. What strategy did the king of Moab devise? Was this a "top-down" or "bottom-up" strategy (i.e., a solution attempted at the management level or among the grass roots—the common people)?

3. How did God tell Balaam to answer the king's request?
   Why was Balaam motivated to press the matter? (cf. 2 Peter 2:15)

4. This motivation prompted him to make a number of wrong decisions. List all you can find.

5. In verse 24:11 Balaam is denied his reward, but he may yet have gained it. What advice did he evidently give the king of Moab on how to defeat Israel? (Numbers 25:1-3; 31:7-9, 14-17)
   Was it a "top-down" or "bottom-up" strategy? Was it successful in the short run? What about the long run?

6. In the Numbers passage Israel was drawn away from the Lord to worship foreign gods. How are we (especially our young people) being tempted by the media to leave our faith today? (1 John 2:15-17)

Who profits if we turn away from God (both monetarily and in our culture wars)?

7. In Matthew 4:8-10 Satan tempts Jesus with images that appeal to His imagination. In our culture what are some of the main messages the media gives us about "all the kingdoms of the world and their splendor"?

How did Jesus respond to the call to "go for all the gusto you can!" or "if it feels good, do it"?

BIBLE STUDY #12:
"A TIME TO LAUGH . . . DANCE . . . AND BE SILENT"

A Bible study about developing a strategy
to "guard our hearts"

Read Romans 12:1-2; 14:1-12. Instead of the example of meat versus vegetables, substitute the idea of going to movies versus never going to movies.

1. How can we learn to distinguish between matters of freedom and matters of command?

2. According to the Romans passage, as Christians, sometimes our practices may differ. But Paul exhorts us never to differ on what? (Galatians 1:6-9)

3. On debatable issues how do we arrive at our own convictions? (Romans 14:5)

4. Scripture speaks to convince our minds both positively and negatively about the ideas and images on which we set our thoughts and affections. From the following verses list some of the positive (Colossians 3:1-2; Philippians 4:8) and the negative (Psalm 101:3; Philippians 3:18-20; Colossians 2:8).

In what ways does the electronic media express "hollow and deceptive views of life"?

5. Matthew 6:21 tells us that "where our treasure is, there our heart will be also." We can tell what we treasure, not just by how we spend our money, but also by how we use our time and mental energy. Read Ephesians 5:15-16 and Psalm 90:12. Do you think your time spent

consuming electronic media squares with the intent of these verses? If not, why not? What about your children?

6. *Suggestion:* Pray through the verses in this study that were most meaningful to you and ask God's Spirit to affirm or convict you concerning your use of the electronic media (TV, music, movies and computers) and your oversight of your children's use. Talk to your husband; share your concerns. With him, discuss strategies and guidelines to reinforce or adopt concerning media use. Consider how you can be good stewards of your family's time and imagination with regard to each kind of media you consume.

BIBLE STUDY #13:
ABOUT DONKEYS AND ELEPHANTS

A Bible study about citizenship, freedom, and justice

1. Read Romans 13:1-7. According to this passage, where does government get its authority to govern? Is the ultimate source of power "the consent of the governed," i.e., "we the people"? (v. 1)

See also Daniel 4:29-37. (Note: Nebuchadnezzar was king of Babylon, the country that conquered Jerusalem and took the Jews into captivity.) And Isaiah 45:1-7, 13. (Note: Cyrus was king of the Persians, who conquered Babylon and freed the Jewish exiles.)

2. In addition to Romans 13, read Matthew 22:17-22. Besides paying taxes, what else should we "render to Caesar"? Or, in other words, as a United States citizen, what are the responsibilities that we should fulfill as unto the Lord? (See also 1 Timothy 2:1-2; 1 Peter 2:11-17; 3:16-17.)

3. Should we always submit to the governmental authorities as Paul exhorts in verse 2? (Acts 5:17-20, 27-33) Explain your answer.

4. I believe strongly that our freedoms and democracy are a trust given to us by God. How does 1 Corinthians 4:2 speak to our stewardship of this trust? What actions should we take to preserve that trust?

How can believers be "salty" salt and bright light in national affairs? (Matthew 5:13-16)

5. Paul was a citizen of _____ (Acts 22:25-29). But he valued his _____ (Philippians 3:20-21) citizenship even

more. In Acts 22 Paul claims his right as a citizen to be free from
_____, but he talks to the church in
Rome (6:15-23) about a greater freedom. What is it?

He talks about this freedom as a kind of slavery. What does he
mean?

On the main building of the University of Texas is inscribed John
8:32. In what way is this true of education and yet, at the same time,
missing the point of Romans 6?

6. According to Romans 13:3-5, what kind of justice should the government administer? Is God also concerned with economic justice
(the just distribution of money and wealth)?

Should the State help the truly needy in material ways? (Psalm
72:1-4, 12-14; 82:2-4; Ecclesiastes 5:8) Should the individual?
(Proverbs 22:9; 31:20; Amos 3:15; 4:1; 5:11-13)

Do you think that the principle "from each according to his ability,
to each according to his need" is a biblical principle?

Why, or why not? (1 Corinthians 9:7-10; 2 Thessalonians 3:10)

For a long time we have relied on our tax dollars to provide welfare
for the poor. As welfare is scaled back, what creative projects can our
families undertake to help the poor?

(*The above quote was taken from *The Communist Manifesto*.)

Readers may contact the author
by writing or E-mailing:

LAEL ARRINGTON
400 N. Walnut
Tomball, TX 77362
jkajr@flash.net

INDEX